Grand Coteau

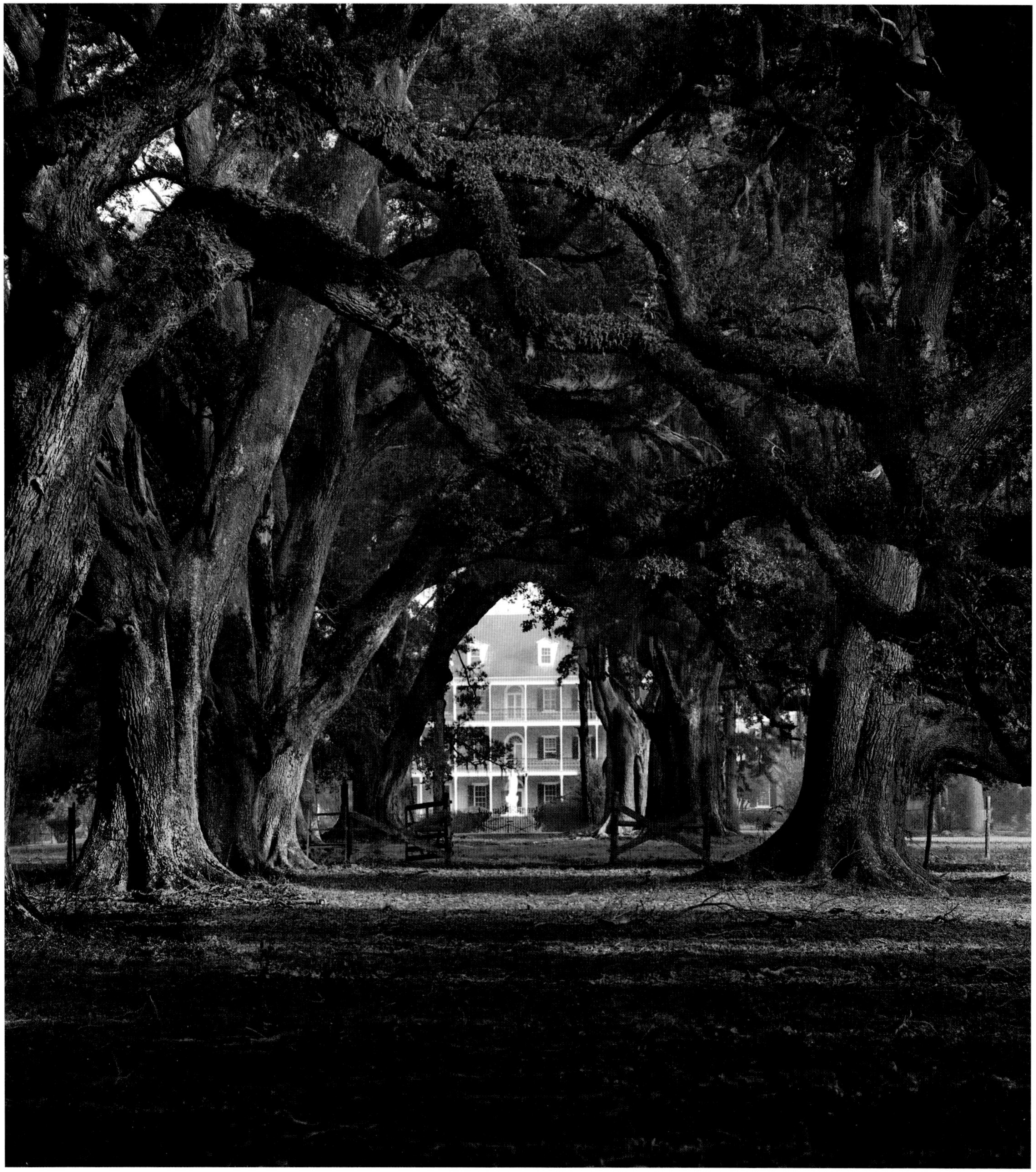

Oak Alley – Academy of the Sacred Heart
1983

Grand Coteau

John Slaughter

University of Louisiana at Lafayette Press
2012

University of Louisiana at Lafayette Press
P.O. Box 40831
Lafayette, LA 70504-0831
http://ulpress.org

ISBN 13 (hardcover): 978-1-935754-19-0
Printed in China

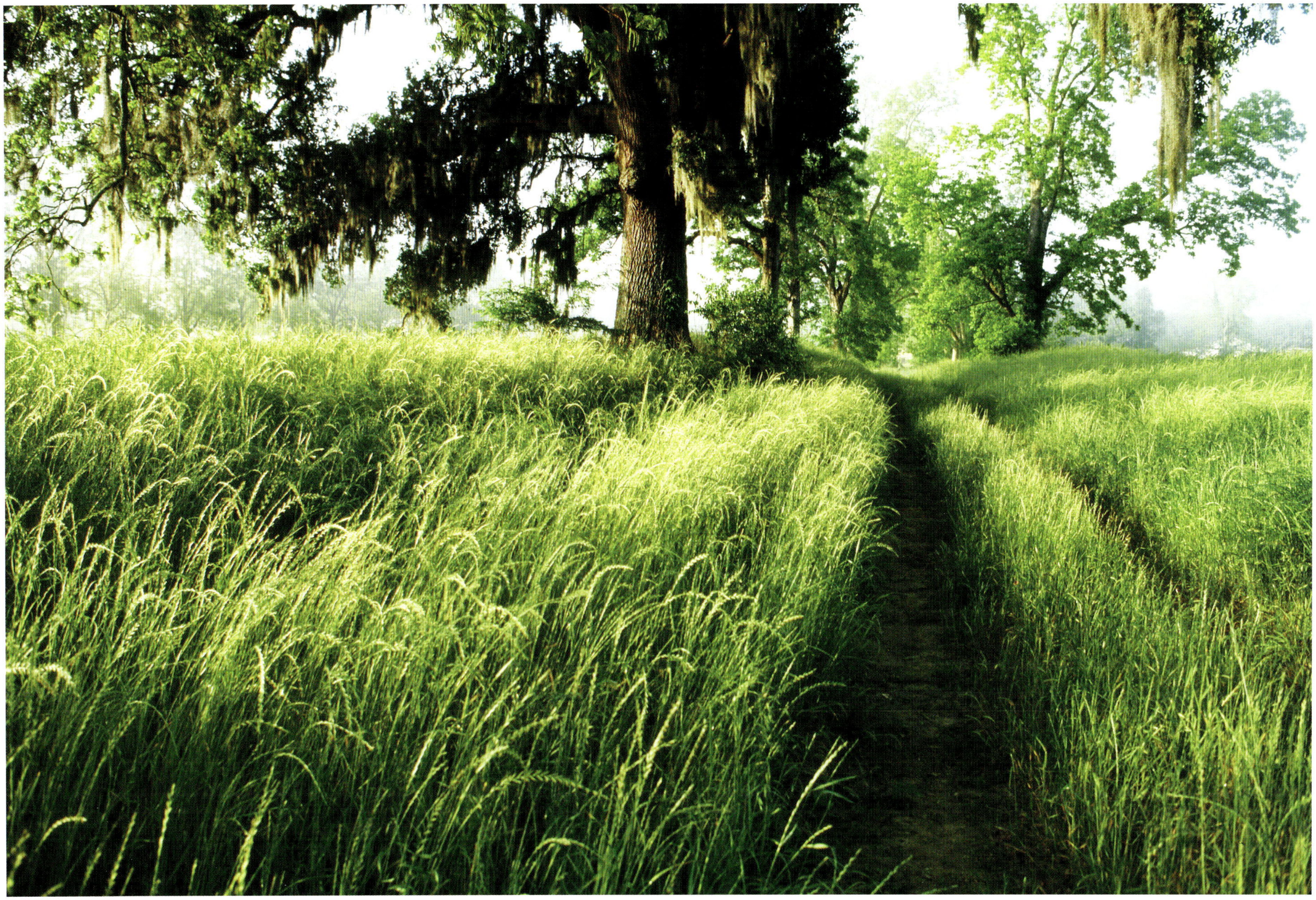

Preface
by John Slaughter

Included among the photographs presented in this book are quite a few depicting the efforts to preserve, restore, or renovate historical structures in Grand Coteau. By American standards Grand Coteau is an "old" settlement with many pre-Civil War buildings. The south Louisiana environment—with its heat, humidity, insects, varmints, occasional downpours, and, of course, hurricanes—demands vigilant maintenance for both buildings and grounds.

Grand Coteau is not Williamsburg. It's a lived-in town. Occasionally a visitor will comment on the "tin" roofs. Underneath many of those tin roofs are wood shingles. Covering wood shingles with tin (actually steel) is now part of the town's identity. The rusted tin roofs are frequently heavy-gauge material that may last longer than a new roof.

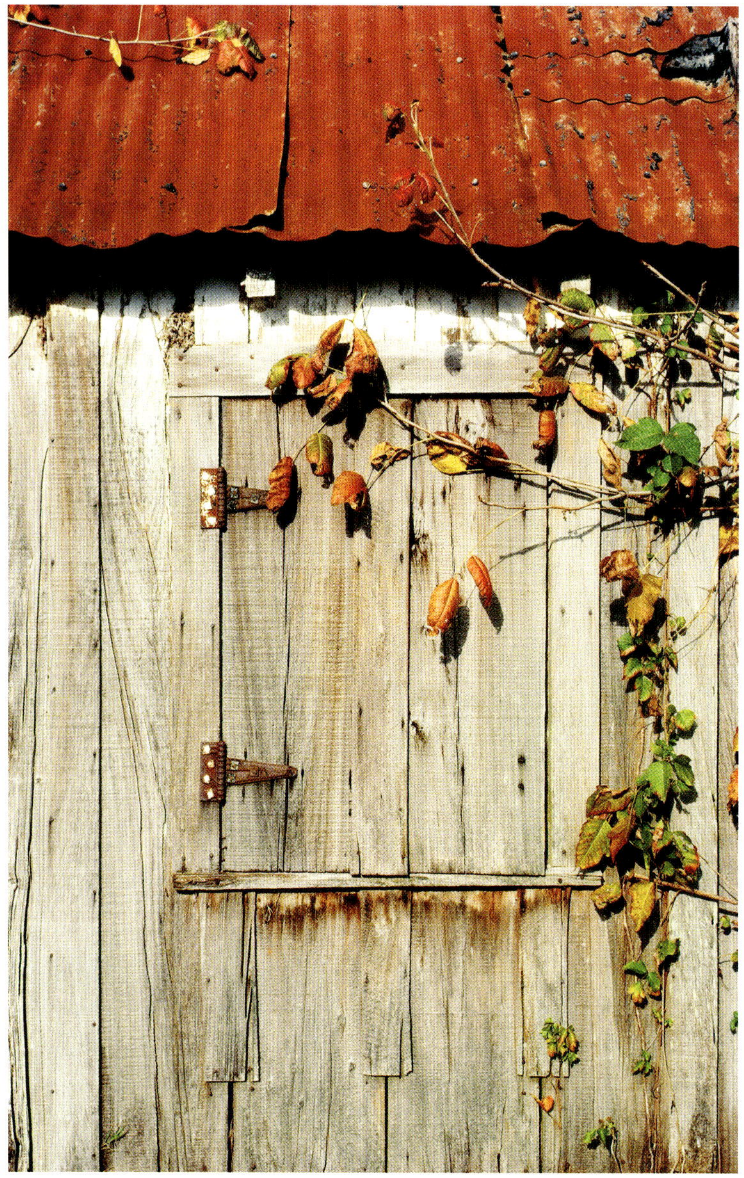

Large tracts of undeveloped land lie within the town limits of Grand Coteau, lending it a bucolic atmosphere. The Jesuit and Sacred Heart orders have extensive pastoral acreage as well as generous gardens surrounding their main buildings. Additionally, there are large tracts belonging to families who prefer vistas to suburbia. When the town was placed on the National Register of Historic Places in 1980 it included many of these areas, even taking note of important tree alleys.

Zoning has never been prescribed in Grand Coteau. Residents, like many Americans, don't want to be told what they can or can not do with their property. Zoning, or at least building guidelines, could have prevented some unsightly construction, especially in historic areas; however, good fortune has generally prevailed.

Interstate 49 and the town's proximity to Lafayette have stabilized or increased property values, but also have altered the dynamics of the "small town." Recent commercial development has focused around I-49's Exit 11, but the benefits of increasing sales taxes are tempered by demands for extra vigilance from a community with limited resources. The activity generated by being in the peripheral orbit of a growing metropolitan area is affecting a community that for two hundred years has been mostly quiet.

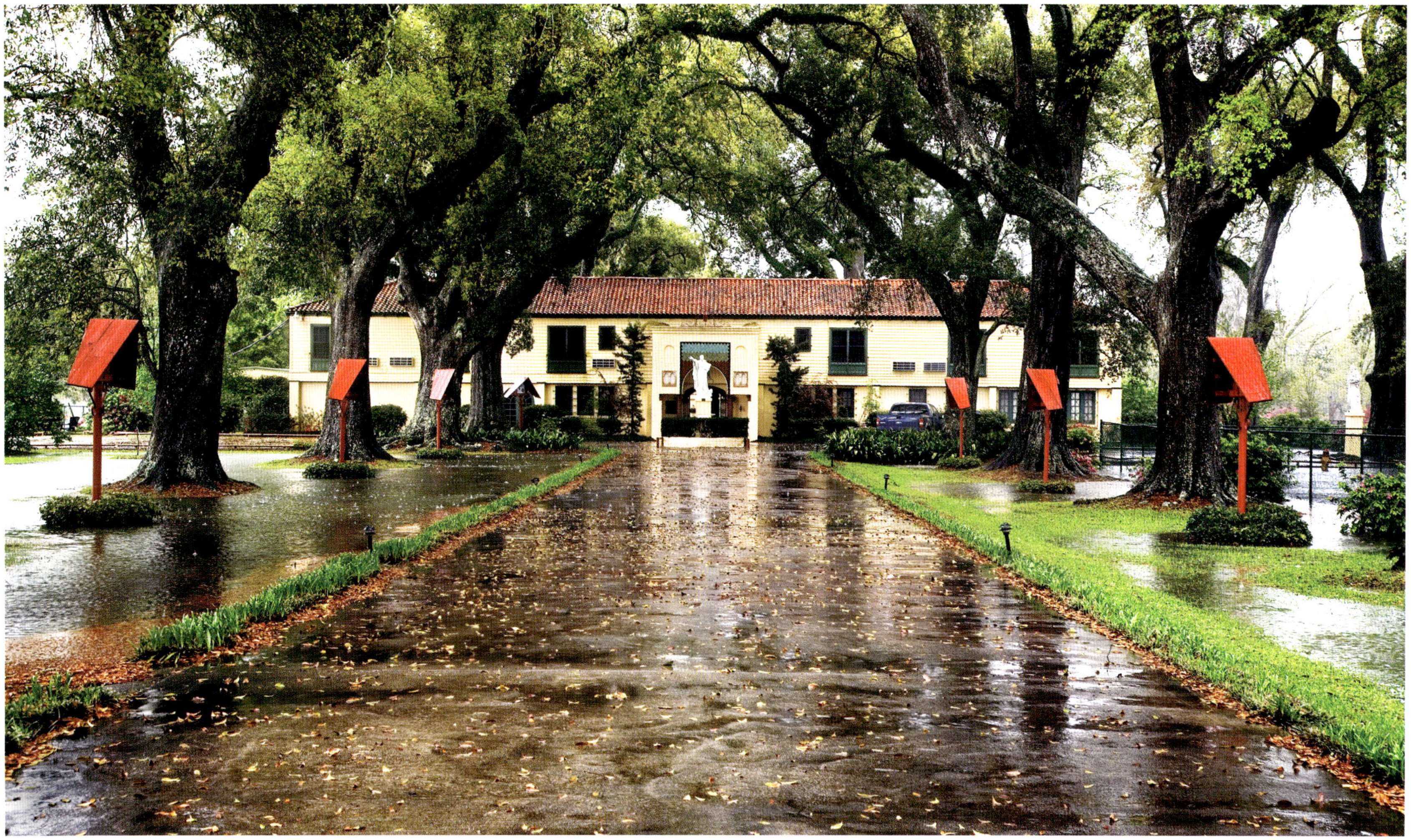

With its history, architecture, schools, and spiritual services, Grand Coteau has connected to many people beyond its residents. Students, retreatants, and tourists come and go, but the memory and the existence of this special place remains.

How did I end up in Grand Coteau?

It was 1976. My wife Hilary and I had just returned from a two-month odyssey to Guatemala and back in a 1968 Ford station wagon. We wanted to move from where we had been living north of St. Francisville. Hilary was looking for a teaching job, preferably in her field of Spanish. Checking with the Catholic Youth Organization in Baton Rouge, she learned of an opening for a Spanish teacher at the Academy of the Sacred Heart in Grand Coteau. Arriving at the school, we found a venerable and elegant institution in a picturesque rural town. It was an easy decision for Hilary to accept the job offered by Headmistress Sister Lucie Nordmann, RSCJ.

The photographs in this book were taken over a thirty-five-year period (1977–2012). In a sense they present a visual history. People died, structures changed, and views were altered. Take the cover shot of St. Charles Church: the water tower on the left has been removed, porticos have been added to the front and side entrances, and an oak tree has matured. What's remarkable is that Grand Coteau has lost no significant historical structures in that period and has seen improvement to many others.

Nancy Brewer (page 134) suggested in 2011 that I do a book on Grand Coteau. With this encouragement for a project that I had periodically considered, I began selecting the images. Sifting through thirty-five years of transparencies and negatives took some doing. Some were easy to locate as they had been previously exhibited. Others I forgot I had ever taken. The criteria for inclusion was multifaceted: aesthetic quality, historical significance, subject importance, and social value. Covering the marquee scenes, while revealing the life of a small town, was the sought-after balance. The decision to arrange them chronologically seemed only natural.

Introduction
by Patrice Melnick

On an early spring morning in Grand Coteau, the land lies draped in folds of fog that obscure low-lying areas. Acres of green lawn accent the center of town. On these verdant expanses stand almost ten Catholic institutions, including the three-story brick structure of St. Charles Jesuit College; the double-steepled wooden St. Charles Borromeo Church; Our Lady of the Oaks Retreat House, dressed in Spanish tile and maize-hued stucco; and the grand Academy of the Sacred Heart. These religious grounds are punctuated with azalea and camellia bushes beneath tall, swaying pines and sprawl-limbed, two-hundred-year-old live oaks. Sleepy-eyed cows meander in a field with a butter-yellow Midwestern-style barn in the distance.

In the old cemetery, a steady wind shifts the arms of oaks that shade headstones with names like Olivier, Meche, Thibodeaux, and Senegal. Trees matter in Grand Coteau. Oak Alley, planted in the early 1800s, stretches from St. Charles College to the Academy of Sacred Heart. Several double rows of live oaks and pecan trees bisect fields, creating canopied walkways and roads. The presence of nature, captured so clearly in many of John Slaughter's photographs, contributes to the spiritual calm that characterizes Grand Coteau.

Throughout the 1800s, Grand Coteau served as a stopping point for travelers between Washington, Louisiana, and St. Martinville, Louisiana. However, the town was difficult to reach. A traveler would have to take a boat to Washington or Port Barre along Bayou Teche. From there, one would travel to Grand Coteau by horse-drawn carriage, or wagon, or for those without means, by foot. By the time of the Civil War the community had two bakeries, a cobbler shop, a millinery, a blacksmith shop, a post office, and an inn where stagecoaches changed horses.

In 1821 the Religious of the Sacred Heart arrived. With the support of Mrs. Charles Smith, the widow of a wealthy planter, two nuns traveled to Grand Coteau to found a convent and the first Academy of the Sacred Heart in the United States. Mrs. Smith had donated land and a two-story building. Eventually, the Sisters of the Sacred Heart urged the Jesuits to come to Grand Coteau—they needed priests to conduct mass. The nuns promised land and a donation of 200,000 slave-made bricks. The Jesuits accepted, and in 1837, St. Charles College was built. New settlers arrived in Grand Coteau including Acadians, French, Irish and German immigrants, and African slaves.

The sisters at the Academy of the Sacred Heart, following the values of the order's founder, Sr. Sophie Barat, made it a priority to educate young women. They believed that women could change the world for the better, independently and through their husbands. Women were not routinely offered education at the time. The Academy in Grand Coteau has remained in continuous operation through fire, epidemics, and war—longer than any of the other two hundred Sacred Heart Schools.

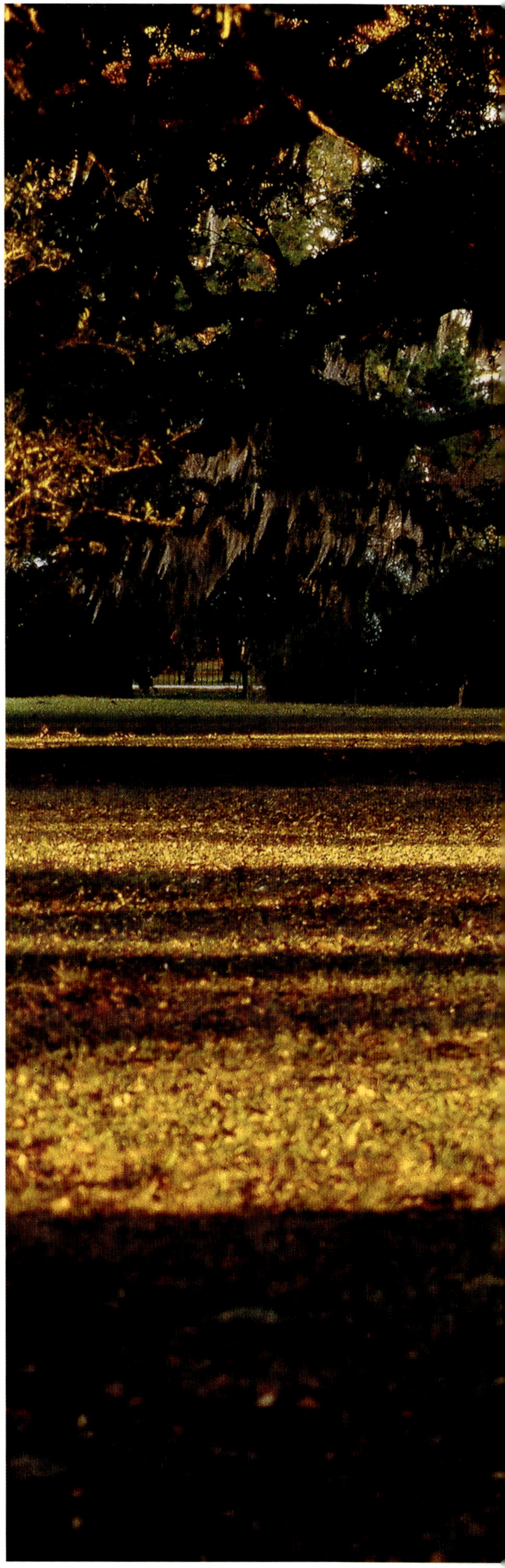

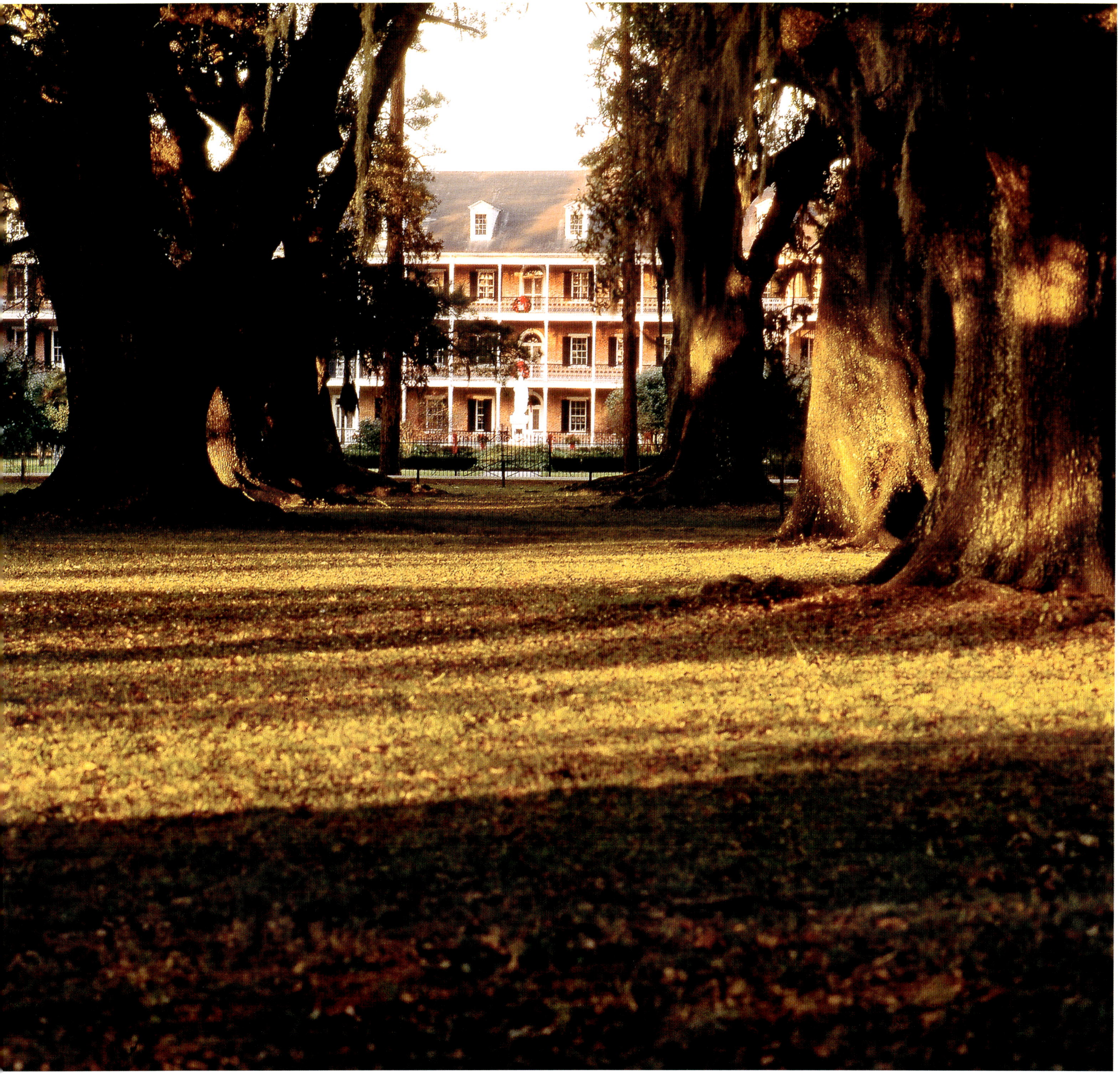

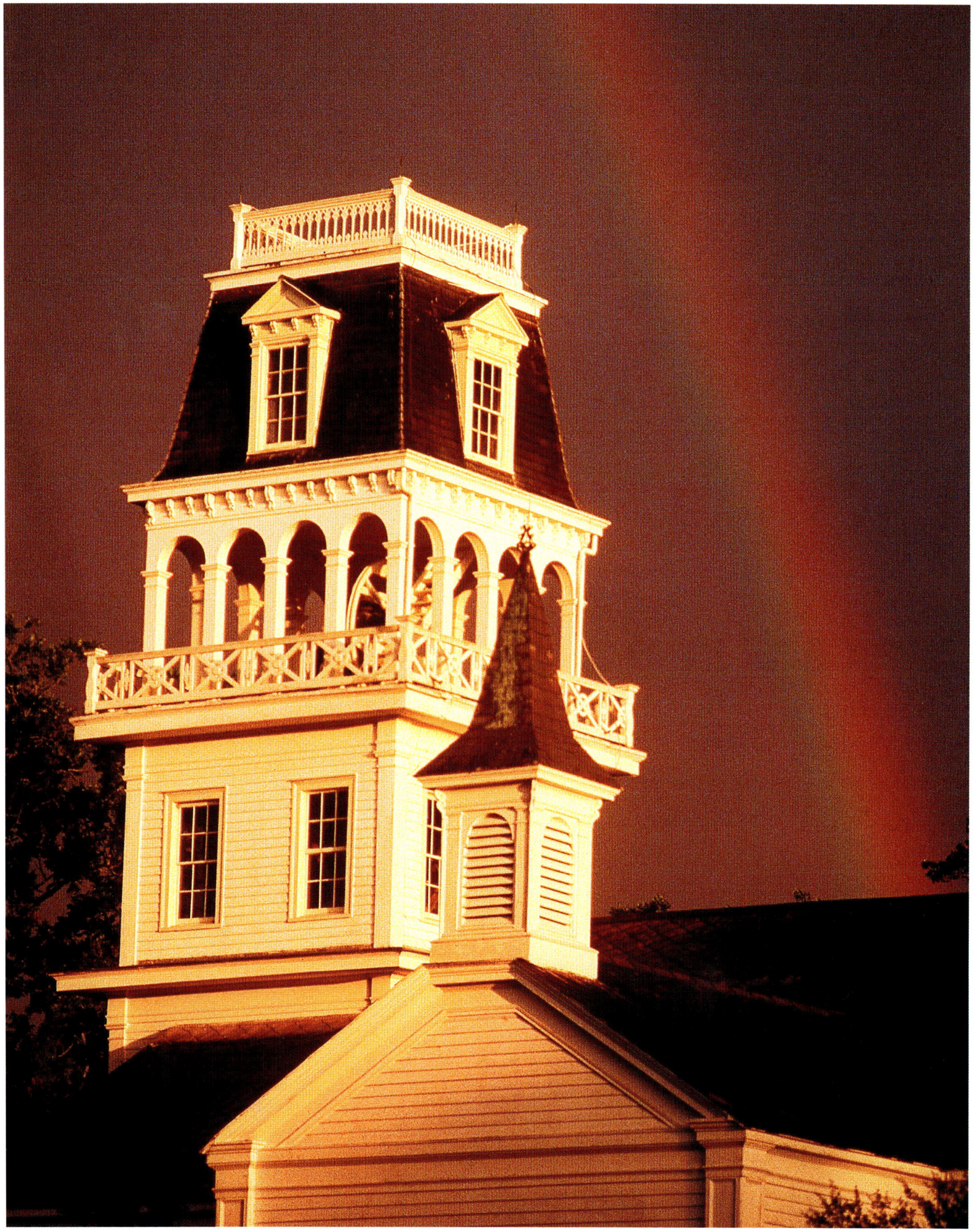

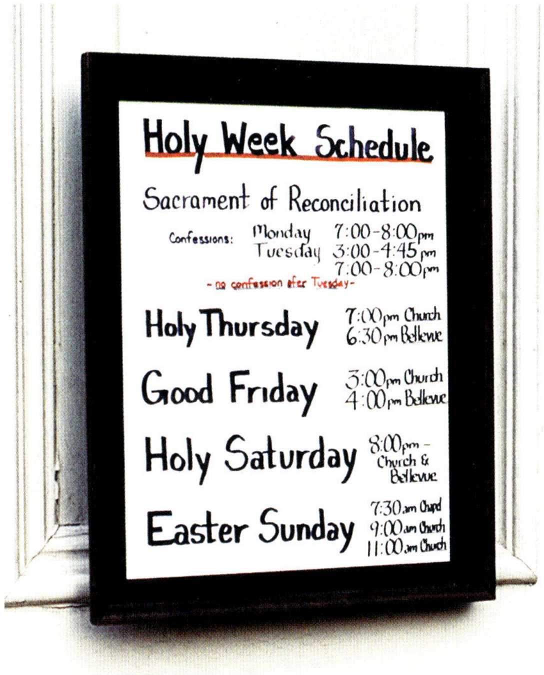

Like most institutions at that time, the Academy of Sacred Heart owned slaves, and the school functioned like a plantation. Slaves cultivated and harvested crops and tended the livestock, all of which helped the nuns, and the school to thrive. Ironically, the Sisters of the Sacred Heart were also the first to educate blacks in the area, who had virtually no access to education in the 1800s.

On April 7, 1890, the Religious of the Sacred Heart founded the Sacred Heart Parochial School, which later became St. Ignatius. Today, St. Ignatius offers education from pre-kindergarten through eighth grade.

From these beginnings grew many schools, including St. Peter Claver Elementary and High School for black students, Grand Coteau Elementary, and most recently St. John Berchmans, a new boys' school on the grounds of the Academy of the Sacred Heart.

For some families education remained elusive in the early part of twentieth century. Local landowners, who had sharecroppers living on their property, expected the children to work alongside their parents. The children might attend a few years of elementary school, but often were absent, especially during harvest, and some remained illiterate. Over time, however, the presence of multiple educational institutions helped each generation gain a stronger economic foothold.

Some come to Grand Coteau in search of self or to grow closer to God. It is not unusual to see men and women on retreat meandering the grounds of St. Charles College or strolling along quiet streets in town. They remain silent, perhaps with wooden rosary beads intertwined between fingers. Retreatants can be seen sauntering through green pastures, praying, standing before statues or the Grotto, or leaning back in the Adirondack chairs reading prayer books. The presence of Catholicism permeates life for residents and visitors alike in Grand Coteau.

One of Grand Coteau's most significant historical religious moments occurred in 1866, when an ailing novice, Mary Wilson, was cured upon having a vision of Jesuit novice John Berchmans. This Miracle at Grand Coteau was the third documented appearance of Berchmans, leading to his subsequent canonization.

Today, Grand Coteau's culture, economy, historic preservation, and tourism are flourishing. The town's historical district charms tourists and locals with unique gift shops, a café, a cake shop, a beauty salon, and more. An array of annual festivals take place in the town including the Sweet Dough Pie Festival, the Festival of Words, Le Grand Noel, and Sacred Heart's Christmas at Coteau and Congé.

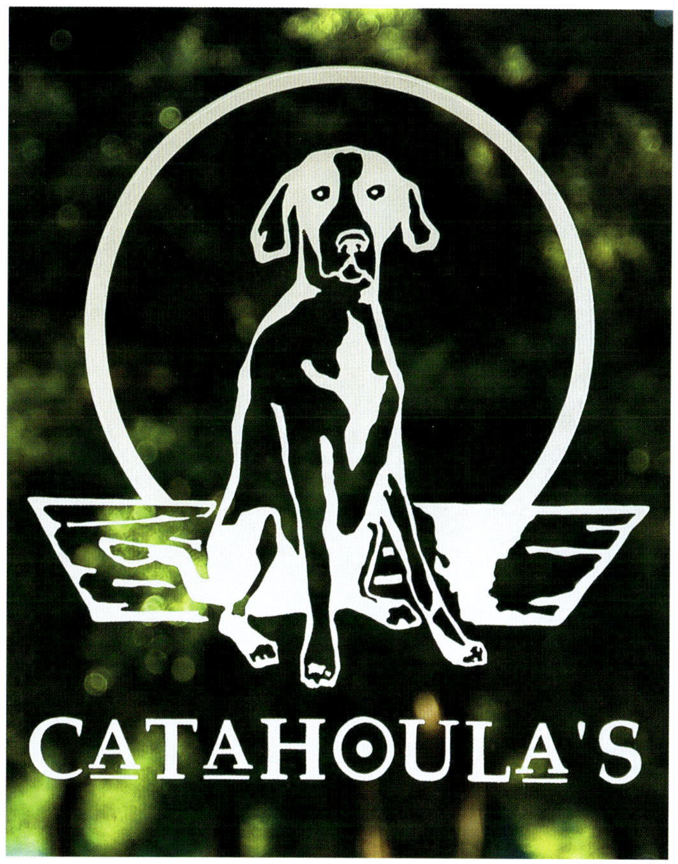

With over seventy buildings included on the National Register of Historic Places, almost anywhere one roams in Grand Coteau, historical buildings meet your gaze. As many of the gift shops are housed within these structures, just browsing the shops gives one a sense of history—from the tall ceilings, to wavy-glass transoms, to cypress-planked floors.

Grand Coteau brings together elders who hold memories and traditional culture; newcomers such as artists and others seeking inspiration; and natives who earned a living in other towns such as Houston or Atlanta, but have returned in retirement.

In researching this book, I made many appointments with residents in order to gather information. Often, when visiting with the elderly, I would arrive to find a woman who had put on makeup, jewelry, and a dressy blouse in anticipation of my visit. Settling into a chair, what began as a fact-finding mission quickly evolved into an hour of stories detailing childhood mischief, doing laundry on a washboard, or going to school; I was also educated on terms like "hack," which I now know means a traveling general store. Often people appeared to be stimulated by the fond memories. I am told that in the past neighbors visited for hours on porches or around kitchen tables, and these conversations evoked in me a similar sense of this social spirit. Grand Coteau residents are full of stories, hospitality, and heart.

Many of those I interviewed were African Americans, who currently make-up over seventy percent of the town's population—947 according to the 2010 census. They discussed difficult lives of harvesting crops, scrubbing floors, or cooking while raising seven, ten, or twelve children. And yet, the storyteller almost always expressed gratitude for his life, for fresh food, for family love, and for the nuns and priests who shared faith and education.

When John Slaughter first approached me about writing text for this book, I was glad for the opportunity to share thoughts and observations on a town that has grown dear to me and to work with a fine photographer. I looked through the photographs and appreciated the combination of landscape, architecture, photojournalism, and portraits. John has beautifully communicated the small-town ambiance along with the majestic grace of this spiritual mecca. Before I even saw the photos, I anticipated inspirational images of the Academy of the Sacred Heart, St. Charles Borromeo Church, and St. Charles College—in different qualities of light and seasons. But images of these buildings are rendered more relevant by inclusion of the surrounding neighborhood with small cottages where farm workers once lived and vestiges of former businesses—a meat market, a cobbler shop, a general store. In the portraits we see into the eyes of the people who helped develop Grand Coteau spiritually, culturally, and economically. Those portrayed range from the clergy, like Father Joe Doyle (page 50) and Father Ben Wren (page 96), who nurtured spirituality; to people like Mayor Mary Murray (page 84), who invested her wisdom into education and politics. The residents of Grand Coteau and their relatives of the past two hundred years envisioned, and then built the schools, churches, businesses, and homes; they measured angles and shaped bricks that created the spaces within which we still gather, learn, and pray.

It was a privilege to interview the people who generously shared memories and information. And I am honored to write about John's enlightening images. As his photographs reveal, Grand Coteau is all about its history, its architecture, nature, education, religion, and residents.

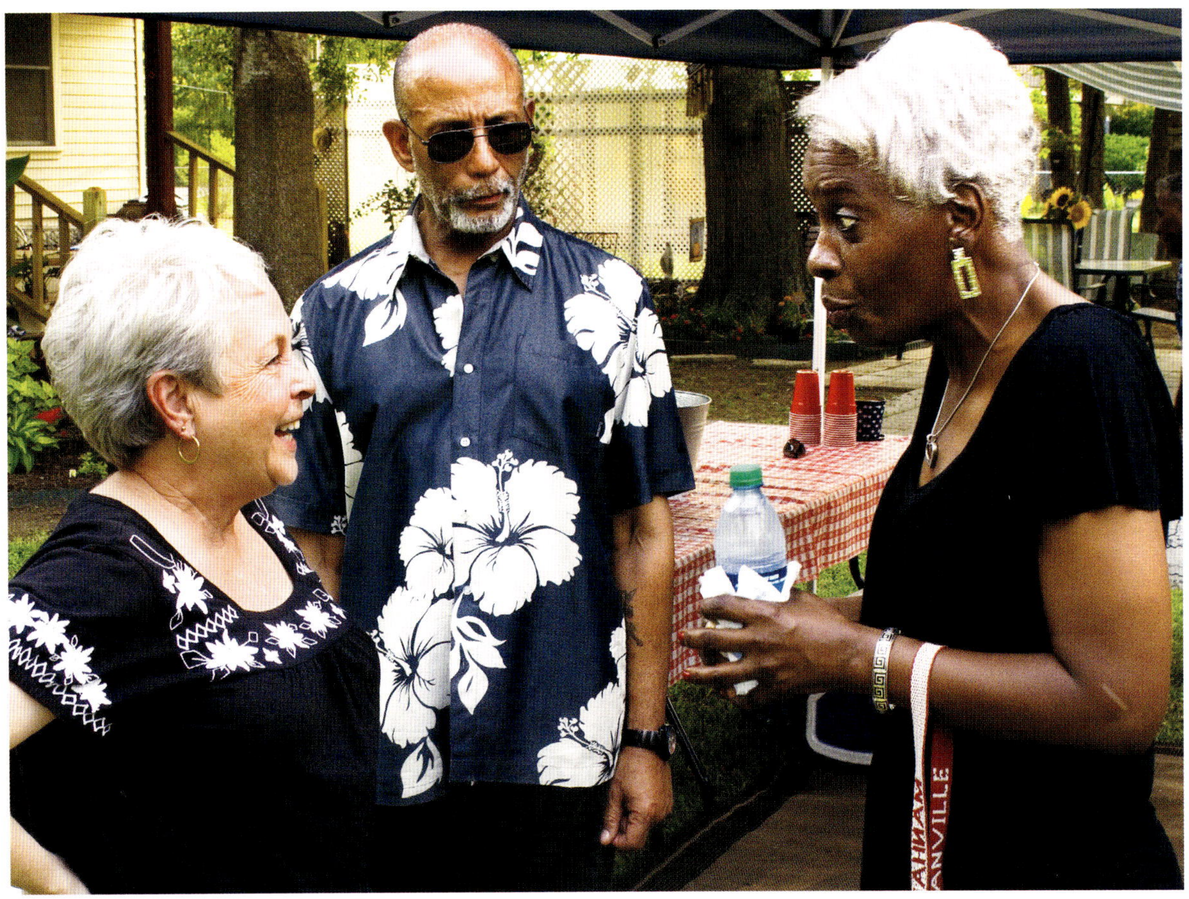

Gail Lark, Elbert Lee Guillory and Julia B. Richard.

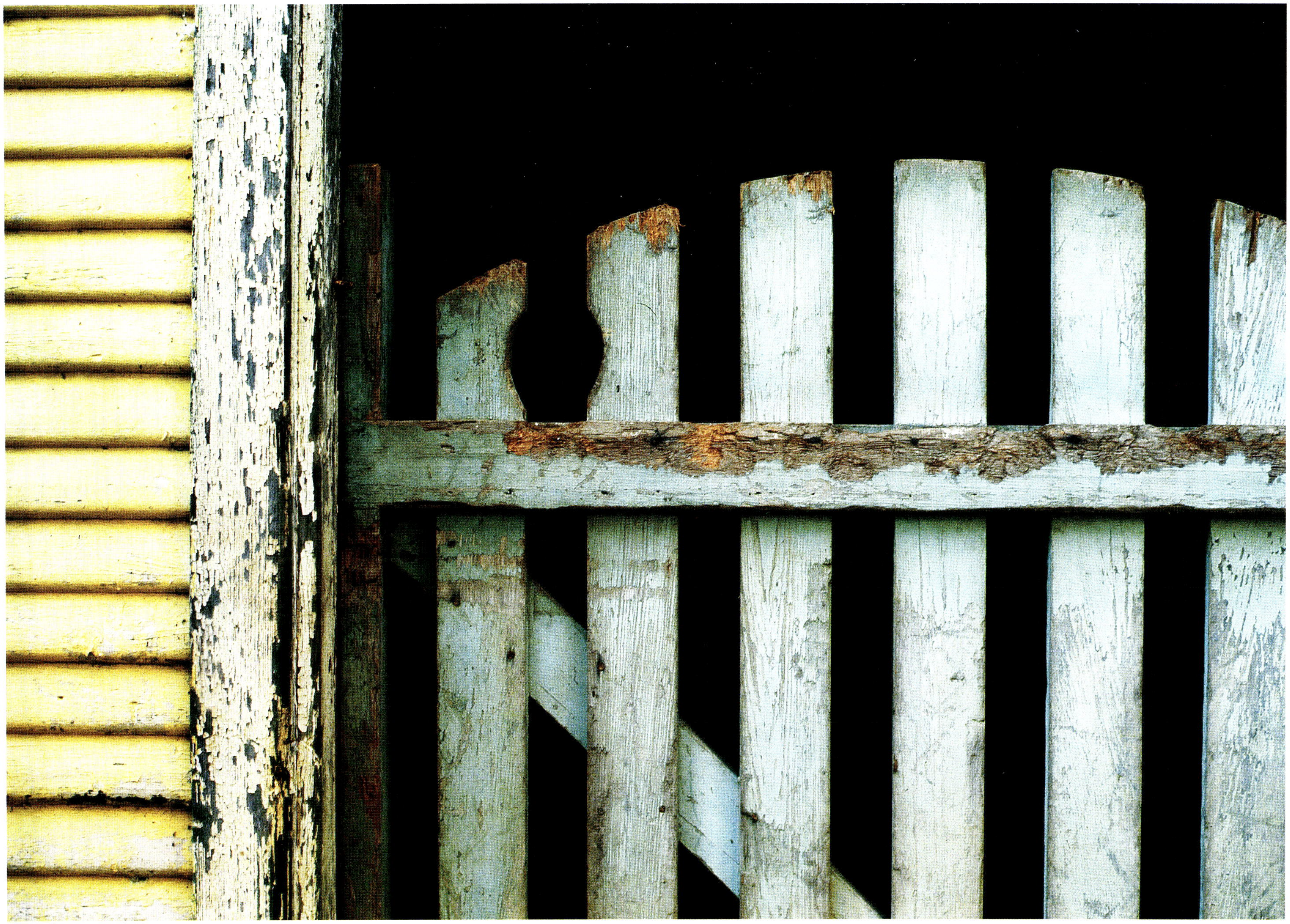

Influential Citizens of Grand Coteau
THE LEGACY OF MADAME CHATRIAN & FATHER THENSTED

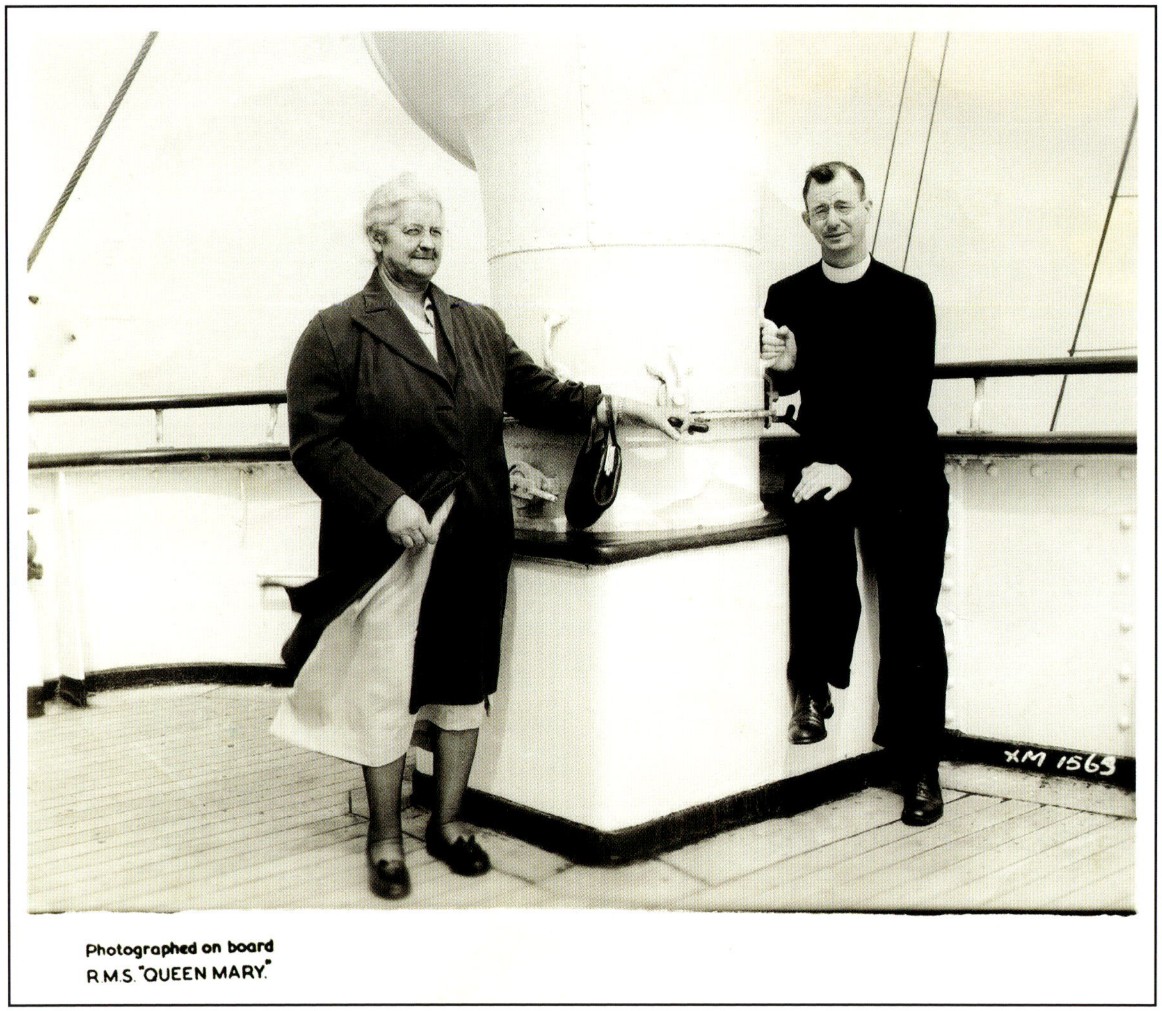

This was the first and only overseas journey for both Madame Chatrian and Father Thensted. Madame's live-in domestic, Mary Louise Charles (page 84), had also been invited, but opted to stay home. Many report that Madame Chatrian, who was a native of South Louisiana, commented on the beauty of the "Bayous of Venice."

Madame Chatrian (1888–1978), a native of Grand Coteau, was married to Frenchman Martin Theodule Chatrian (1867–1942), who owned a farm and a great deal of land in the area. After her husband passed away, she operated the farm. Madame owned two black Cadillacs: one to ride around in town, and another to drive to the field to oversee work on her lands. She had great affection and respect for the Jesuits, especially Father Thensted. Almost daily, Jesuits gathered around the large wooden table in her kitchen to share coffee and homemade pastries for an afternoon of stories and camaraderie.

Originally from New Orleans, Father Thensted was known for his work in the black community from the 1940s through the 1960s. He raised funds for many black institutions, including Grand Coteau's St. Peter Claver Elementary and High School and Christ the King Church. People called Father Thensted "Stepper" because of his high-stepping rapid walk as he scurried off to different projects. As one of his biggest supporters, Madame Chatrian never turned down Father Thensted's requests for donations to cover financial shortfalls to build the church or school.

In this black and white photo a grey-haired woman and a priest pose on opposite sides of a cruise ship smokestack. At the bottom of the photo are the words RMS "Queen Mary." The stout, middle-aged woman stands with hair pulled back, one edge of her dark coat blown open by the wind, and a black purse dangles from one arm. Her solid stance suggests confidence and stability. The slender priest who is dressed in black except for the white collar, appears younger than the woman. Half-perched on a ledge, one leg extends to the floor. His posture suggests restlessness, as though with the click of the shutter, he might stride off in another direction. However, both offer the relaxed smiles of a trusting friendship.

In 1949, Father Cornelius J. Thensted (1903–1981) gave this photograph of himself and Madame Theresa Bajat Chatrian to his friend Lawrence Xavier Taylor, Sr., organist at the local African American church, Christ the King. Thensted had just returned from a cruise to Italy with Madame Chatrian to visit the Pope Pius XII.

Many in the white community disapproved of the efforts that Father Thensted invested in the African American community. In the 1960s, Father Thensted waged a campaign for equal pay for blacks who worked the sweet potato kilns–they received less compensation than their white counterparts. In response, a secret meeting was called for whites in the community to discuss a way to drive Father Thensted out of town. Madame Chatrian got wind of the meeting and showed up, threatening that if they so much as touched him, she would call in all of the many loans she had made to white farmers in the area. This threat quieted the room, and the drive to get rid of Thensted faded.

In 1982, the year after Father Thensted's death, Sister Margaret "Mike" Hoffman, RSCJ, founded the Thensted Center in order to continue his legacy of helping the disadvantaged. The Thensted Center strives to empower the community through after-school tutoring and summer enrichment programs for youth, educational programs for the elderly, and many other services.

Acknowledgments

Thanks to the Citizens of Grand Coteau, past and present. Without them, there would be no book.

Special thanks to Patrice Melnick, Phil Schneider, Hilary Slaughter, and James Wilson for their generous help in producing this book.

In appreciation for their assistance and/or encouragement: Nancy Brewer, Darrell Burleigh, Jimmy Dauzat, Philip Gould, Hunt Greene, Robert Guidry, Dosier Hammond, Leroy Hillyard, Sister Lynne Lieux, Elizabeth Lyles, Michael Martin, John Mikell, Jesse Poimboeuf, Cynthia Prather, Melissa Teutsch, Olan Thibodeaux, and Jeanette Williams.

Finally let me express my gratitude to everyone who appears in *Grand Coteau* and to all who helped along the way.

John Slaughter

Thank-you to the following people who have generously shared their time and knowledge of Grand Coteau and the community:

Etha Simien Amling, Charles Andrus, Pamela Barriere, Cynthia Bellemin, Margaret Brinkhaus, Darrell Burleigh, Sidney Creaghan, Joseoh Eaglin, Mavis Fruge, Jane Gagner, Ruby Gardner, Charles James, Anne Marie Jean, Rose Johnson, Ulysses Johnson, Father James Lambert, Gail Lark, Cecile Laurence, Brother Alcide Joseph Martin, Rosalyn Garrett Mayfield, Gregory Miller, Sister Alice Mills RSCJ, Mary V. Murray, Father Jerome Neyrey, John Olivier, Julie Olivier, Eleanor Ramirez, John Tate, Father Mark E. Thibodeaux, and Olan Thibodeaux.

Patrice Melnick

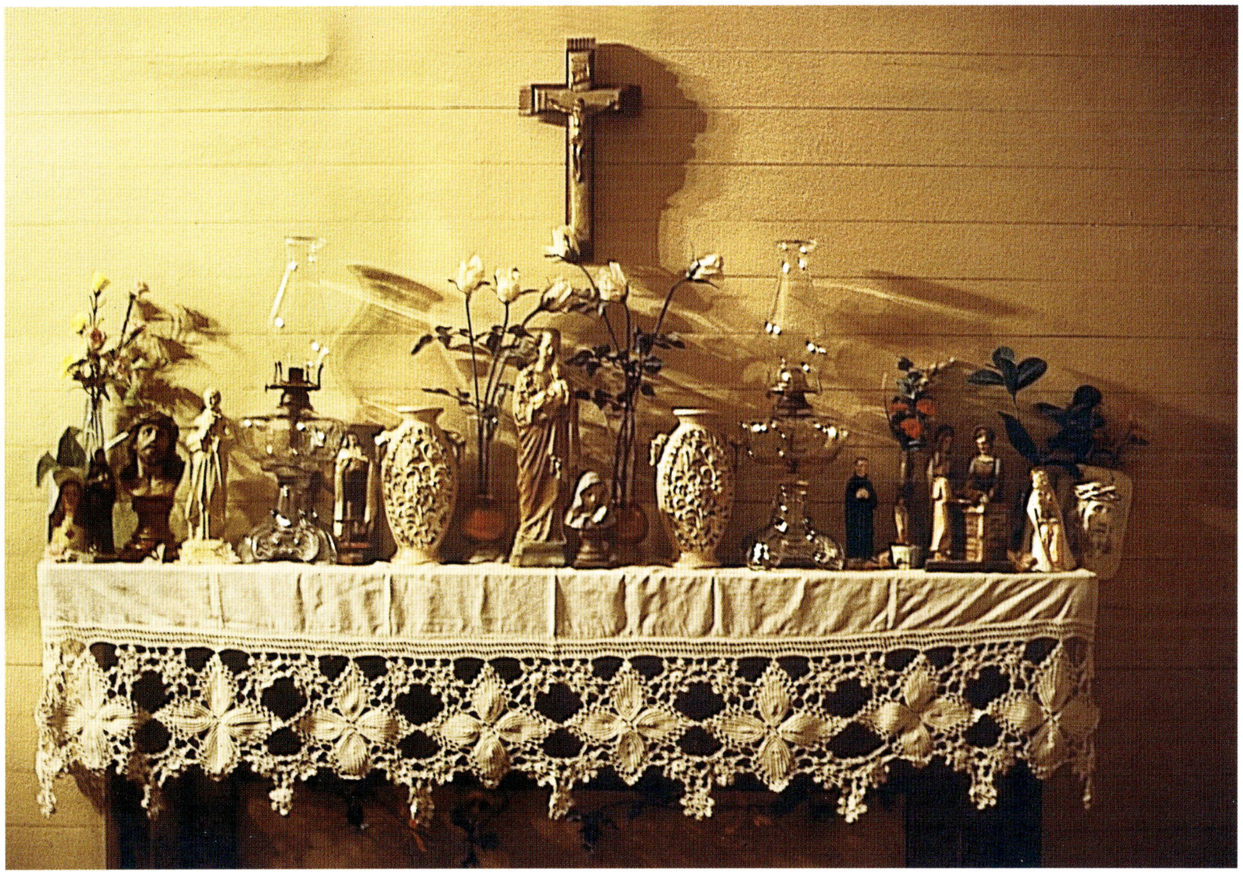

Madame Chatrian's Mantle
1990

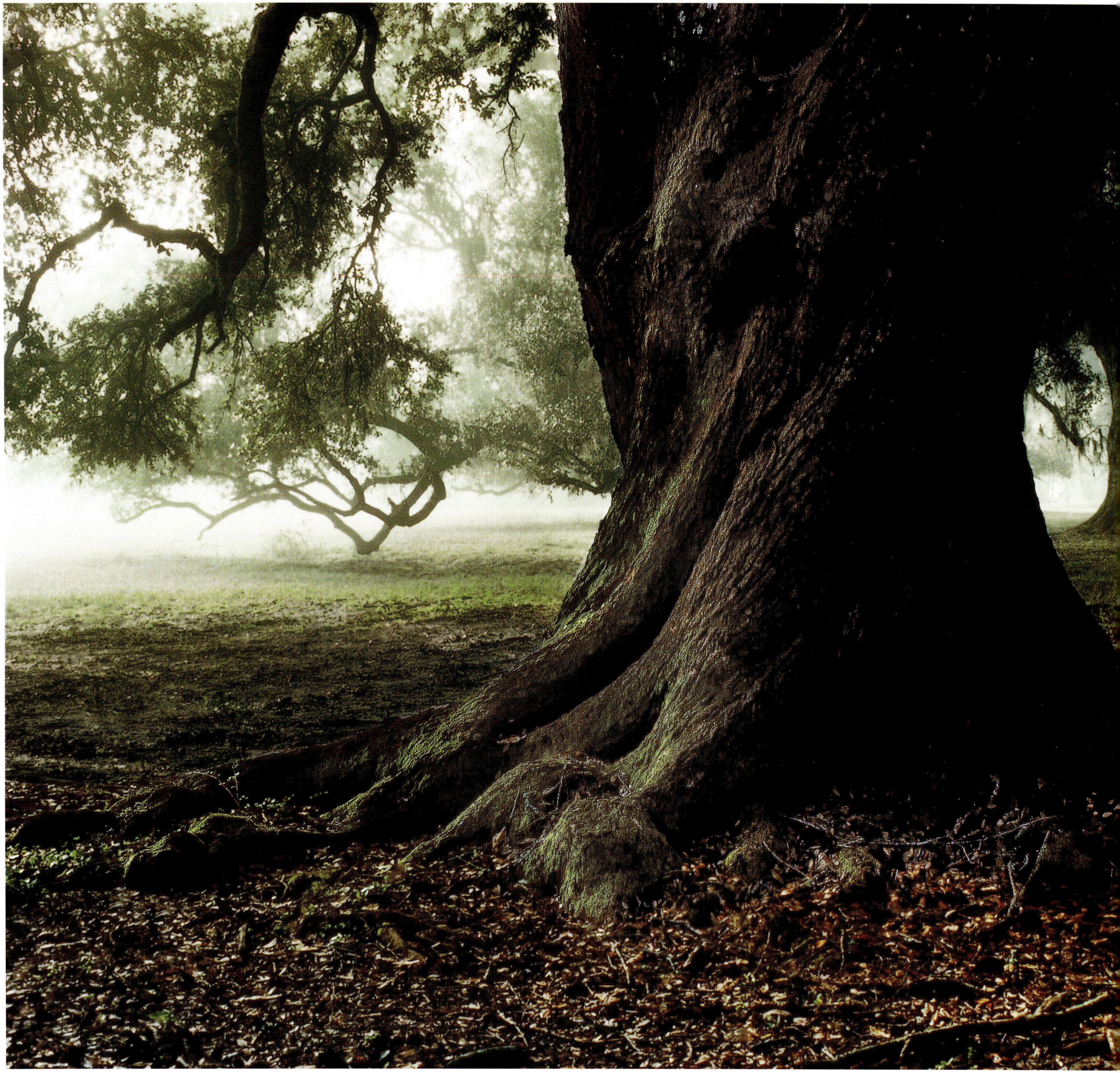

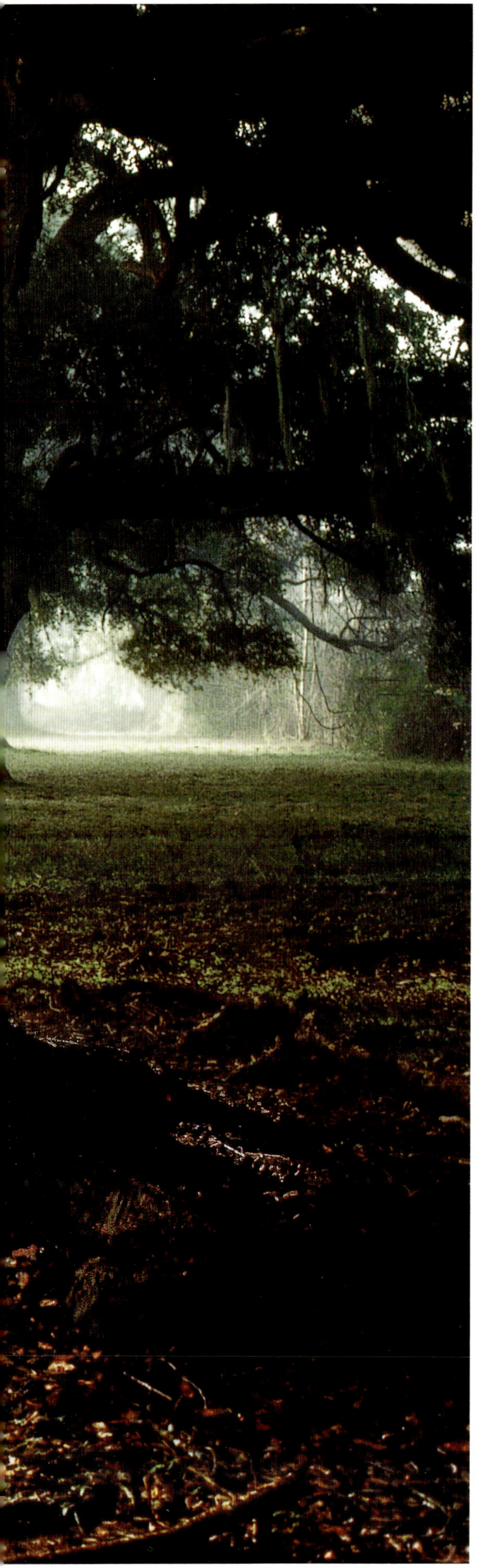

Grand Coteau

Big Ridge

Ruby and Bill Foraz
1977

Ruby Prudhomme Foraz (1919–1987) and William Anthony Foraz (1906–1983), are shown working on an addition to their home, which was originally built in 1869 by Bill's grandfather, Andre David Meche. The majority of the material came from a house near Gradnigo Island that Ruby inherited and which they subsequently dismantled. A carpenter was hired to do the framing, but the couple wanted to do the finish work themselves. Bill's second cousin Robert Guidry and his wife Lubie currently live there and have maintained the home's unpainted rustic elegance. (Also see pages 18 and 24.)

PHOTOGRAPHER'S NOTE: Ruby and Bill seemed to be from a former age; they were the proverbial "salt of the earth" types—hard working, self-reliant, and proud of their heritages. Ruby once told me they "had capital." If you visited them, you most likely would be offered some homemade wine.

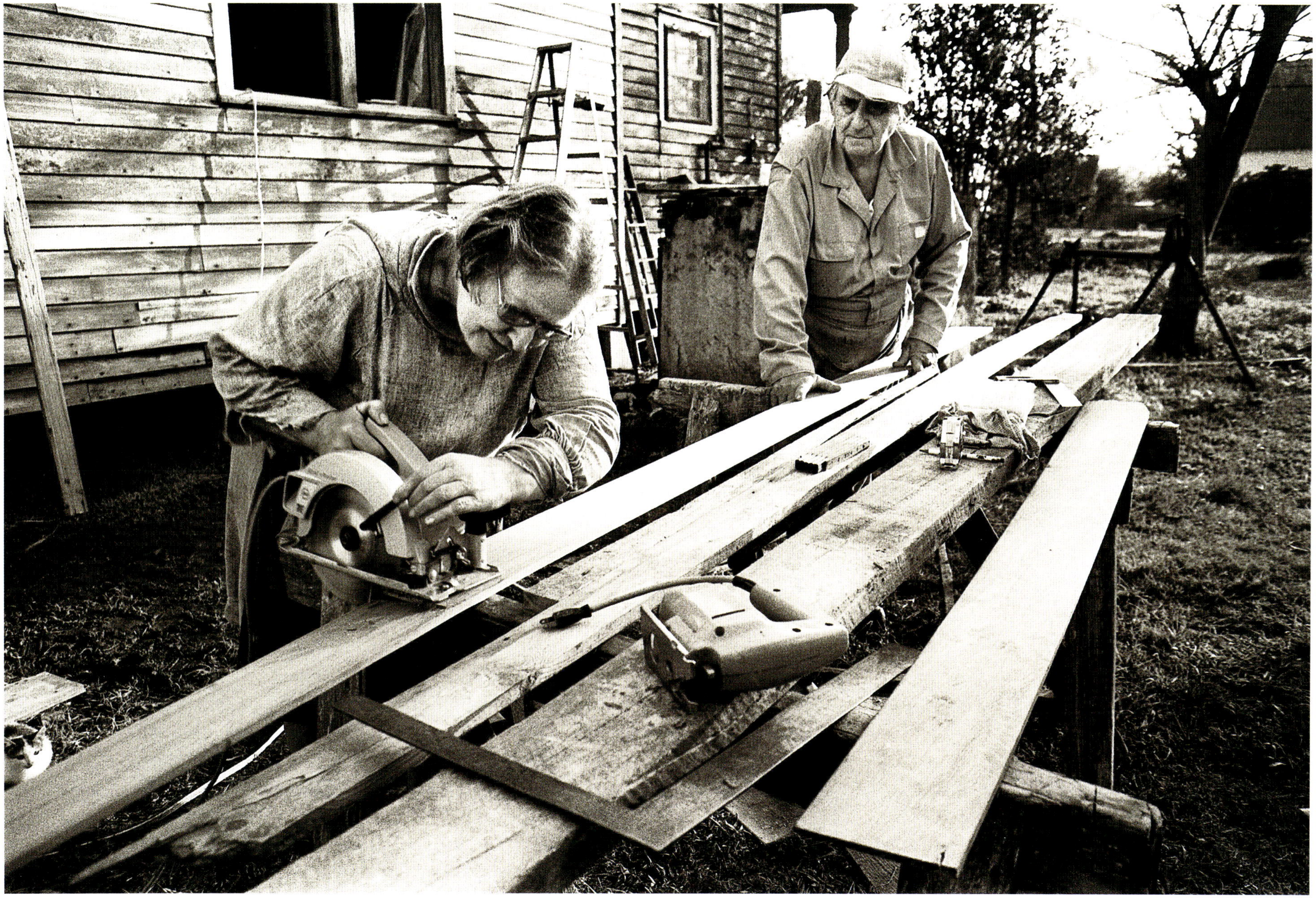

GROTTO – ST. CHARLES COLLEGE

1977

The Grotto on the grounds of St. Charles College is a replica of the original in Lourdes, France. Jesuit Scholastics constructed the Lourdes Grotto in honor of the Blessed Mother who appeared eighteen times to the young peasant girl, Bernadette Soubirous, between February and July in 1858.

The grotto project in Grand Coteau began May 20, 1926, and was completed on the Feast of Our Lady of Lourdes, February 11, 1928. Materials used include brick columns for support and a network of gas pipes attached at different angles. Finally, the structure was overlaid with sturdy wire and cement to form the "mountain." The statues of the Blessed Mother and Bernadette in the grotto came from St. Stanislaus College in Macon, Georgia, after it closed.

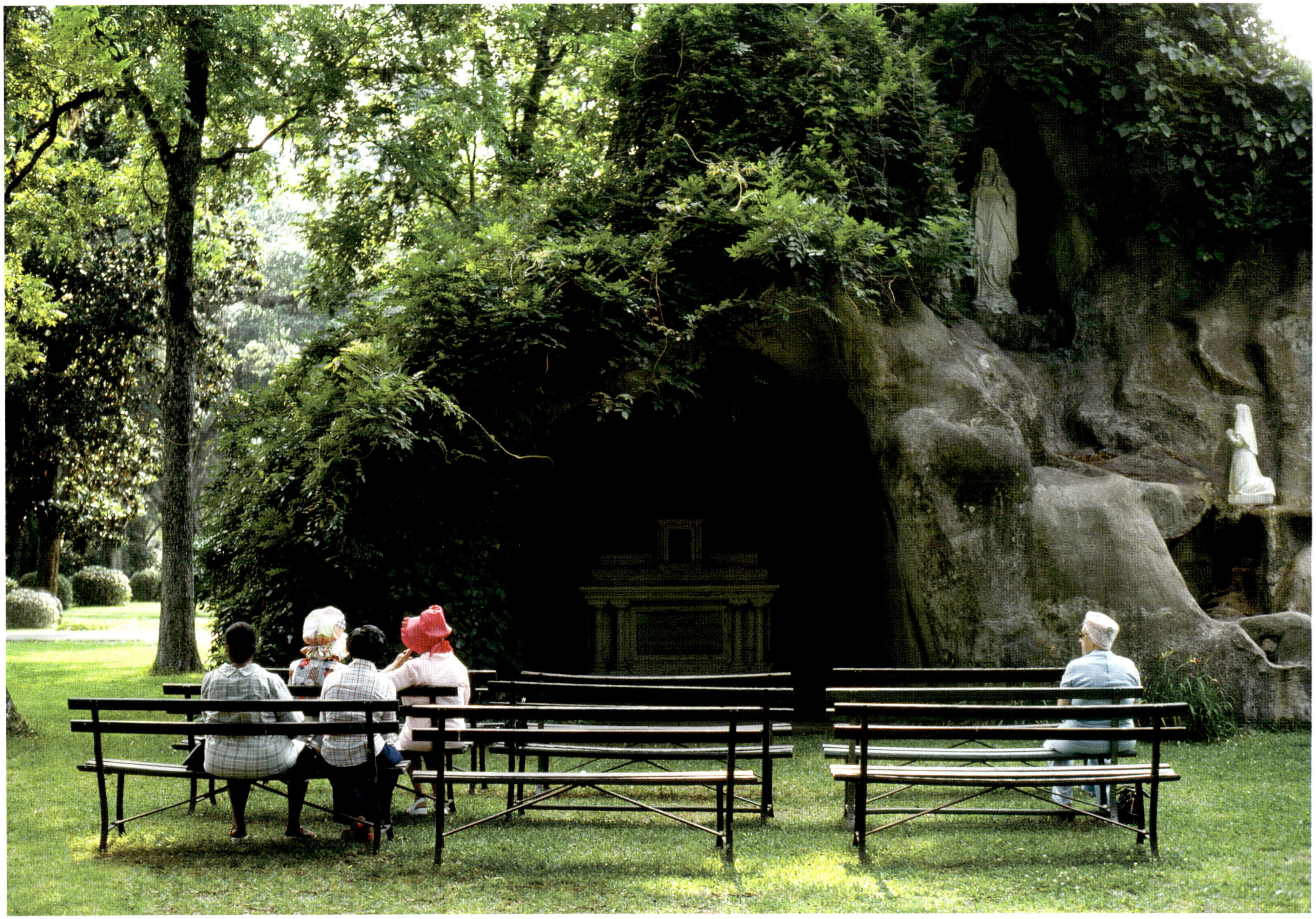

Shooting Marbles – St. Ignatius School
1978

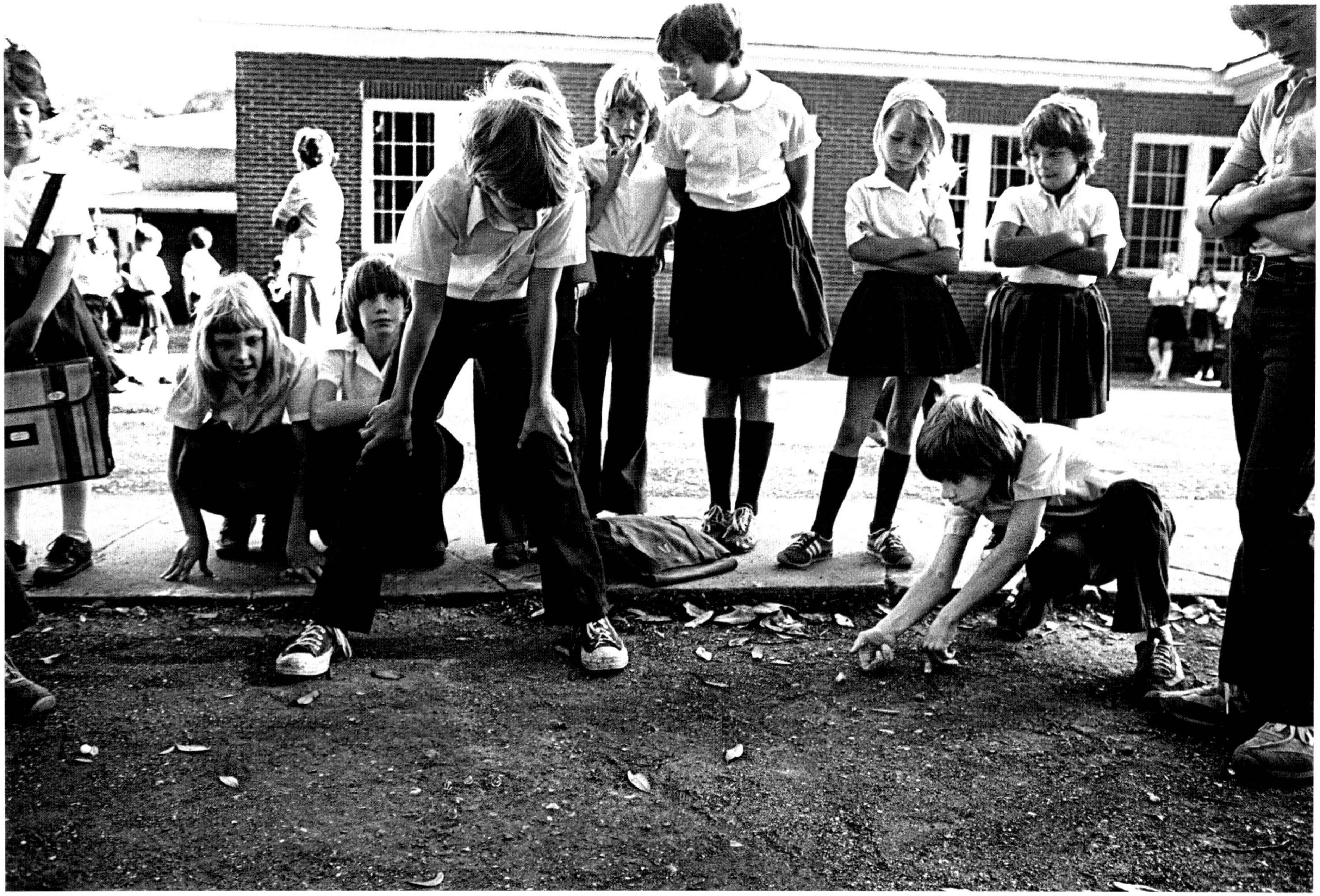

Congé – Academy of the Sacred Heart

1978

Mother Marie Odeide Mouton (1896–1993) and Sister Corinne Happy (1901–1984) enjoy the Congé at the Academy of the Sacred Heart. Coming from the French word meaning "holiday," the congé tradition began in the mid-1800s. Held in the springtime, it gives students a break from classes. Traditionally, parents came to visit their daughters and children played games like *cache-cashe*, a form of hide-and-seek. Congé takes place at Sacred Heart schools all over the country. The schools consider the congé an opportunity for fundraising through the sale of art, crafts, books, and food, plus a silent auction.

Sister Mouton (right) was born on the Souvenir Plantation in Donaldsonville, Louisiana. Although most novices enter the convent at age eighteen, she delayed joining the Religious of the Sacred Heart until 1927 after she had helped raise her three younger brothers. Possessing a brilliant mind, she served as President of Maryville College from 1937 to 1956 and as an archivist, retreat director, and leader of school tours at the Academy of the Sacred Heart later in her life. She adored dogs and was known to slip a bone from the dining hall into her pocket to pass on to one of the campus dogs.

Born in St. Charles, Missouri, Sister Happy (left), served as Treasurer at the Academy for a brief time and taught elementary school at Marryville, Louisiana. At the time of this photo, Sister Happy had moved away and had returned for visit.

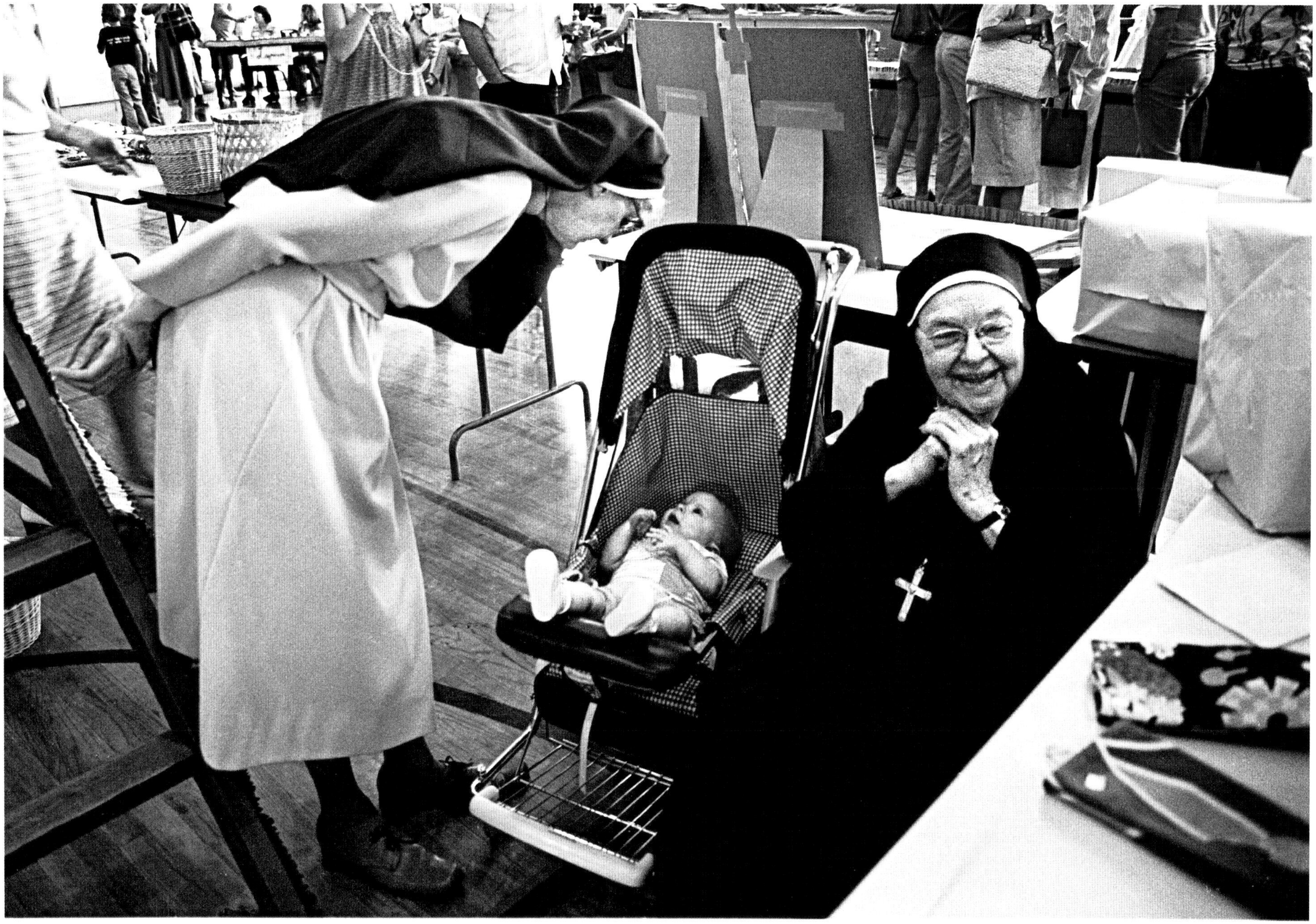

The Red House
1978

There was a fire in the attic, and this photo depicts the reconstruction. Notice the pile of wooden shingles that have been removed. There is evidence that the house may have been moved to its present location. (Also see page 110.)

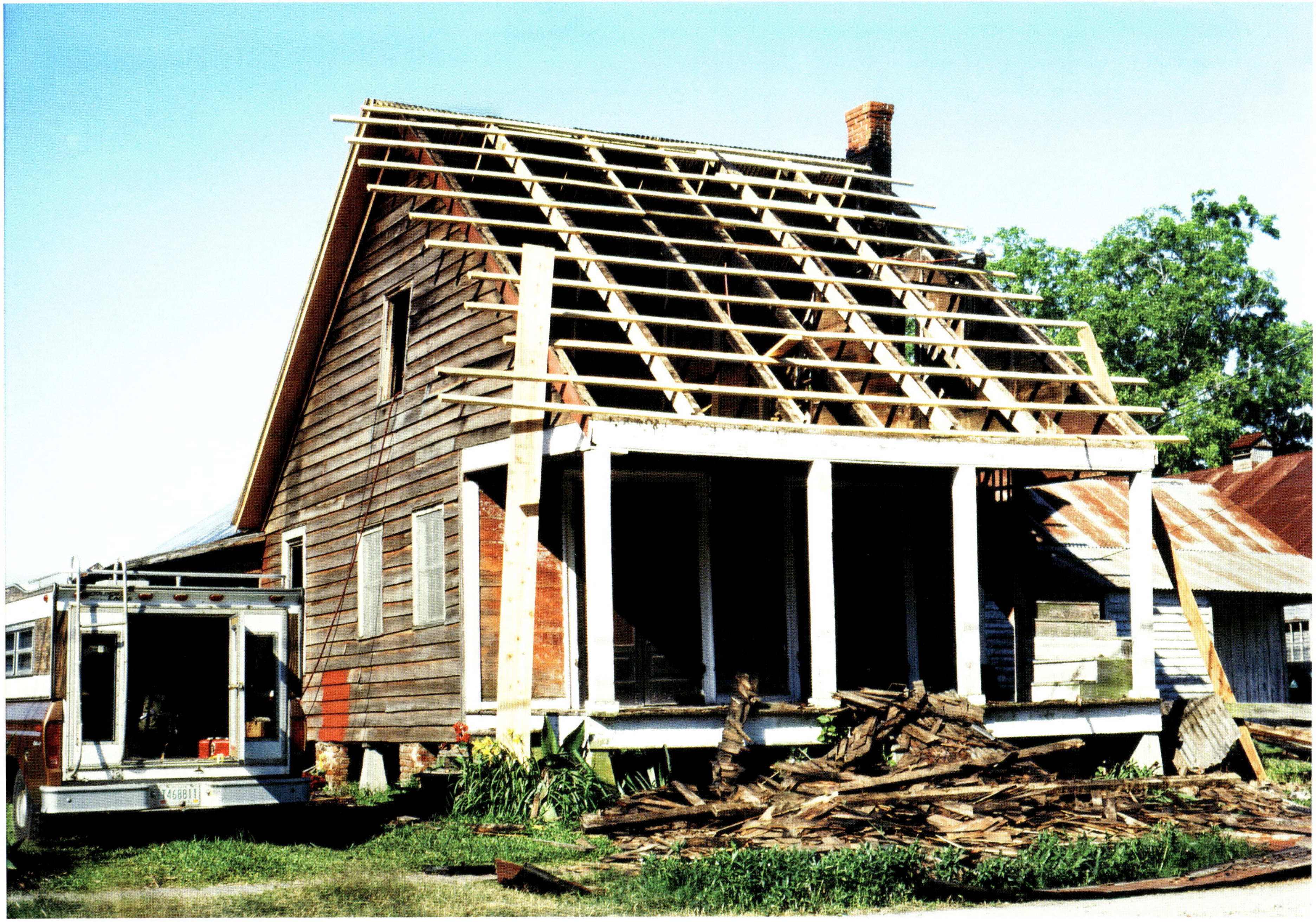

HOUSE FIRE – FEBRUARY 7, 1978
1978

PHOTOGRAPHER'S NOTE: While returning from my job with the *Opelousas Daily World* newspaper, I spotted a huge smoke plume and proceeded to the source. It was a home I had never seen before as it stood a half-mile off the street. With no fire hydrant, the limited on-board capacity of the town's fire truck was no match for the blaze. As you can see in the photograph, the fire truck actually got stuck and a backhoe was used to pull it out. I shot almost exclusively black-and-white for the newspaper, but I usually carried a camera loaded with color slide film for personal use. Thus the front page included the black-and-white, and here we have the color image.

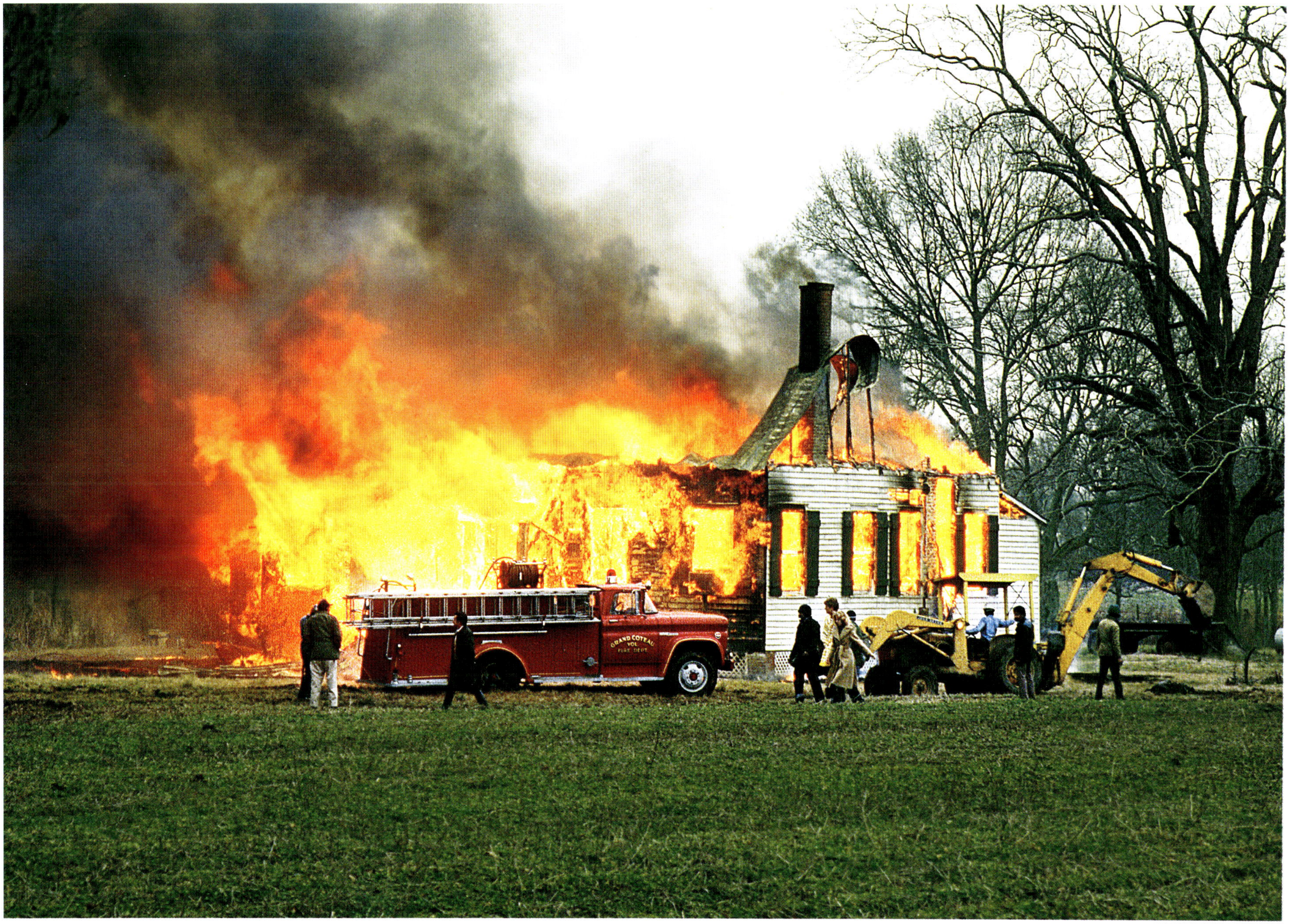
GRAND COTEAU
VOL

ST. CHARLES CEMETERY – OLD JESUIT SECTION
1978

The Old Jesuit Cemetery includes headstones that date back to the mid-1800s. In addition to the graves of Grand Coteau priests, when the St. Stanislaus Koska novitiate located in Macon, Georgia closed in 1927, the remains of Jesuits in its cemetery were reinterred in Grand Coteau.

PHOTOGRAPHER'S NOTE: I recall using a tripod and taking a few shots when for a brief moment the scene became luminescent. I got prepared for the next time it would happen and made this one-second exposure. Thus I learned that when photographing fogscapes in color, the ideal moment often comes when the sun is just breaking through.

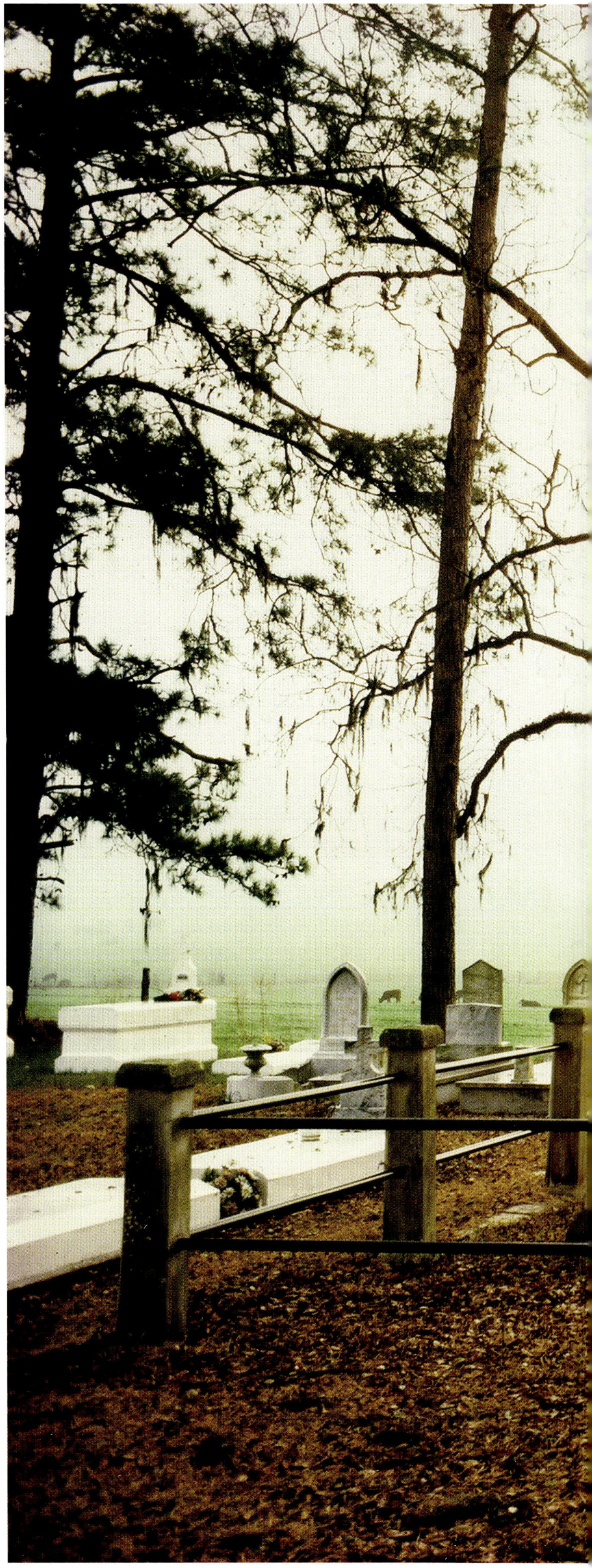

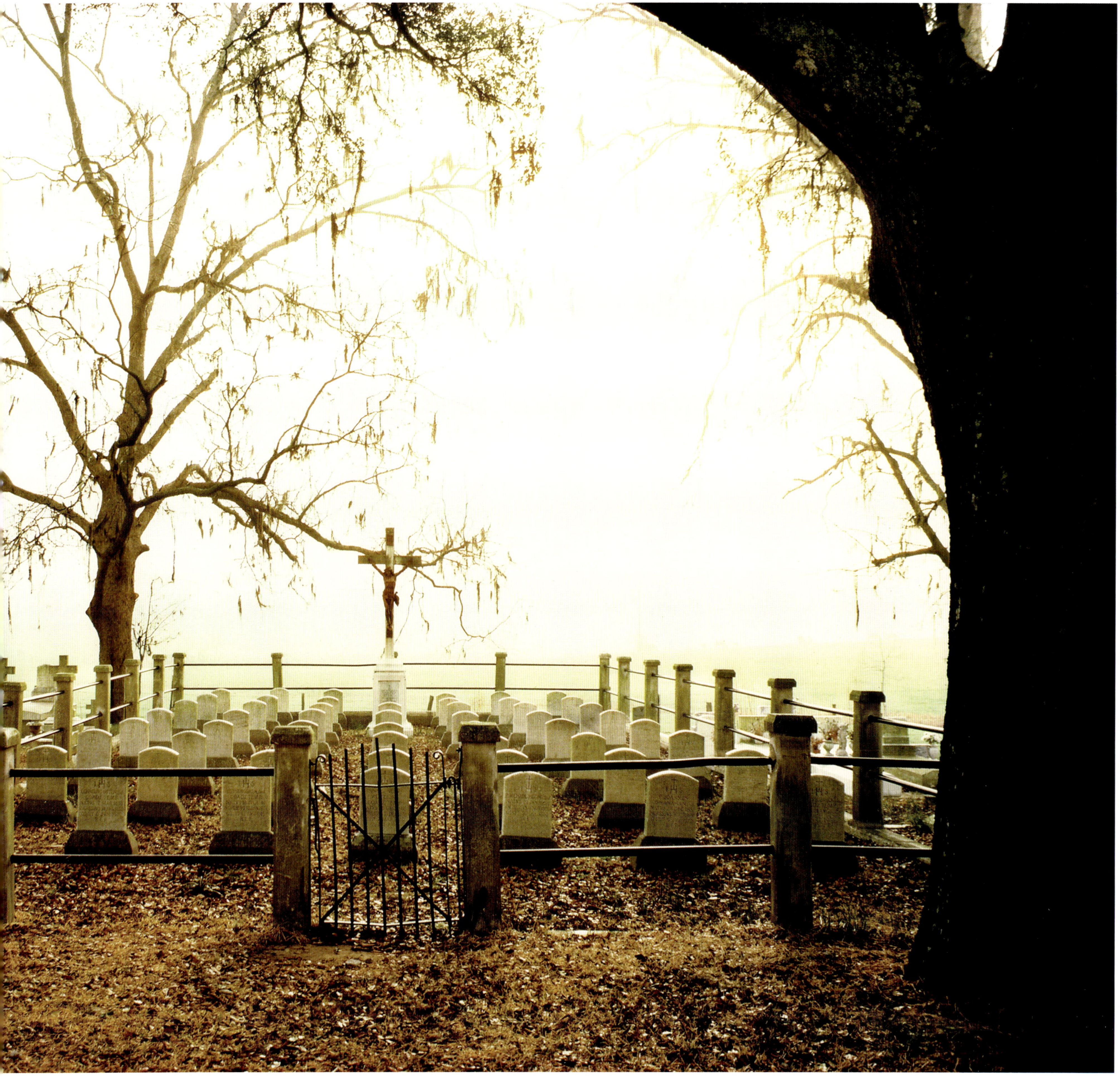

Louise Eugenia Bellemin

1978

Louise Eugenia Bellemin (1916–2011) crochets while watching the family grocery store, built in 1965 by her son Leroy, or "Blue." She often crocheted intricate bedspreads, tablecloths, doilies, and dresses. Locals know the store as Boy Blue's, and it is still operated by her sons, "Blue" and Michael.

Louise was born into the Pelafigue family in Arnaudville, where her family cultivated cotton, corn, and Irish and sweet potatoes, while also raising cattle. During the Great Mississippi Flood of 1927, she came to Grand Coteau, and decided to remain, staying with friends. She eventually met her husband, Michael Claude Bellemin, and had four children. Louise was a devout Catholic and would sometimes visit elderly neighbors to pray the rosary.

She loved gardening and brought rose bushes from Arnaudville. Her yard was filled with flowers like gladiolas and amaryllis. As the plants multiplied, she generously shared bulbs and cuttings with friends and neighbors. Today the front yard still abounds with blooms almost year round.

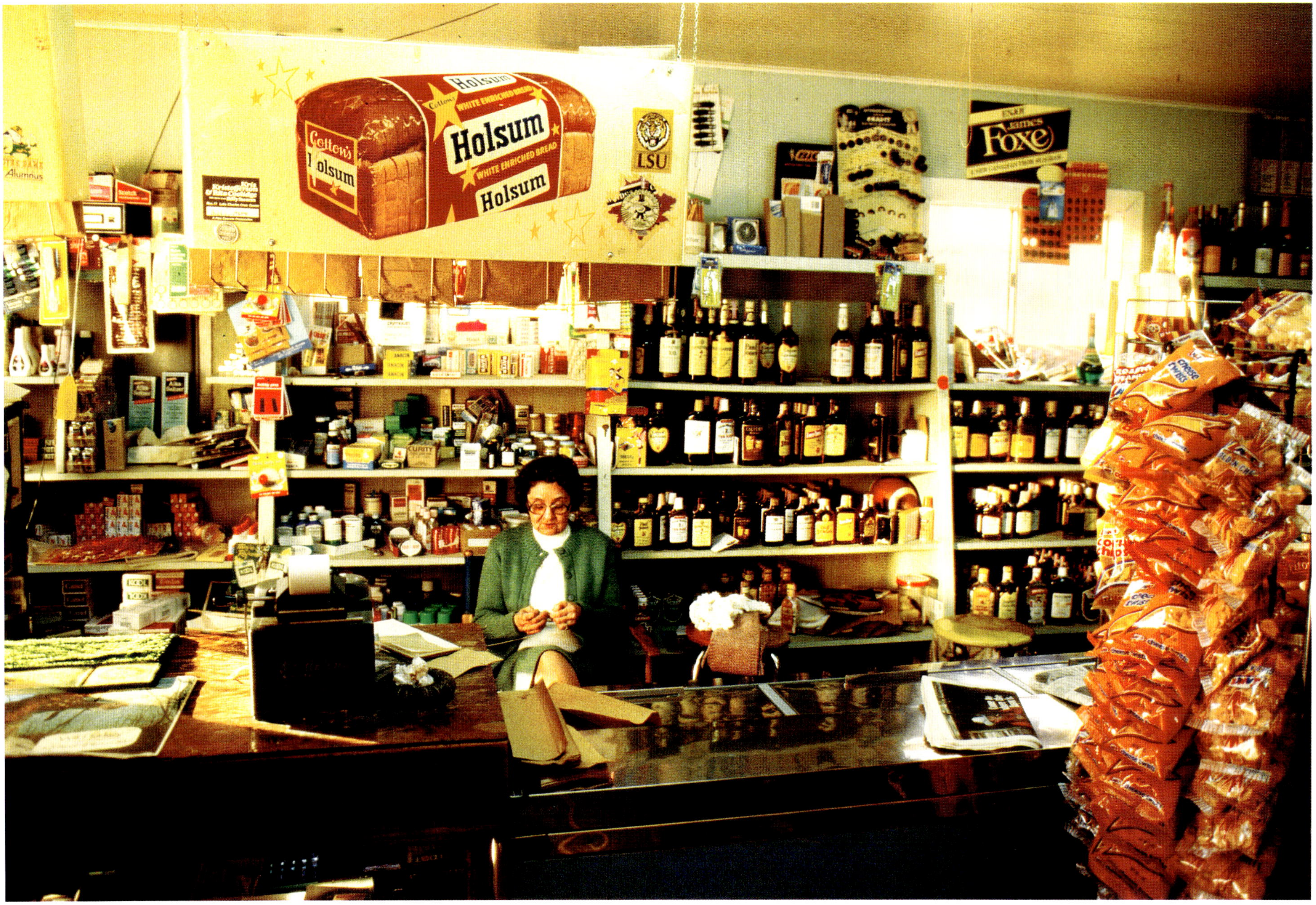
Holsum
Cotton's
Holsum
WHITE ENRICHED BREAD
Holsum
WHITE ENRICHED BREAD
Holsum
LSU
ENJOY
James
Foxe
Alumnus

Foraz House

1979

When entering Grand Coteau from the west, this is one of the first structures that indicates that you have entered the historic district, which encompasses over seventy buildings listed on the National Register of Historic Places. (Also see pages 2 and 24.)

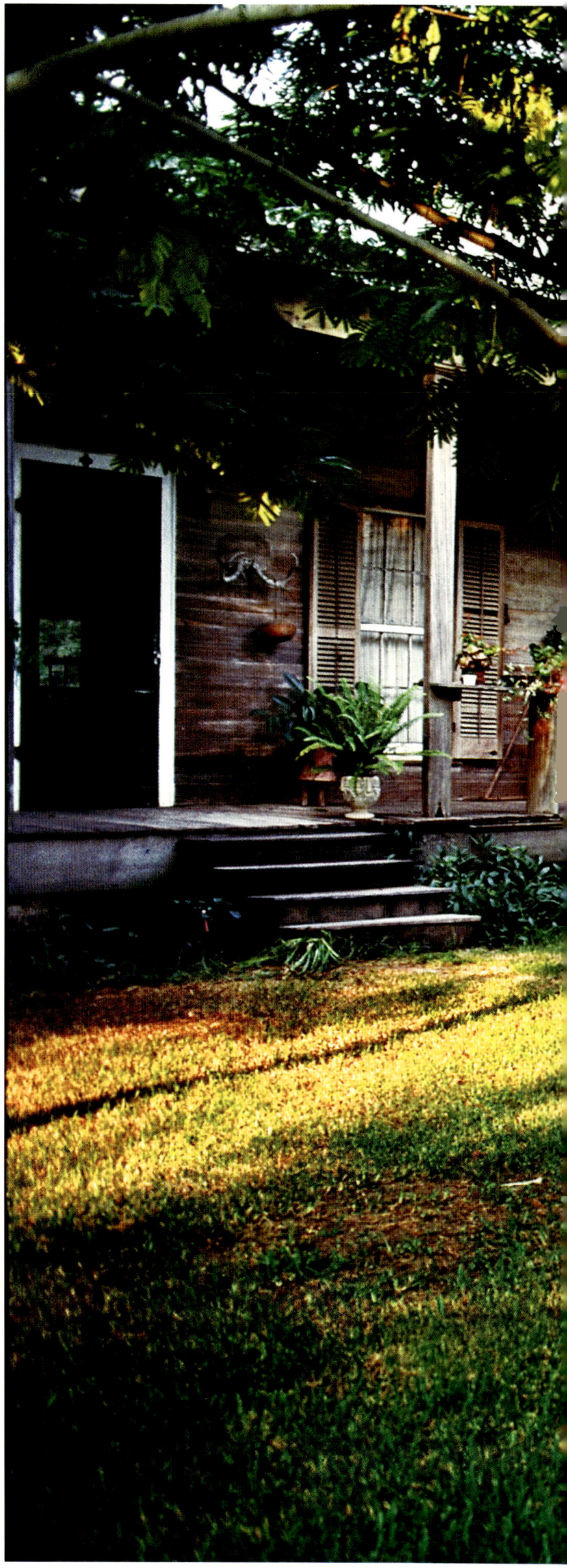

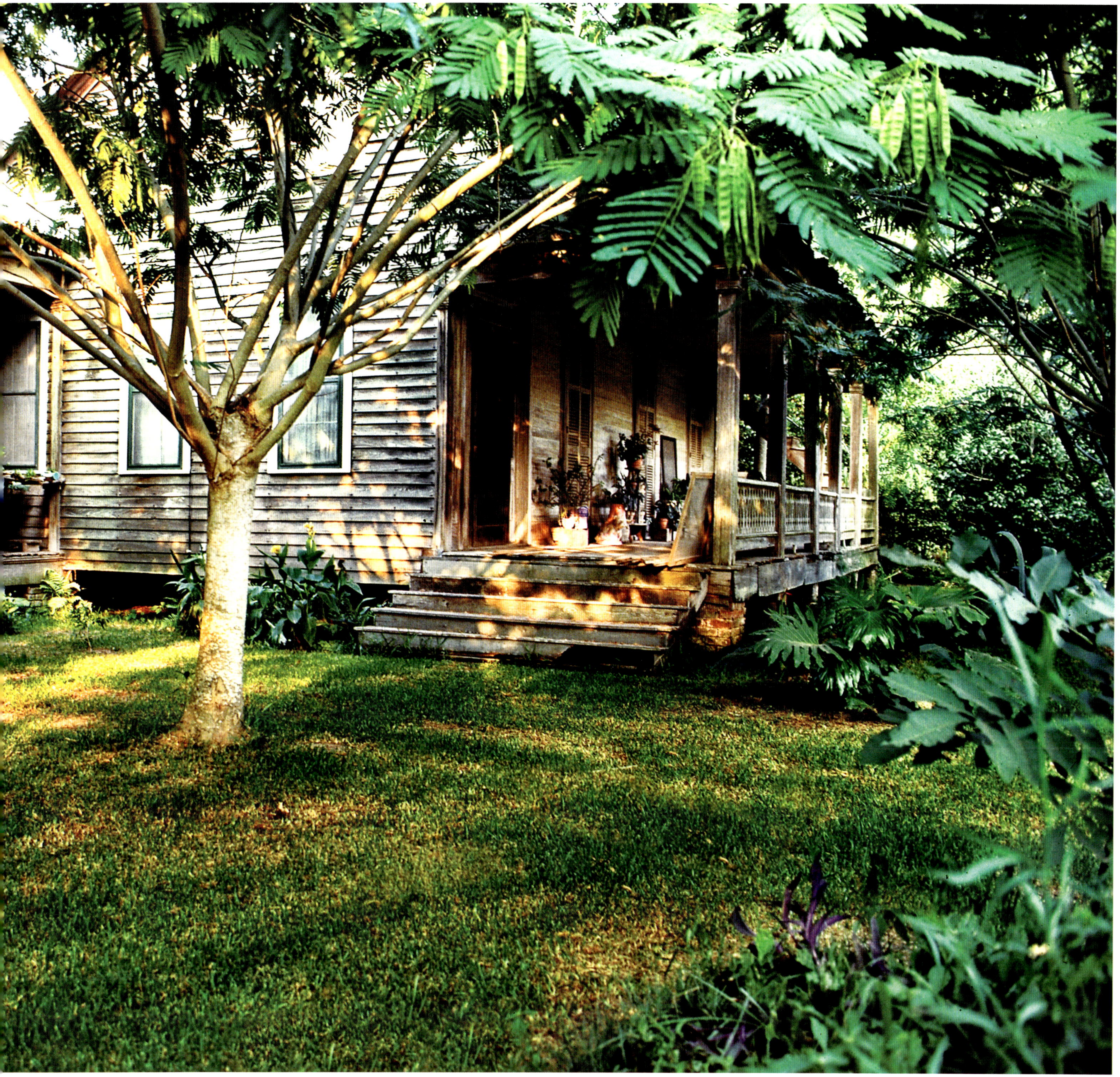

Frances Barriere
1979

While sitting on her porch, Frances Barriere (1909–1989) cleans fish probably caught by her husband, Wilfred "Beck" Barriere (see page 48). She was born in Prairie Basse, one of eleven children, and attended St. Peter Claver Elementary through the seventh grade. She worked at St. Charles College doing laundry for several years before finding employment in the infirmary at Sacred Heart. Barriere was a member of the Ladies Auxiliary of St. Peter Claver and of the Legion of Mary. Humble and soft-spoken, she enjoyed baking pies, cookies, and popcorn balls for her children and their friends. After Barriere retired, her daughter purchased land in Grand Coteau and relocated from New York, moving a house onto the property for her parents.

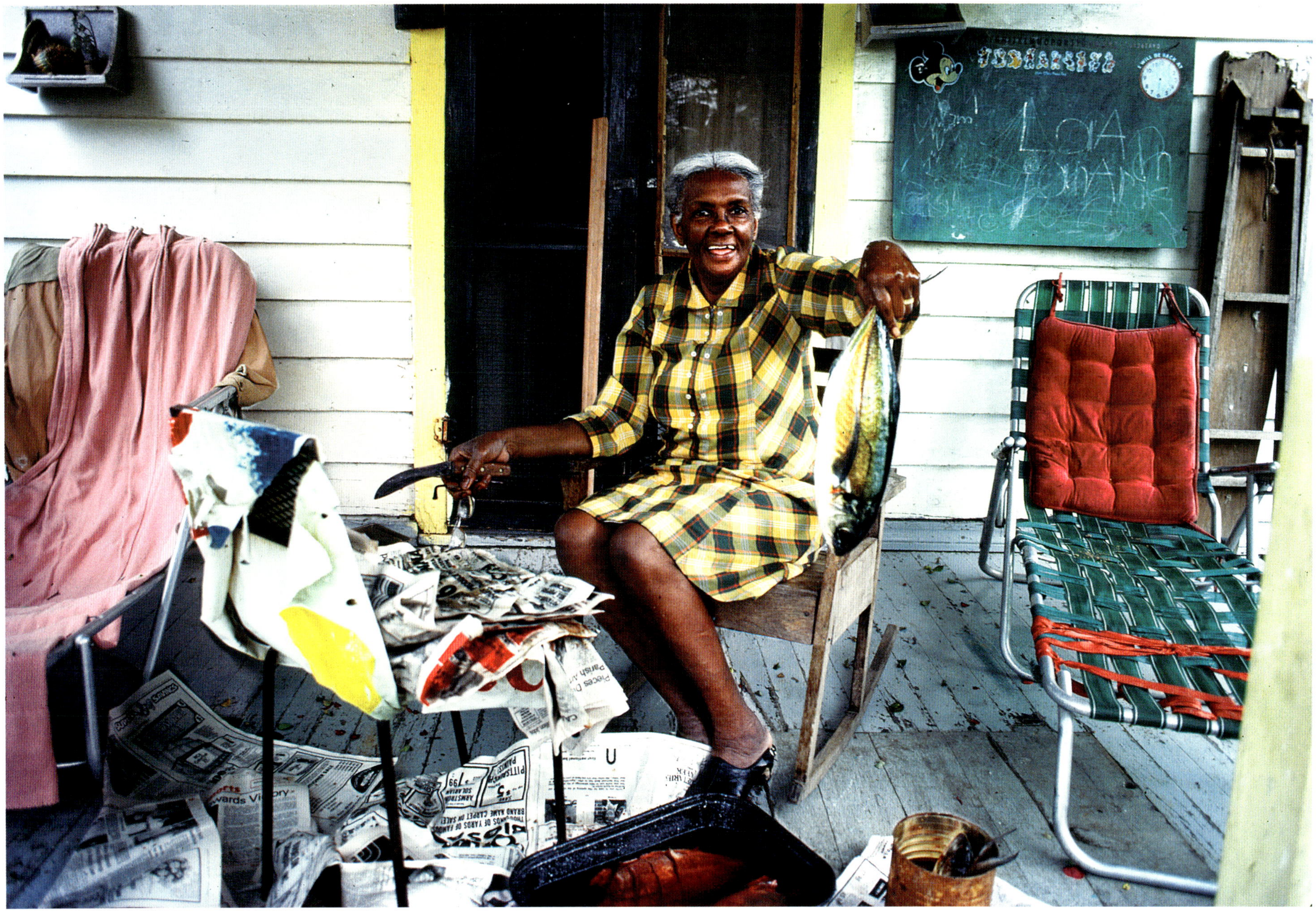

Festival de Grand Coteau
1979

Sister Alice Kock (1893–1985) and Mother Eleanor Adams (1918–2007), sisters of the Sacred Heart, enjoy the antique car show at the festival. In this image of contrast, the older, outgoing Sister Alice stands close beside the younger, soft-spoken Sister Adams.

Sister Kock, also known as "Tante Alice," grew up in Donaldsonville, Louisiana, and claimed to be one of the first women in Louisiana outside of New Orleans to drive a car. She grew up on her family's sugar plantation, Belle Alliance, which was built in 1846 by Charles Anton Kock, a wealthy German immigrant. Alice Kock attended St. Michael's school on River Road near Convent, Louisiana, a popular school for plantation girls, and afterwards she entered the novitiate. Because of her southern belle background, she underwent a difficult transition as a novice. Gregarious by nature, she could no longer socialize in the cloistered culture of nuns who followed a strict rule of silence within the walls of the convent.

Sister Adams, originally from St. Louis, Missouri, was highly educated and served as Academy treasurer for many years. In later years she was Director of the Retired Religious for the convent at the Academy of the Sacred Heart.

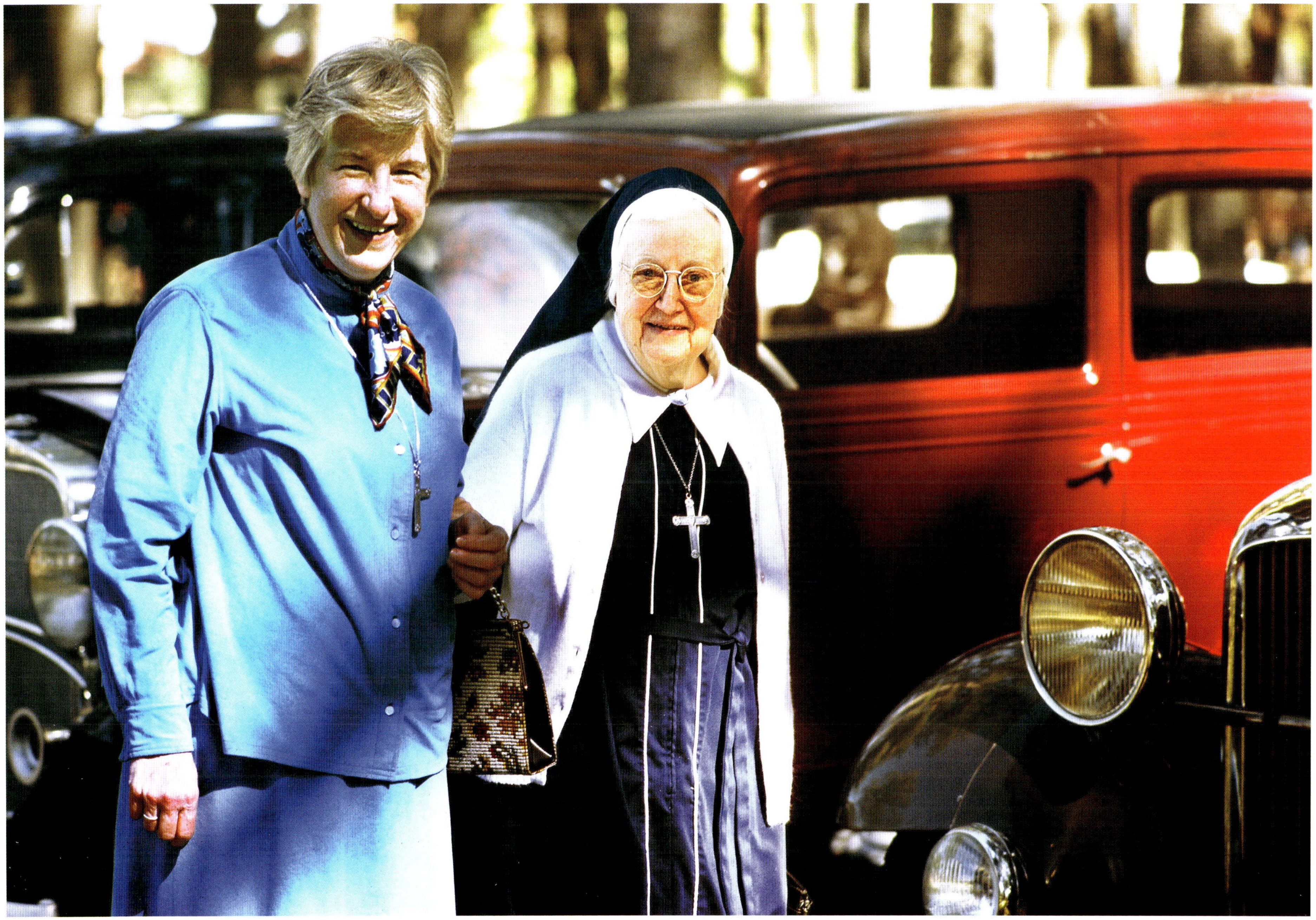

Foraz House Porch
1979

(Also see pages 2 and 24.)

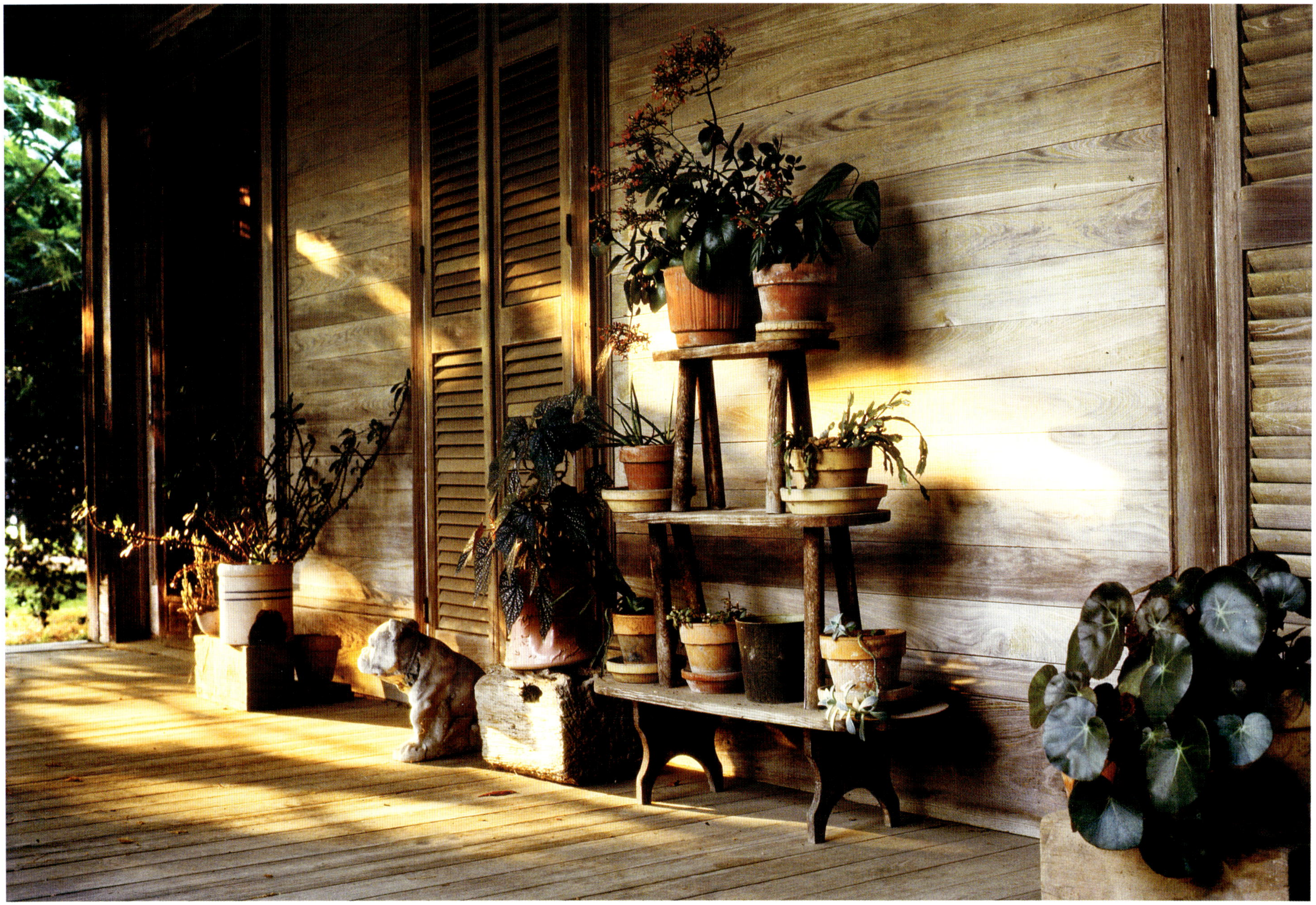

Gardiner Street Store

1979

Emma Meche and her father, Charles, opened their store and butcher shop in 1925. The meat market sold fresh pork and beef, as well as locally made sausage; the store carried items such as beans, rice, peas, and canned goods. Even on sweltering summer days, meat stayed cold and fresh in a metal ice box the size of a walk-in closet. It could hold a one-hundred-pound block of ice, which was delivered from Opelousas several times a week.

Emma married Odell Andrus, who later ran the business alongside his father-in-law. The store and market closed in 1965.

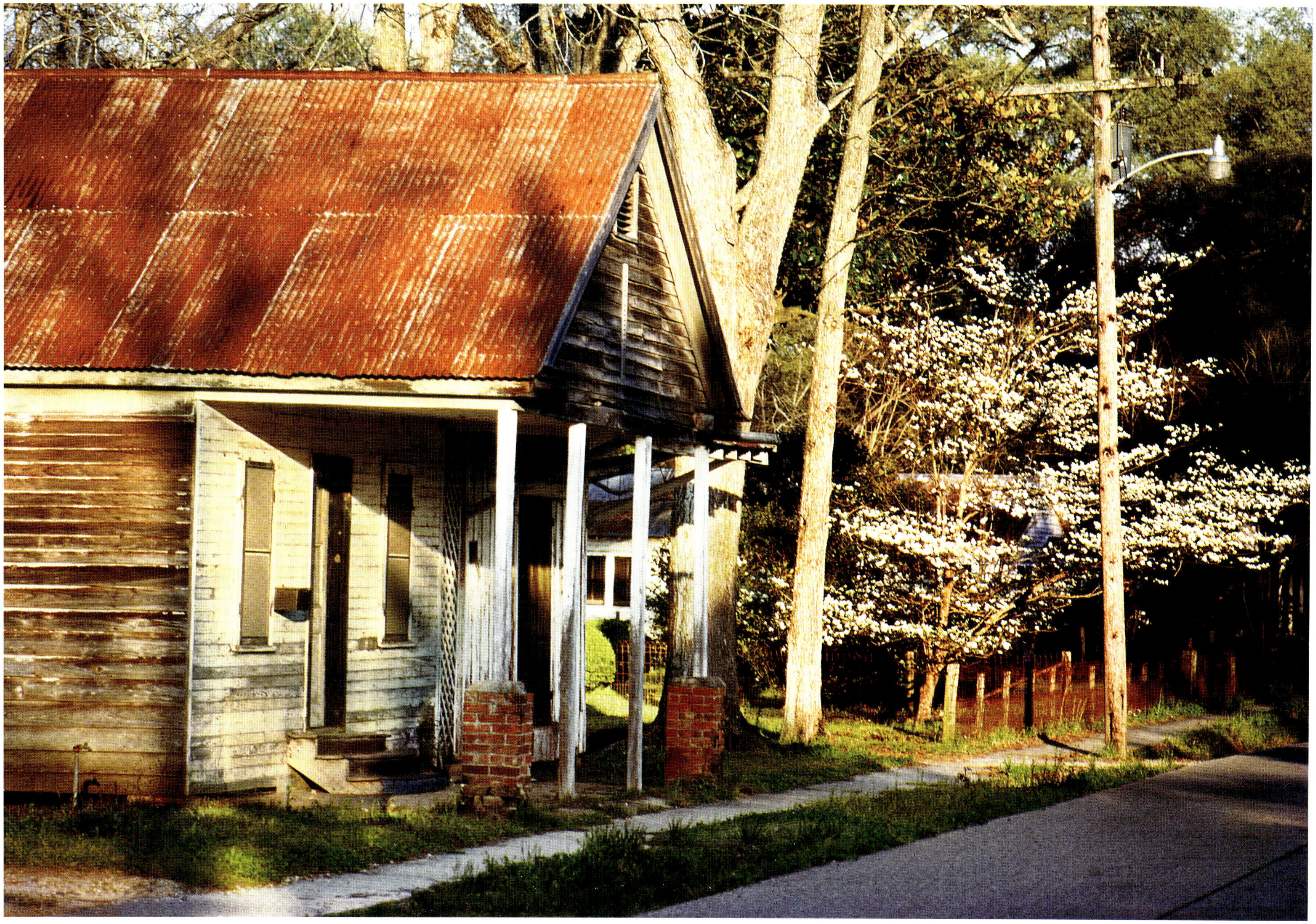

PORCH CAT

1979

PHOTOGRAPHER'S NOTE: We rented this house from 1977 to 1980. It's tucked away at the end of Savoy Lane and up the hill. I surmise that originally it had a bat and board exterior, but in time the bats were removed and replaced by pressed tin. I fixed the termite-damaged floor in one room, rewired the entire house, dug a septic tank by hand, and erected a TV aerial so we could get PBS from Baton Rouge. We made-do with a wood heater and a small fire place when, due to rain, the propane truck couldn't get in. We enjoyed Buster, the horse, even after he ate seven cantaloupes off the backseat of our Volkswagen. It was a wonderful three years despite, or even because of, no phone.

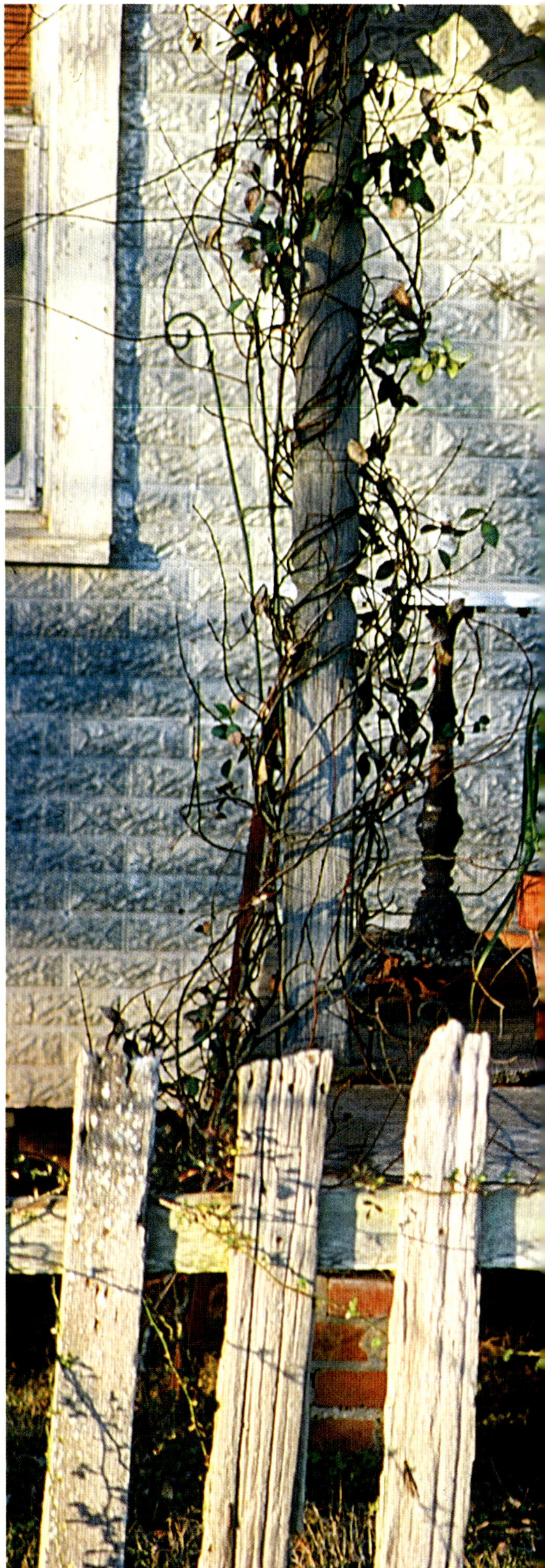

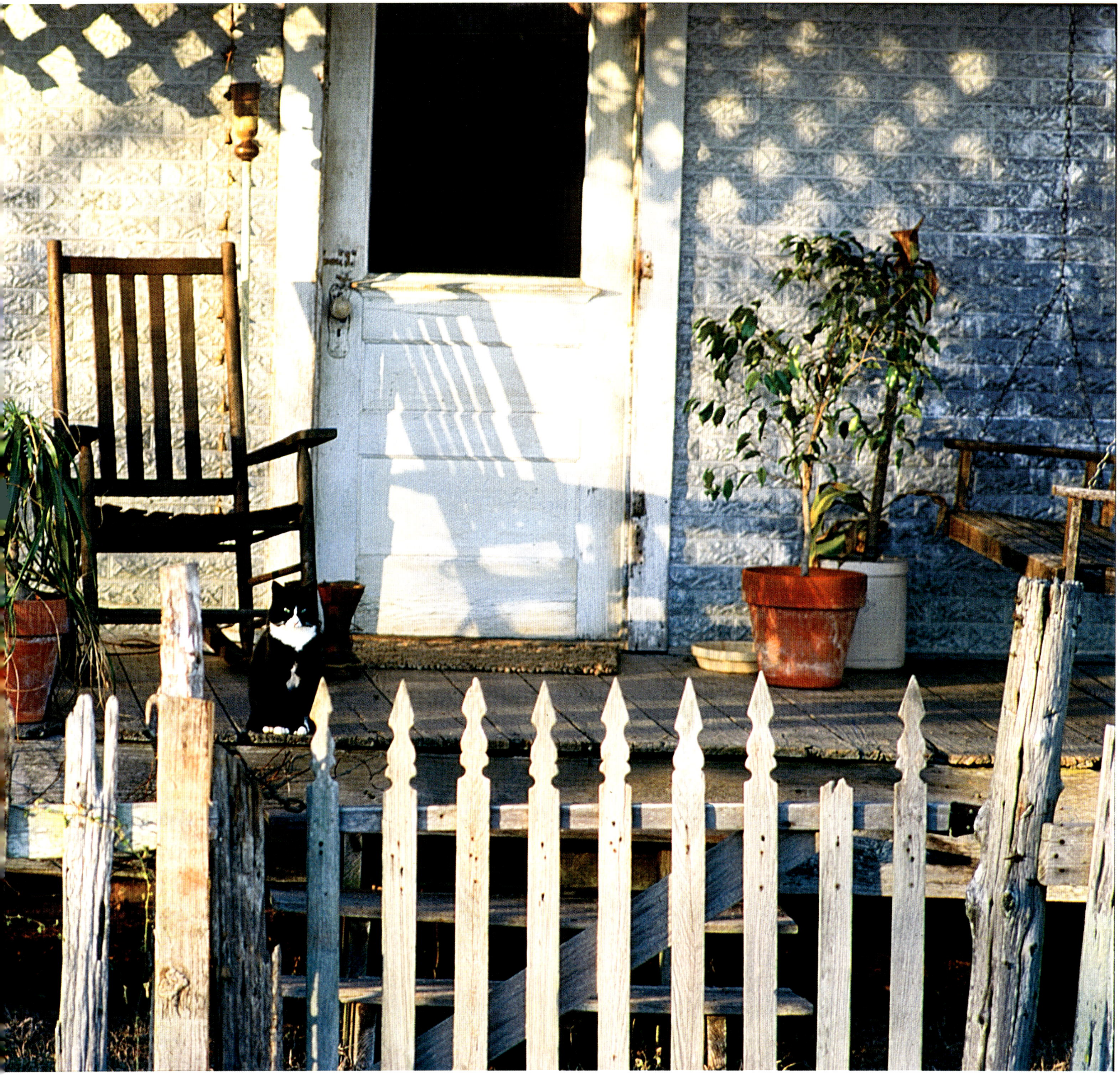

Loren Hurst
1979

Photographer's Note: Our family lived in the house depicted on the previous page. It's in the town's limits, but quite remote. During heavy rains the road would flood. We would anticipate the situation and park the car on the dry side, requiring a wade-out if you wanted to get to school on time.

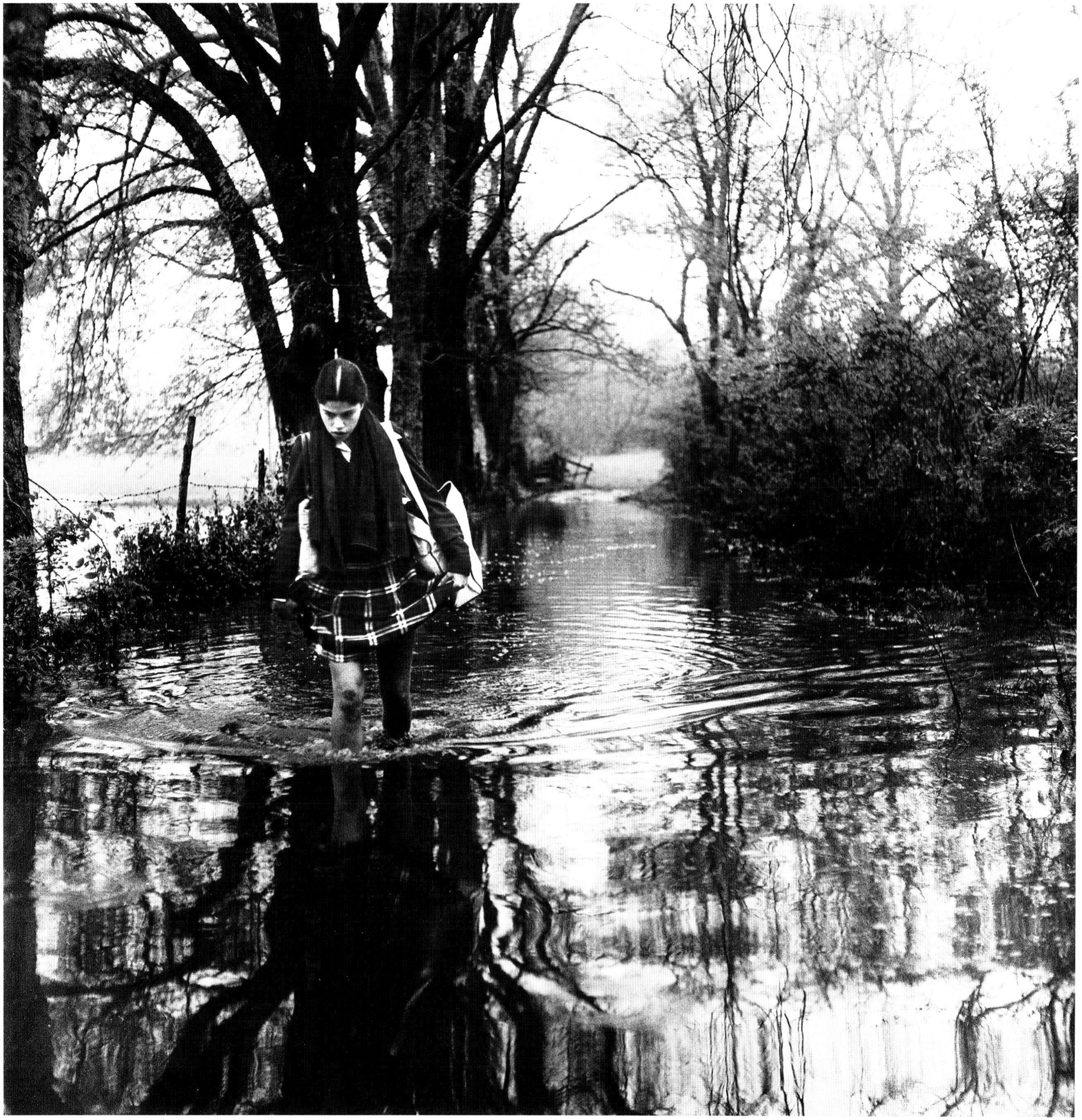

Olivier Store a la Charles

1980

Located in Prairie Basse, "Uncle Charlie's Store" was owned by Charlie and Frank Lawrence Olivier. It carried dry goods, canned goods, fabric, hats, and other items. Charlie Olivier also conducted business from "hacks," mule-drawn wagons that brought his wares to isolated communities. The hacks traveled weekly within a ten-mile range, reaching towns such as Arnaudville and Leonville. The hack carried a myriad of goods: basics such as flour and sugar, soda, shoes, long underwear, fresh shrimp, and fabric. Eventually, the mule-drawn wagons gave way to pickup trucks. Uncle Charlie's Store closed in the late 1960s.

PHOTOGRAPHER'S NOTE: This building is just east of Beau Chene High School on La. Highway 93. Though technically not in Grand Coteau, its proximity, history, and overall feel justify its inclusion. At the time that this photograph was taken, Charles Kimball, a friend and inspiration for many artists, was living in the structure. Kimball was particularly fond of bananas and bamboo.

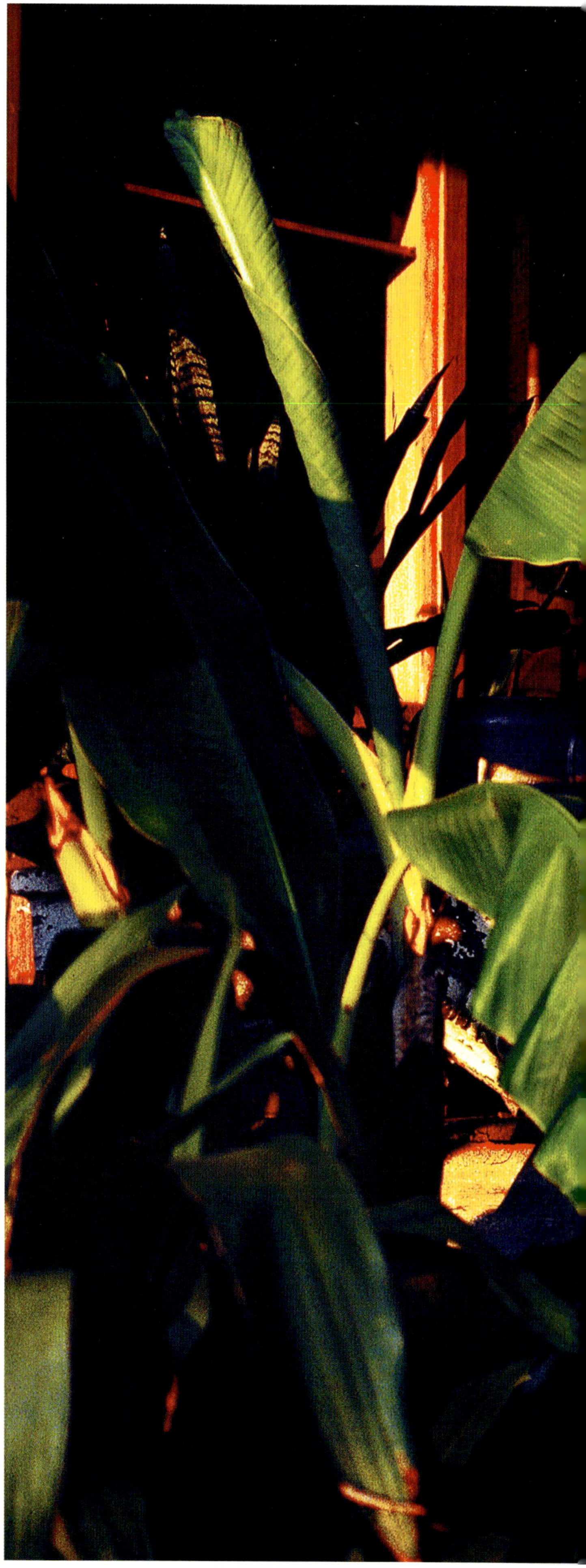

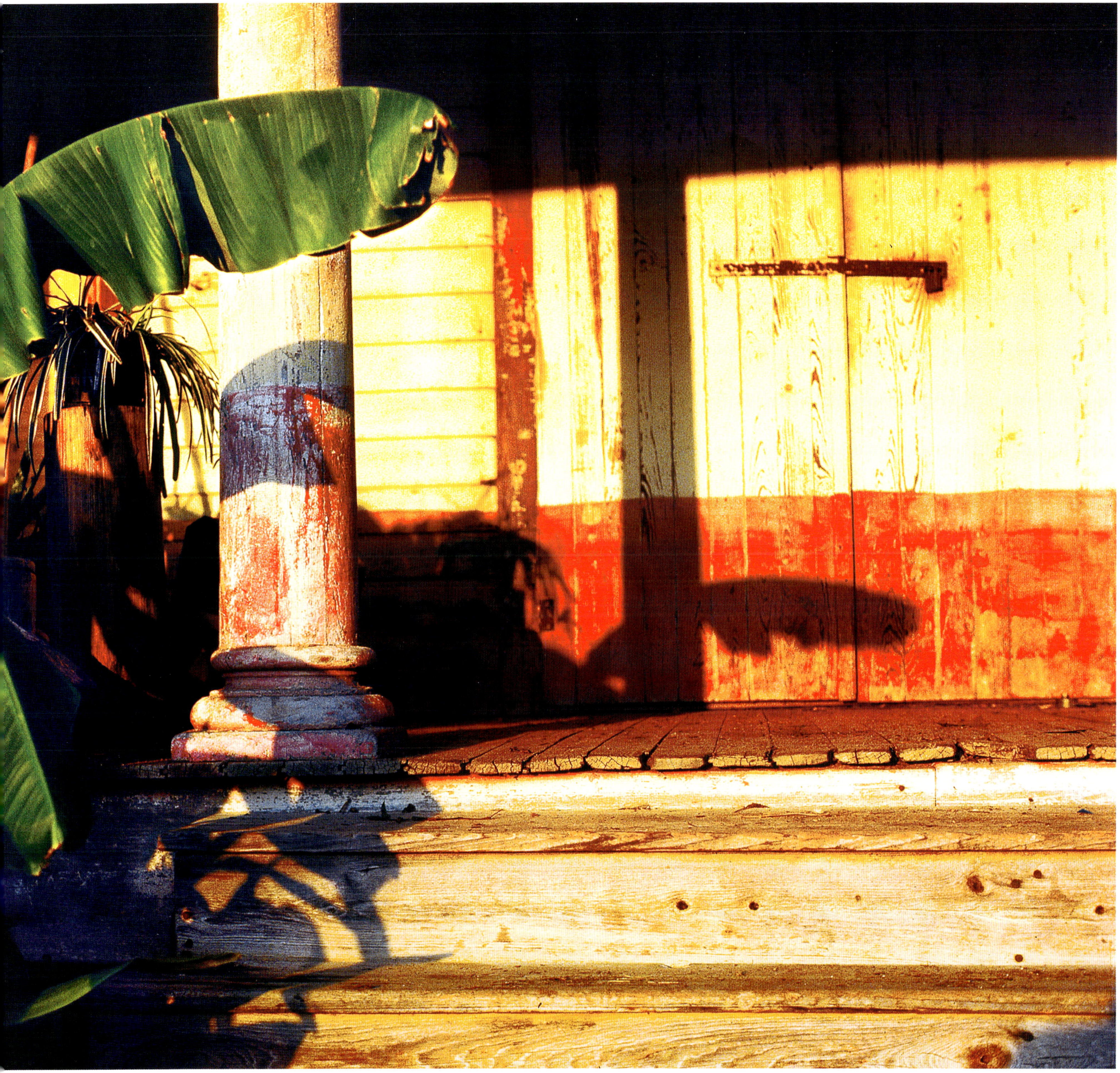

Barnstorming

1981

The yellow Dairy Barn has greeted visitors to Grand Coteau since 1925. Located on the property of St. Charles College, its cruciform shape and architecture are unusual for the Deep South. The style is typical of Wisconsin barns, the home state of the Jesuit priest who built it. It features protruding silos and large gambrel roofs.

From the time of their establishment in Grand Coteau, the Jesuits had to be self-sufficient, which included raising the milk cows housed in the Dairy Barn until the 1960s. The Jesuits milked the cows early each morning, then sent the milk to Opelousas for pasteurization. A portion of the milk was returned to the Jesuits for consumption, while the rest was sold to support the college.

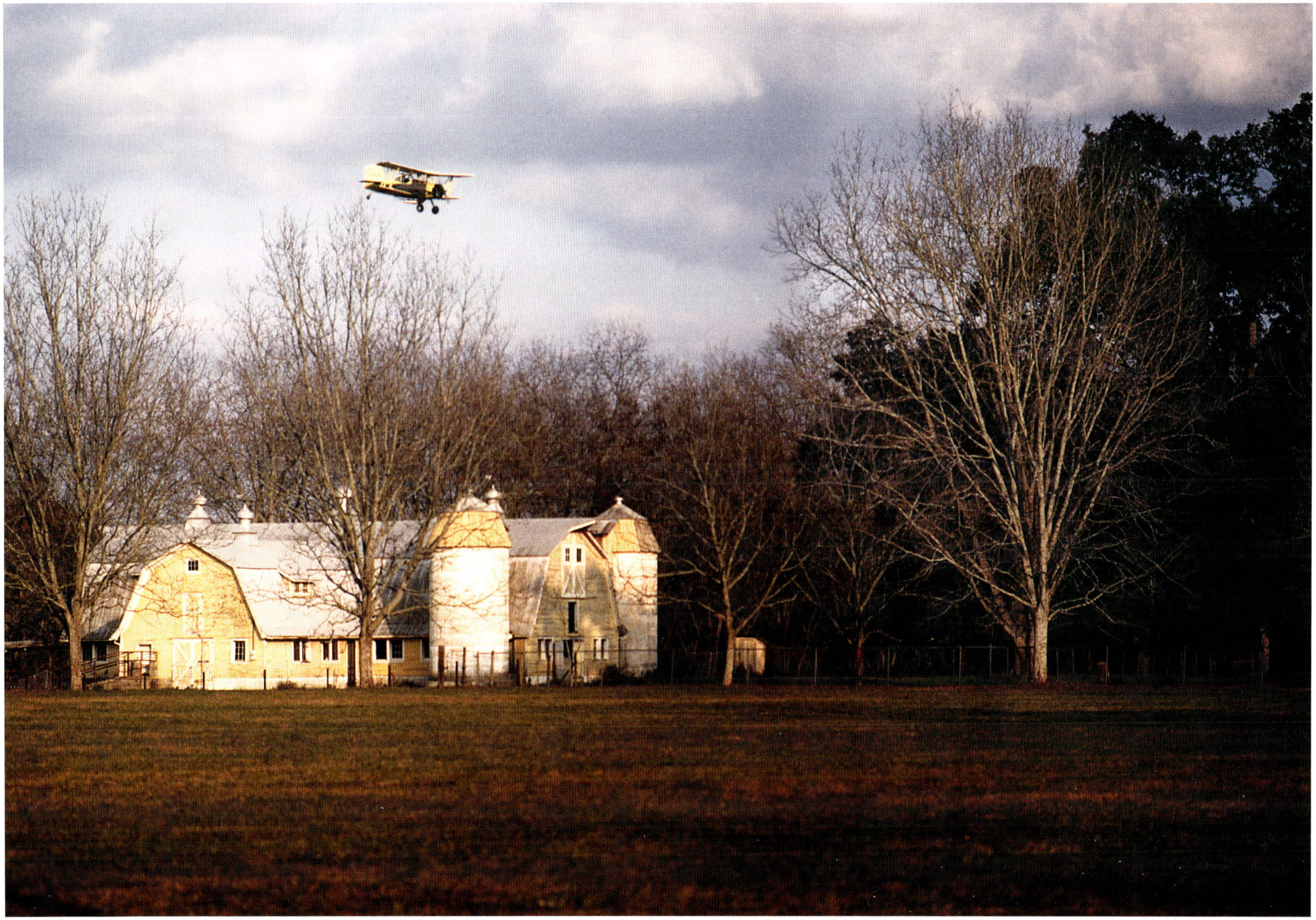

Cottage with Laundry
1981

This cottage caught fire in 2009. (Also see page 122.)

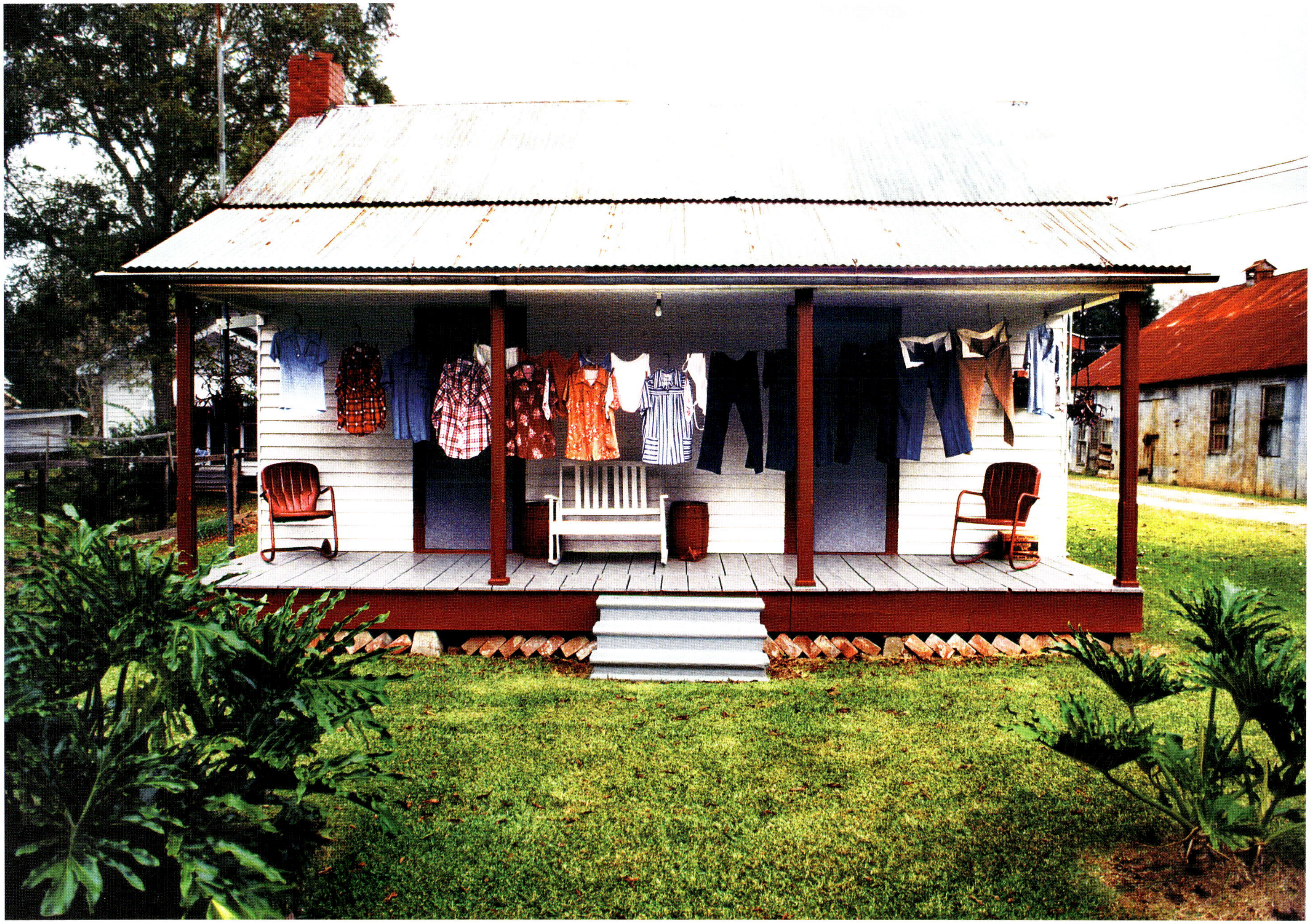

EVANGELINE MAID BREAD BILLBOARD

1982

Little remains of this barn-side advertisement just outside the town's limits on La. Highway 182.

PHOTOGRAPHER'S NOTE: For me there are three kinds of photos: the ones you should have taken, the ones you did take, and the ones you are going to take. I saw the potential of this scene and placed it in the going-to-take category. The grass got red and tall, and it entered the "taken" category.

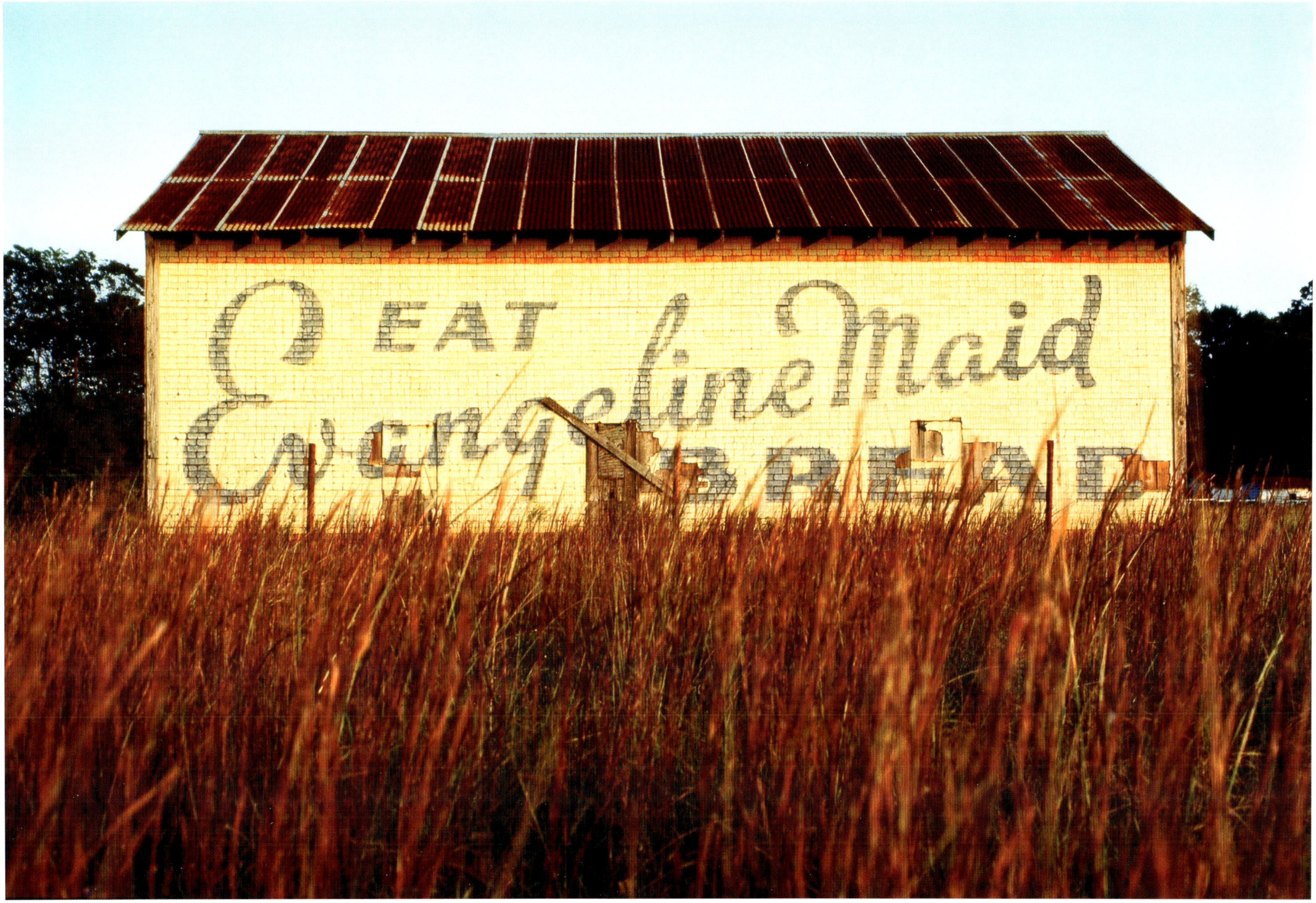
EAT
Evangeline Maid
BREAD

PAINTING – ST. CHARLES CHURCH
1982

PHOTOGRAPHER'S NOTE: Originally the plans called for the church to be built out of brick, but wood was substituted to save money and speed up the process. This resulted in an aesthetic windfall. The choice of wood adds a shine both literally and figuratively to this architectural gem. The delicateness of the trim makes this large building inviting. The lap siding applied in such scale pushes it skyward while at the same time making it home-like and approachable.

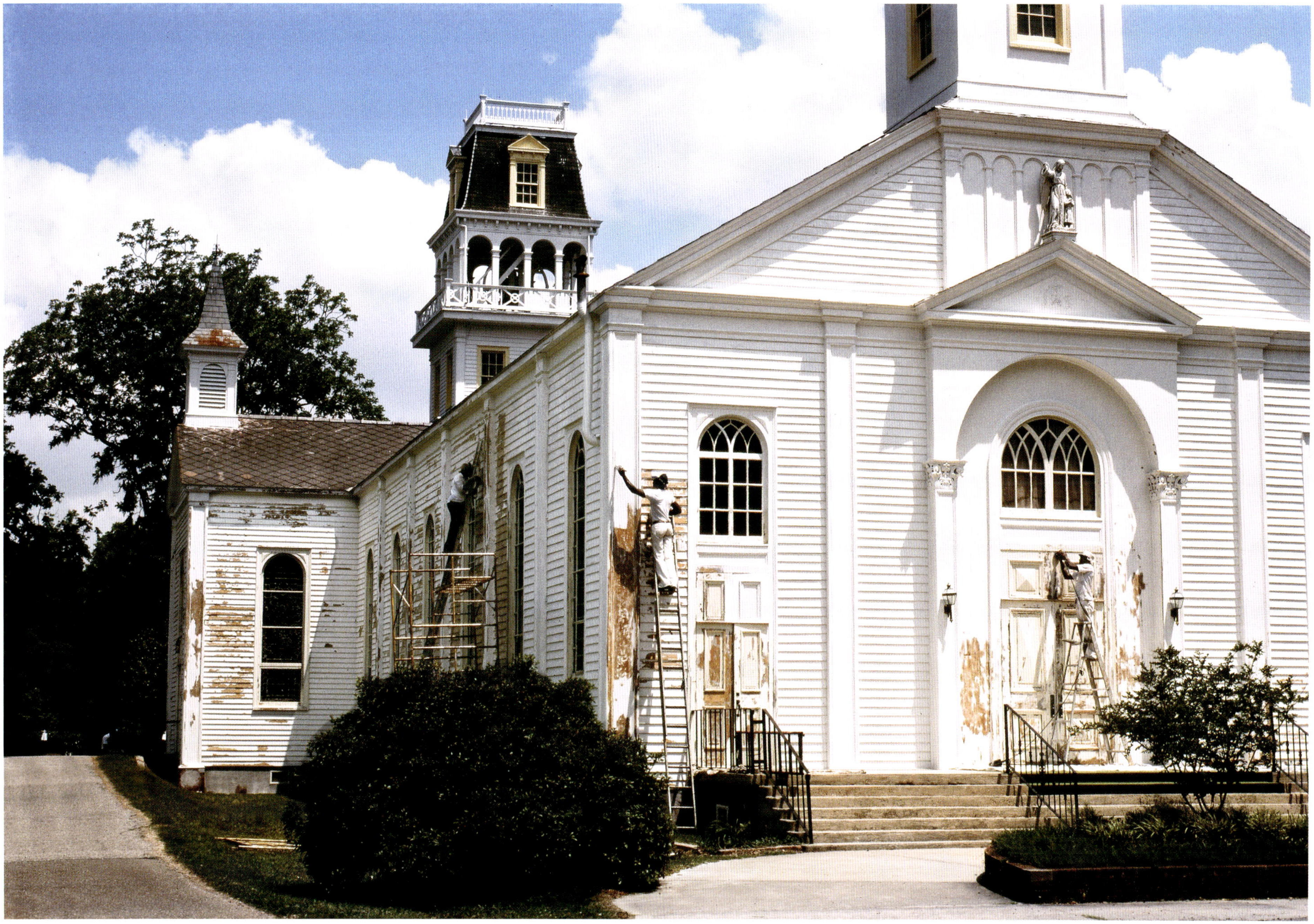

Interior – St. Charles Church

1982

A mass is celebrated in St. Charles Borromeo Church. The "Sacred Heart of Jesus" painting that hangs above the altar dates to 1862 and once belonged to the Duchess of Sagan, a Parisian socialite. She had donated her palace in Warsaw, Poland to the Sacred Heart nuns for a school there. It is not known how the painting was passed on from Poland to Grand Coteau, but it is the oldest in the church.

Following the Vatican II Council, many of the ornaments and symbolic works of art were stripped from the church in order to comply with the council's call for simplicity. It was thought that a simpler interior would create a more welcoming atmosphere for worshipers. In the late 1970s, a trend towards restoring churches to their original elegance swept the country, including Grand Coteau. Lost artifacts were sought and the church hired painter Richard Roberts who dedicated his life to restoring churches after his experience in a Nazi concentration camp.

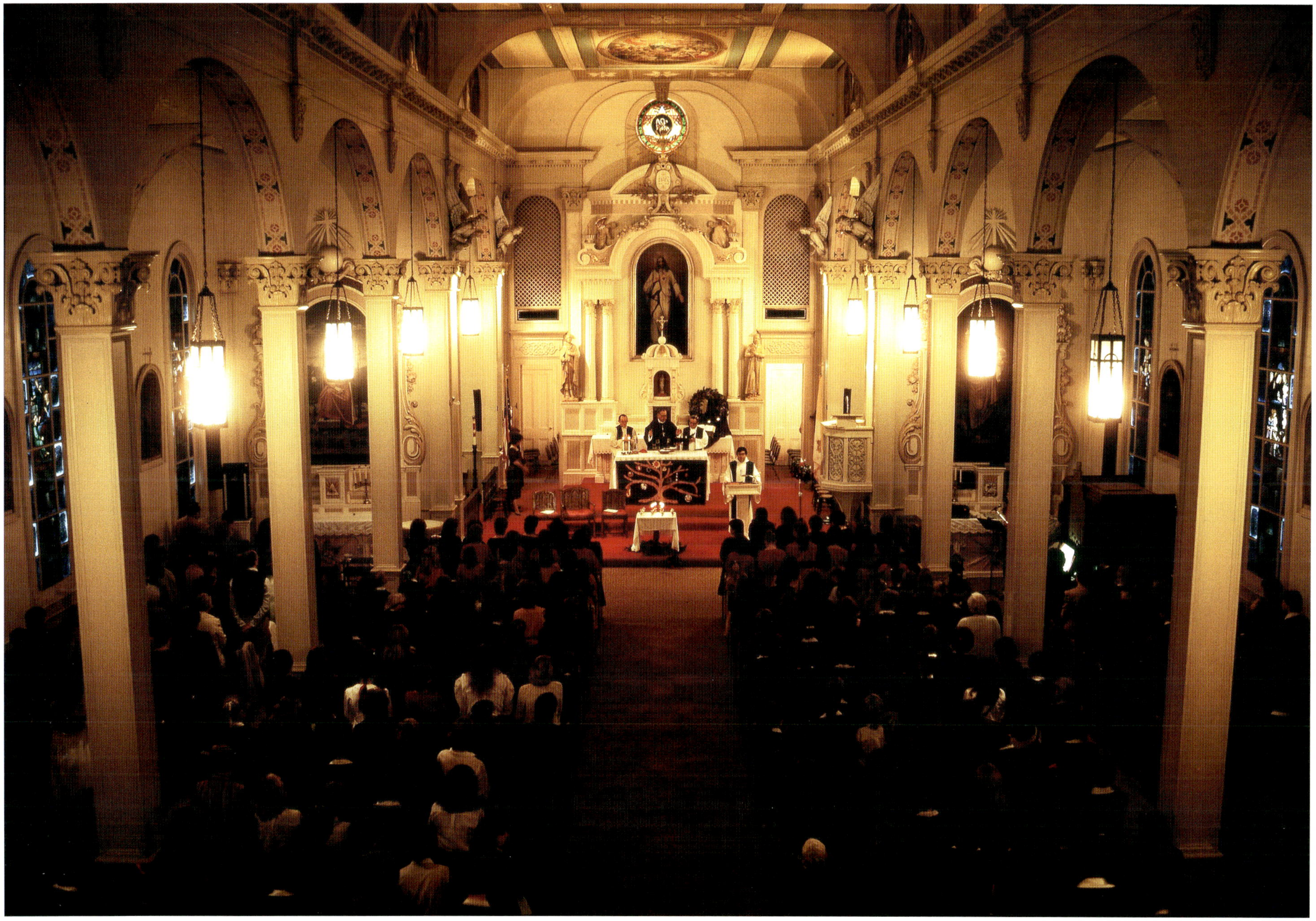

LAWRENCE "BABY" MARTN AND CHESTER SAM
1982

Lawrence Martin (1894–1988), a native Creole French speaker, served in World War I as a cook in France. Known by several nicknames, including "Pie," "Baby," and "Pushoon," he was a charter member of the Knights of Peter Claver and was employed at St. Charles College where he assisted the priests in preparing the altar each morning. He and his wife, Eva, having no children of their own, graciously raised several nieces and nephews, all of whom attended college. Eva was known for her tasty sweet dough pies, which she sold in the neighborhood.

Descended from "free people of color" who immigrated from Haiti soon after the slave revolts, Chester Sam (1930–1995) was born in Prairie Basse. One of five children, his family sharecropped on the Simon-Levy plantation. Soon after graduating from high school at St. Peter Claver, he was drafted into the military and fought in the Korean War. Following the war, he worked at Our Lady of Lourdes Hospital in air conditioning maintenance. Soft-spoken and friendly, he enjoyed horses and was a frequent patron of the races at Evangeline Downs.

PHOTOGRAPHER'S NOTE: "Baby" would often walk down the sidewalk to The Kitchen Shop corner. He had a delightful angelic aura as did his brother Felix. His blue eyes sparkled as he described on several occasions the possibility of nearby treasure that the "Seven Sisters" might know about.

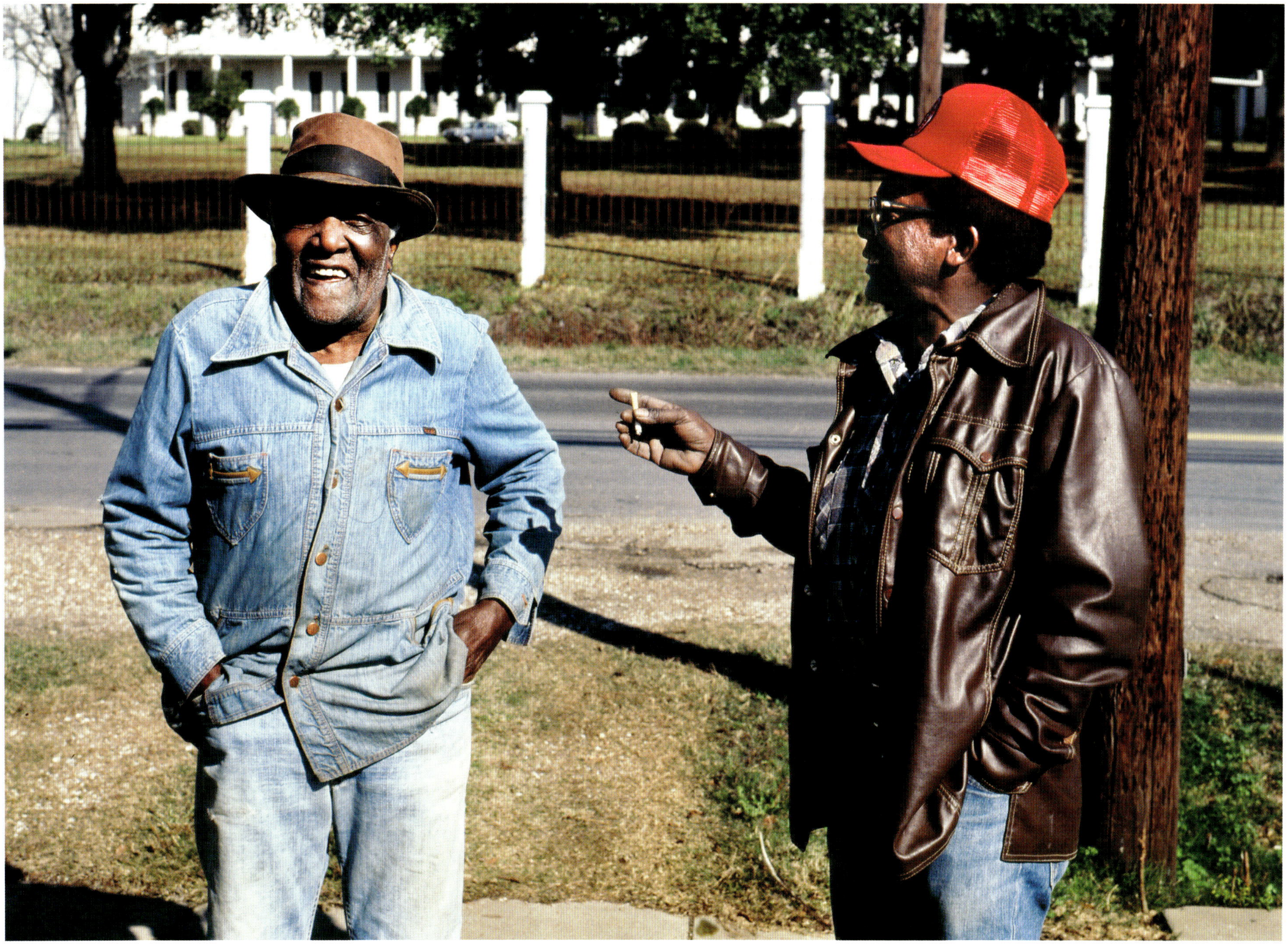

St. Charles Church
1982

St. Charles Borromeo Church was founded in 1819; however, the congregation soon outgrew the original building, and the present structure was built in 1879. The church is an interpretation of Greek Revival style, integrating vertical and horizontal classical elements. New Orleans architect James Freret designed the clapboard structure with its central tower and spire. The primary builders were Brothers Cornelius Otten, SJ and Joseph Armand Brinkhaus, SJ of Grand Coteau. Both clergy and parishioners invested funds, labor and time to create the church. The Sisters of the Sacred Heart financed one-third of the building expenses, the Jesuits financed one-third, and one-third of the funds were raised by area residents through fairs.

The rear belfry, considered Second Empire style, was built six years after the church was completed. The mansard roof on this rear belfry is the building's most unique architectural feature and considered rare in the United States, especially on religious buildings. (Also see pages x and 126.)

Among the over seventy buildings in Grand Coteau on the National Register of Historic Places, St. Charles Borromeo Church ranks as the most architecturally significant.

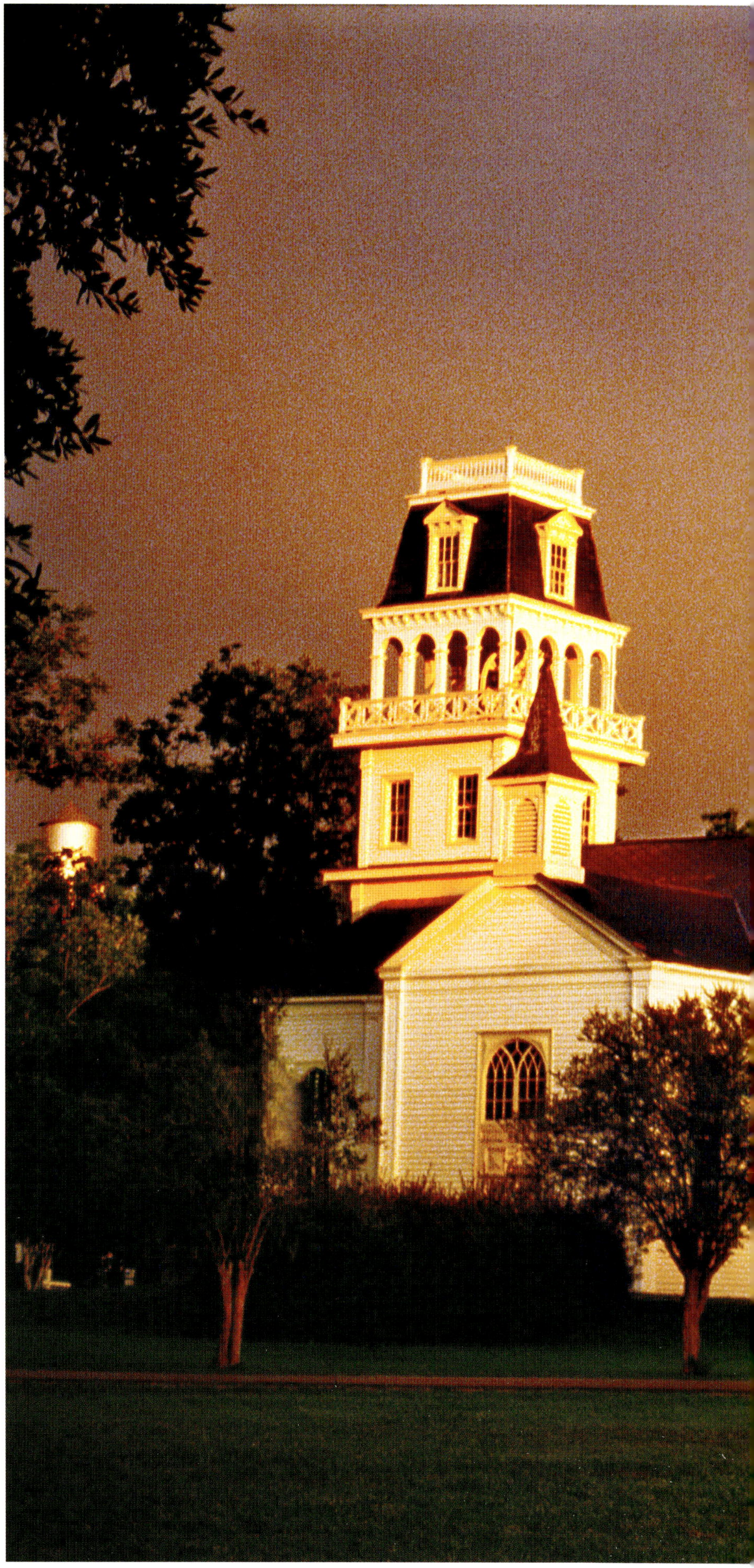

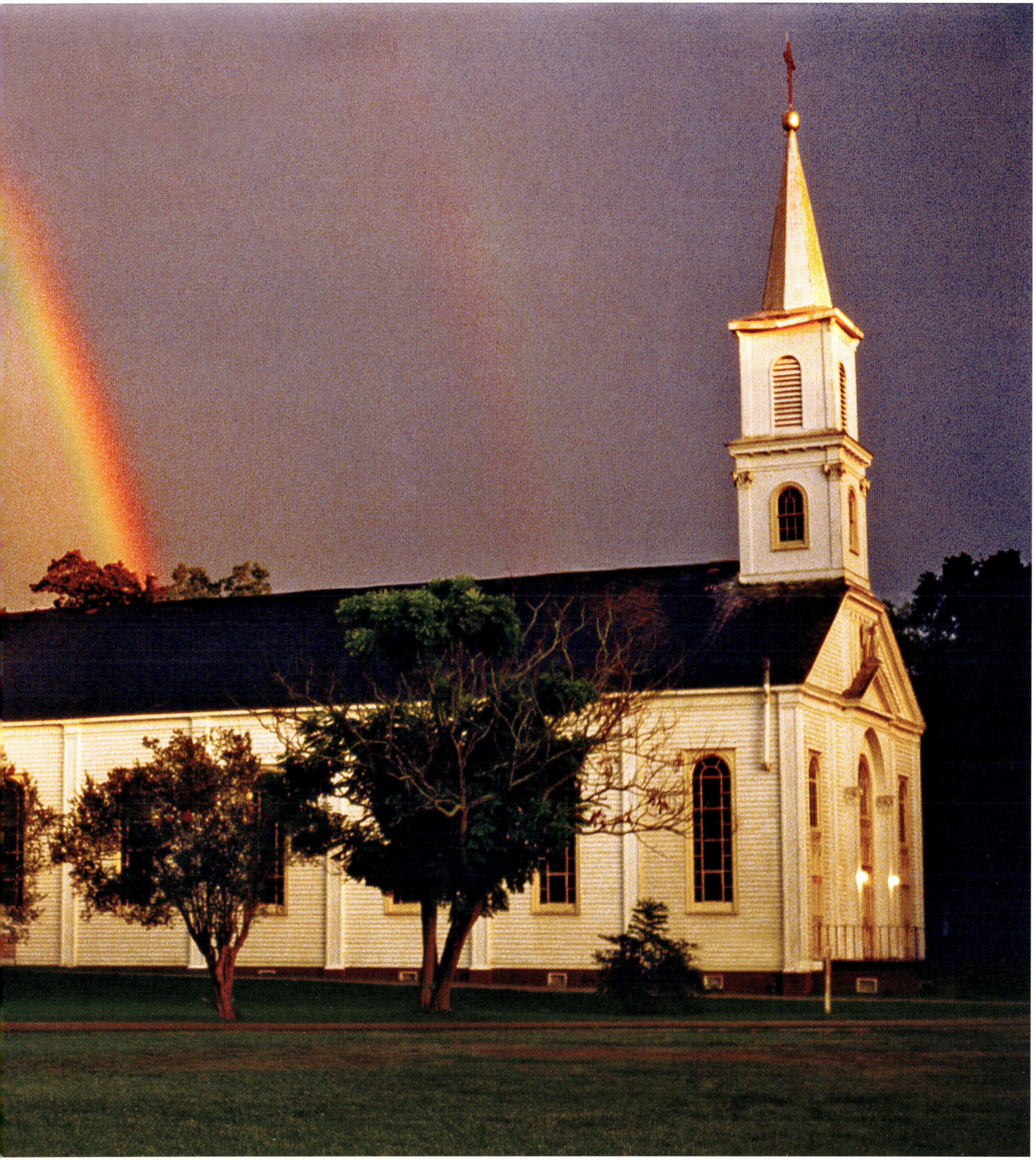

Wilfred "Beck" Barriere
1982

Wilfred "Beck" Barriere (1901–1983) poses with a watermelon balanced on his bicycle. In the background is Our Lady of the Oaks Retreat House. He and his wife, Frances (page 20), raised nine children. Barriere was a sharecropper, the first black deputy in Grand Coteau, and a Grand Knight for the Knights of Peter Claver. He served as a role model for young men and taught local children how to swim in Opelousas. Some say that they occasionally swam in the college pond—among the snakes, turtles, and the alligators.

PHOTOGRAPHER'S NOTE: I was in The Kitchen Shop when I saw Beck riding by with a watermelon he had just purchased from Jimmy Stelly. I ran to my car and sped to intercept him, choosing Our Lady of the Oaks as a background. I liked photographing Beck because he had a certain "country cool" sartorial sensibility which his lanky physique enhanced.

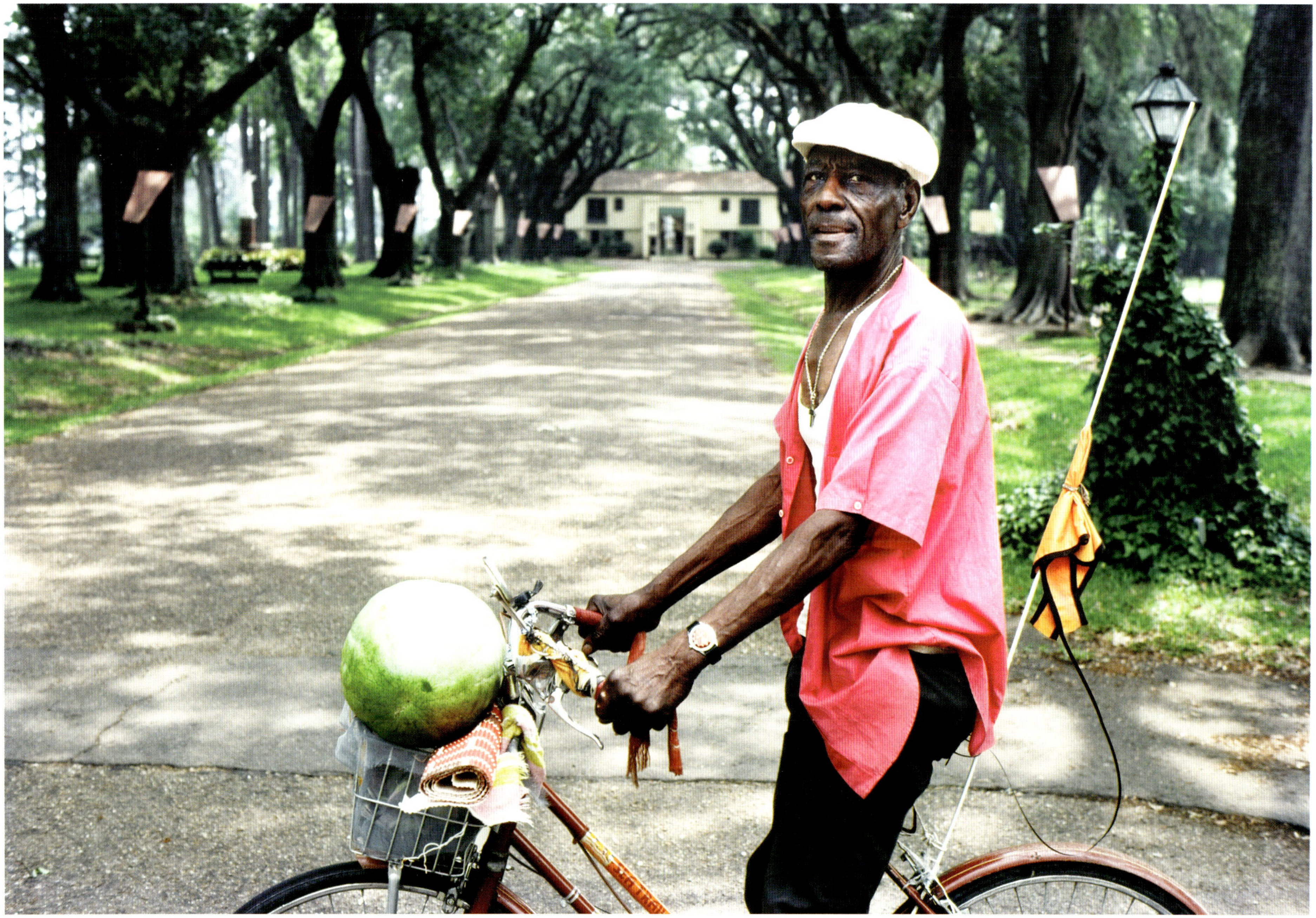

Christmas Mass
1982

Father Joseph Doyle (1936–2008), a Jesuit Priest, holds up the Sacrament for Christmas Mass in the Chapel of the Academy of the Sacred Heart. He is assisted by two students, Kathy Frederic and Mellie Boagni. Fr. Doyle served as Director of the Novitiate Program at St. Charles College from 1976 to 1982. Originally from New York, he attended Fordham Prep High School and Fordham University, graduating in 1958 with a degree in history. When Doyle first applied to the Jesuit Society he was rejected for lack of Greek and Latin. He was encouraged by Father O'Neil, "Come south, we'll take you." Father Doyle was known as a motivating lecturer and loyal friend to the Sisters of the Sacred Heart.

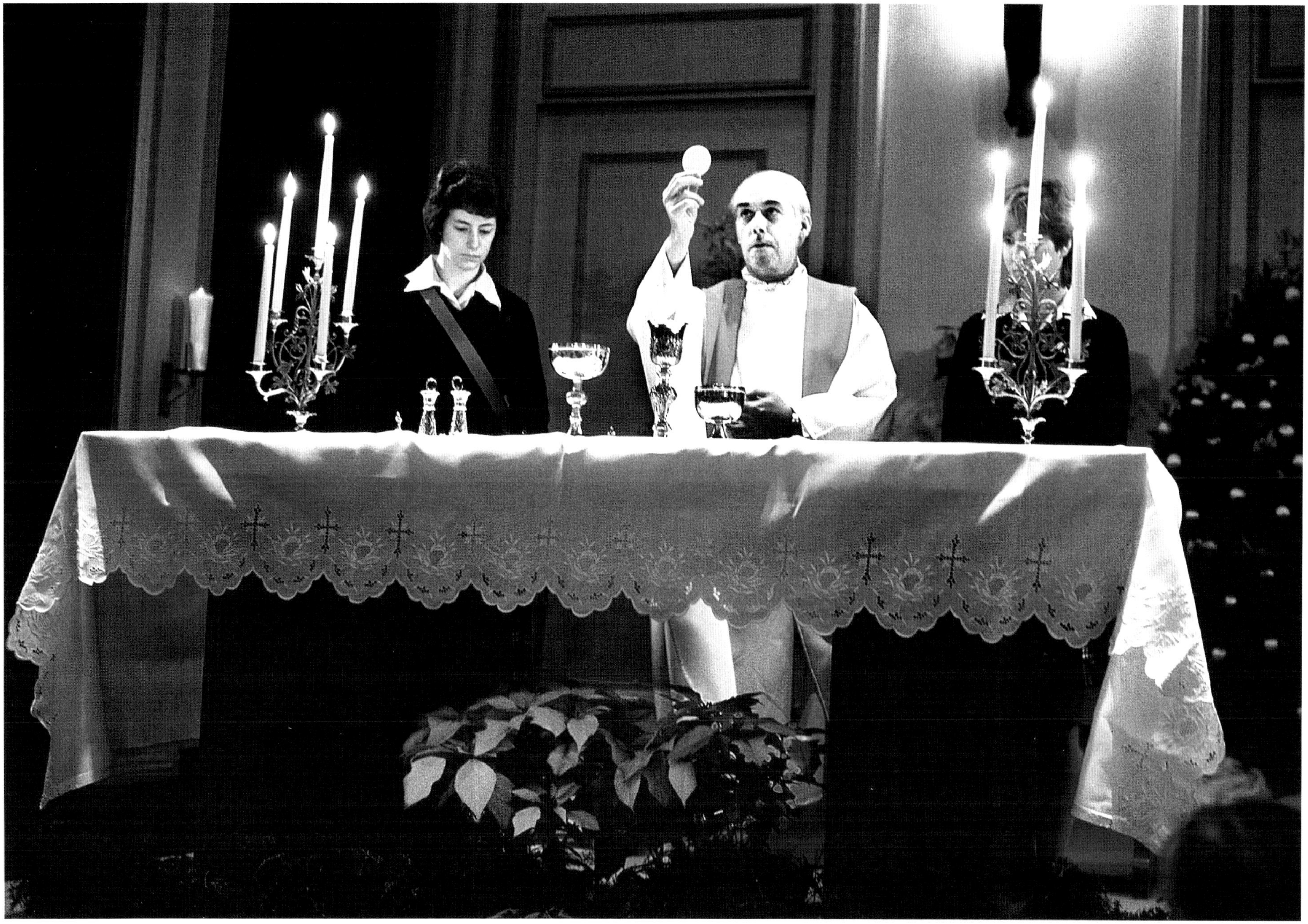

Chief Gilbert "Tossie" Mayfield, Jr.
1982

Chief Gilbert "Tossie" Mayfield, Jr. (1934–2002) was one of twelve children of sharecroppers. His older sisters attended the local school, but as the oldest boy, Tossie had to work in the field with his parents. Despite his lack of formal schooling, he excelled in helping others, whether counseling children, advising parents, or arranging shelter for a battered wife. Chief Mayfield encouraged each of his own children to work hard and to earn the "square hat" of graduation.

Photographer's Note: He knew who the good guys were and who the bad guys were. There are abundant stories about this colorful man, but some things just need to remain local lore. Many people consider Mayfield the best police chief Grand Coteau ever had.

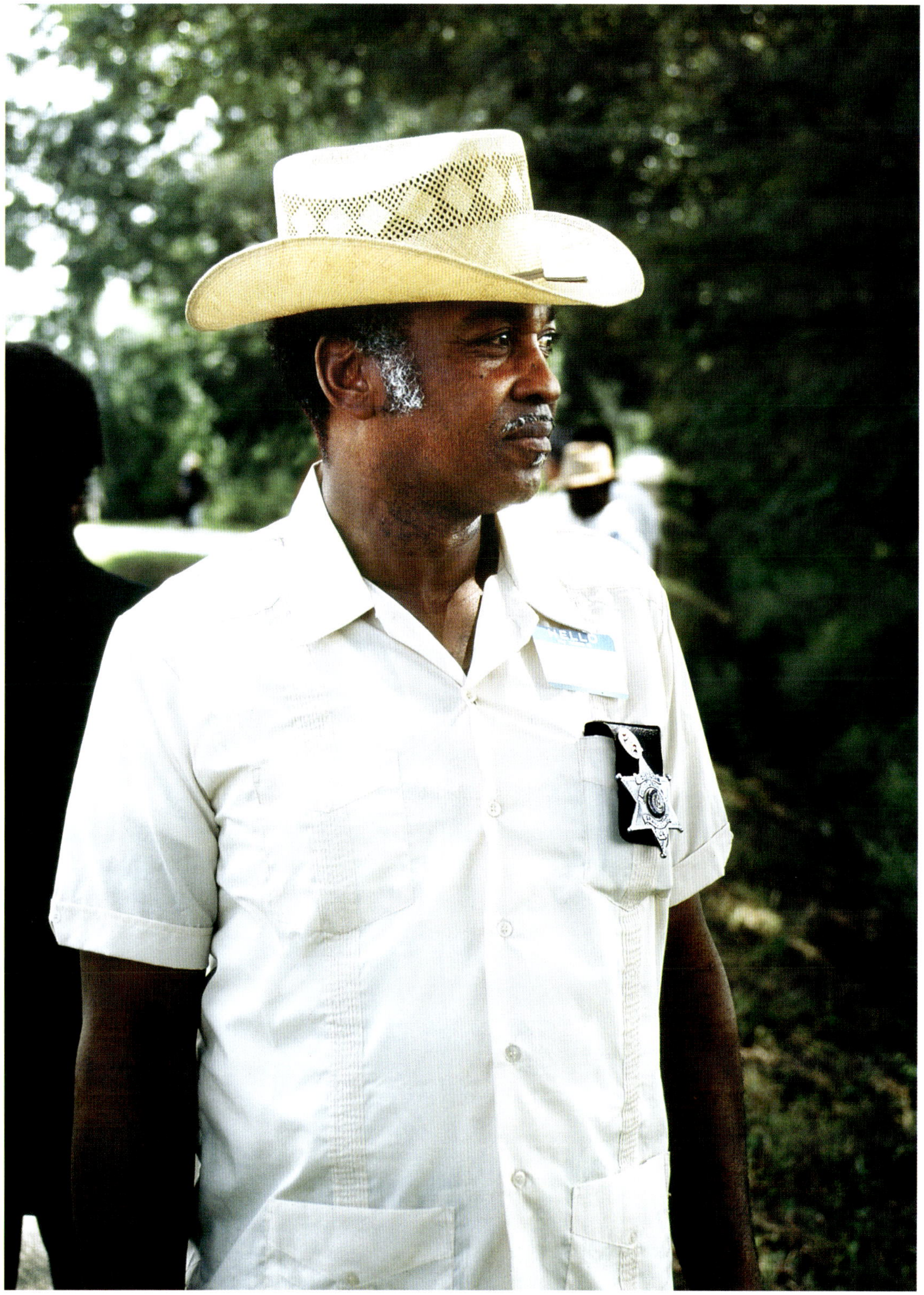

Oak Alley
1983

This double row of grand trees once provided a continuous, light-dappled canopy between St. Charles College and the Academy of the Sacred Heart. Planted during the early years of the college, the alley offered a shady path in the searing summer heat for Jesuit priests who traveled between the College and the Academy by horse and carriage to offer daily mass. Father Nicholas Point is credited with planting the trees.

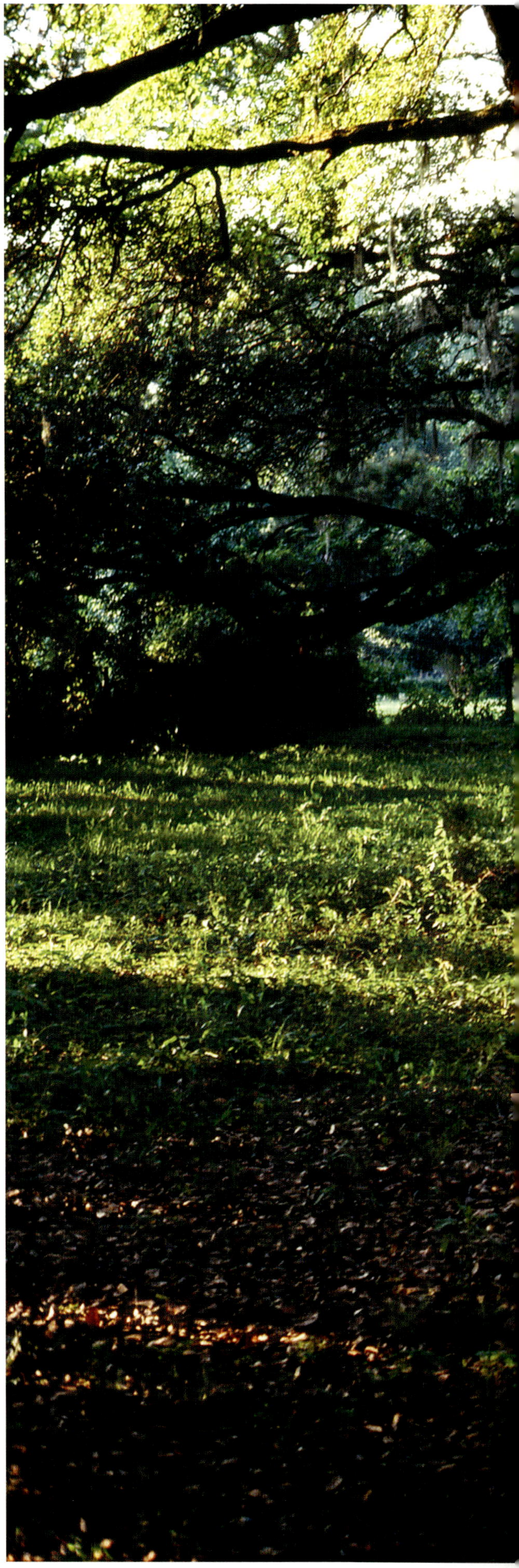

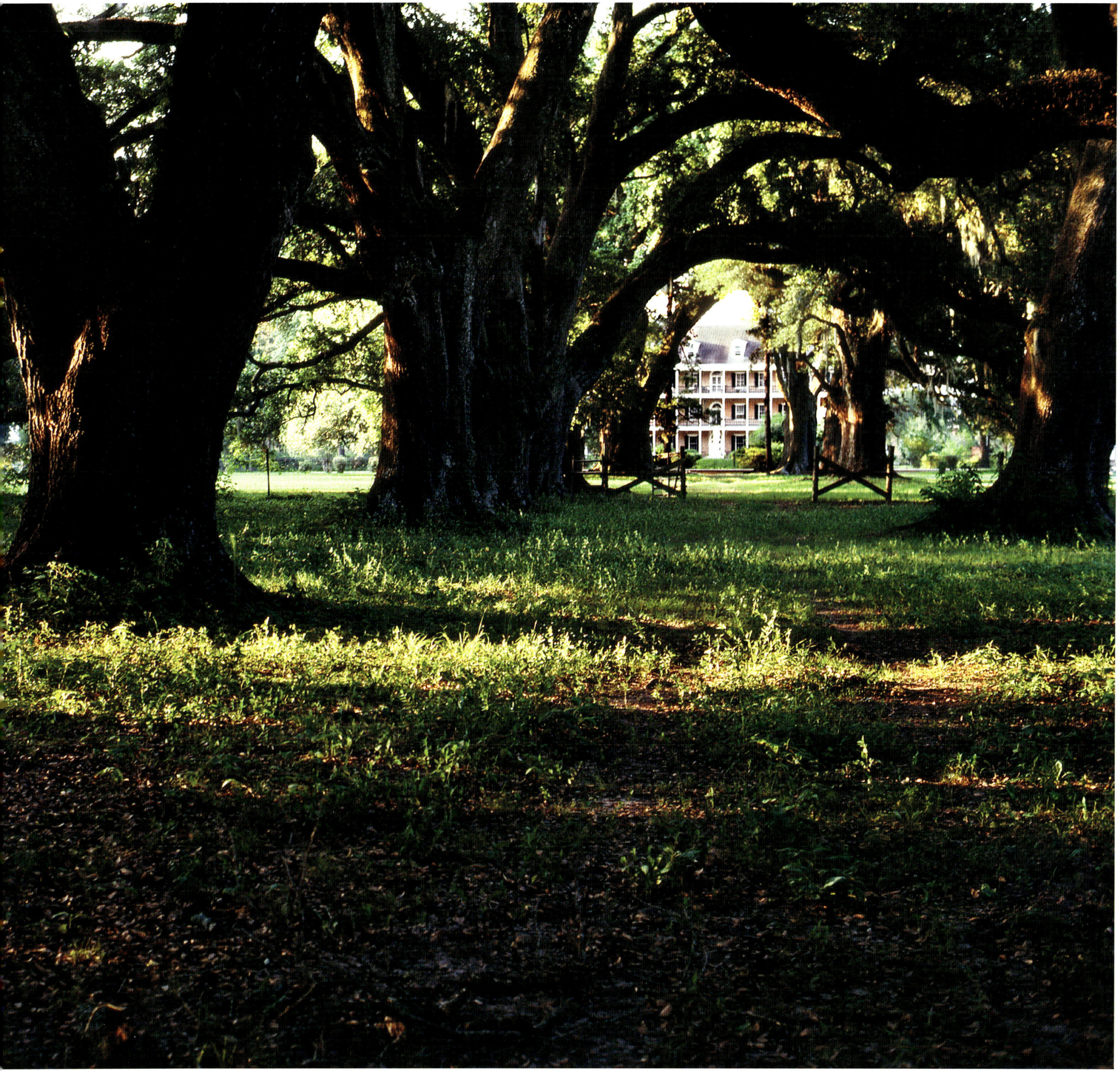

Olan Thibodeaux

1983

Olan Thibodeaux was promoted to Director of Maintenance at St. Charles College in 1983, the first non-Jesuit to become a director at the college. He was mentored by Brother Moore in carpentry and other skills for four years before his promotion. His primary job is to oversee physical plant maintenance, including plumbing, electrical, painting, and carpentry. However, he gladly accepts tasks outside of his job description such as "wildlife removal"—rescuing a lizard from the secretary's office or capturing a disoriented rat snake from a hallway.

PHOTOGRAPHER'S NOTE: Olan is the kindest soul I have ever known. Perhaps having so many siblings—he is one of twelve children—nourished his innate tolerance. I have always prided myself on being resourceful, but many times that resourcefulness has entailed calling Olan for some advice or a helping hand. And let's not forget "Small Time Cinema," the monthly screening of independent films at Casa Azul, which he curates, promotes, and projects.

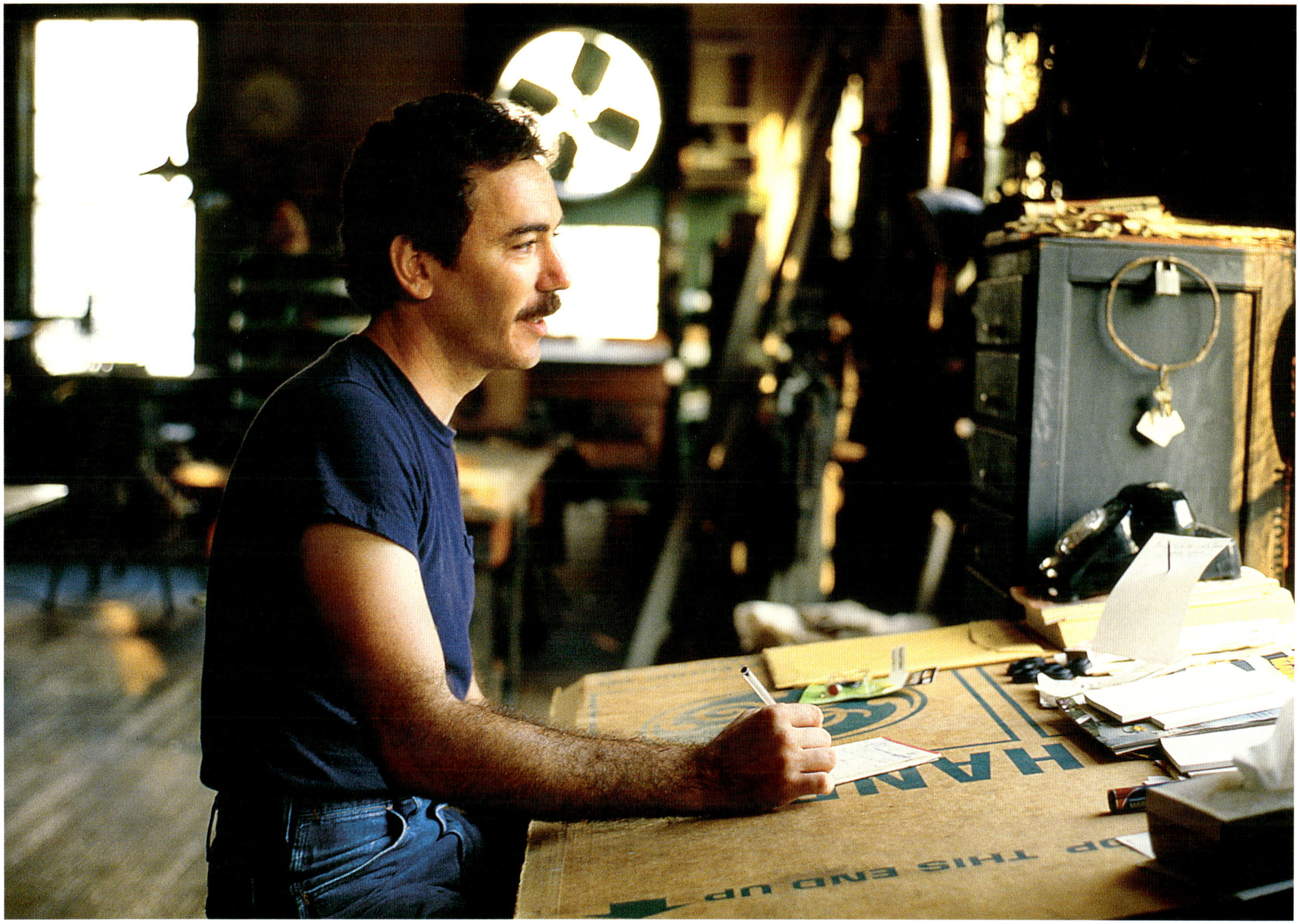
THIS END UP

John Tate

1983

When gazing over soft green lawns, cool groves of pines, and azalea-lined lanes at St. Charles College, you are looking at the work of Grounds Supervisor John Tate. Renowned for his care of all things green, he could revive even the most withered peace lily.

Tate's parents sharecropped for St. Charles College, and when he turned sixteen, the college hired him full-time. He first worked in the Dairy Barn, but eventually became the groundskeeper. Tate planted over one hundred trees on the college grounds and also maintained a green house where he cultivated everything from aloe vera to Louisiana iris to sago palms. Tate tended to the thirty-five acre grounds of St. Charles College for fifty-six years, from 1951 until his retirement in 2007.

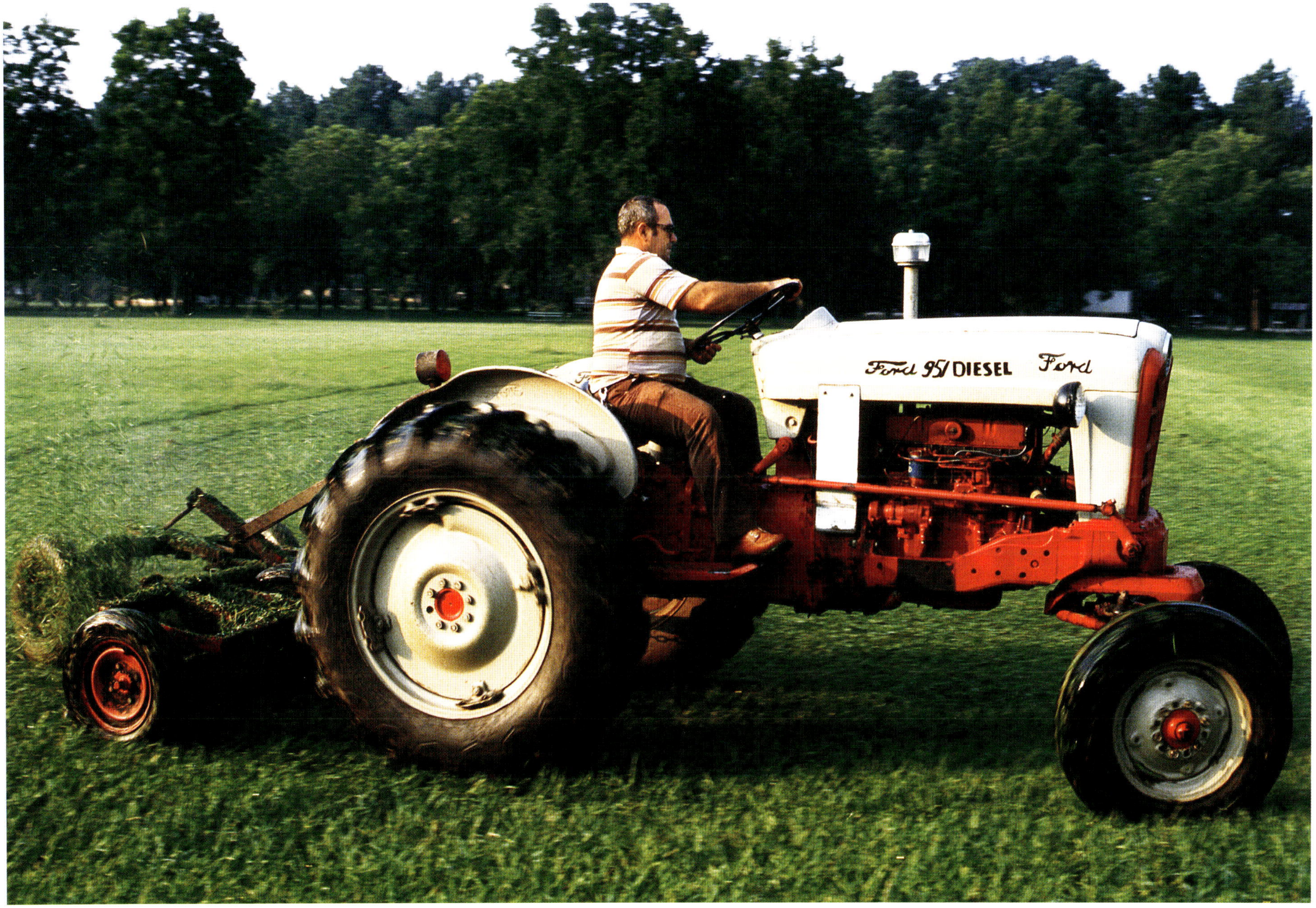
Ford 951 DIESEL
Ford

STEEPLE OF ST. CHARLES CHURCH
1984

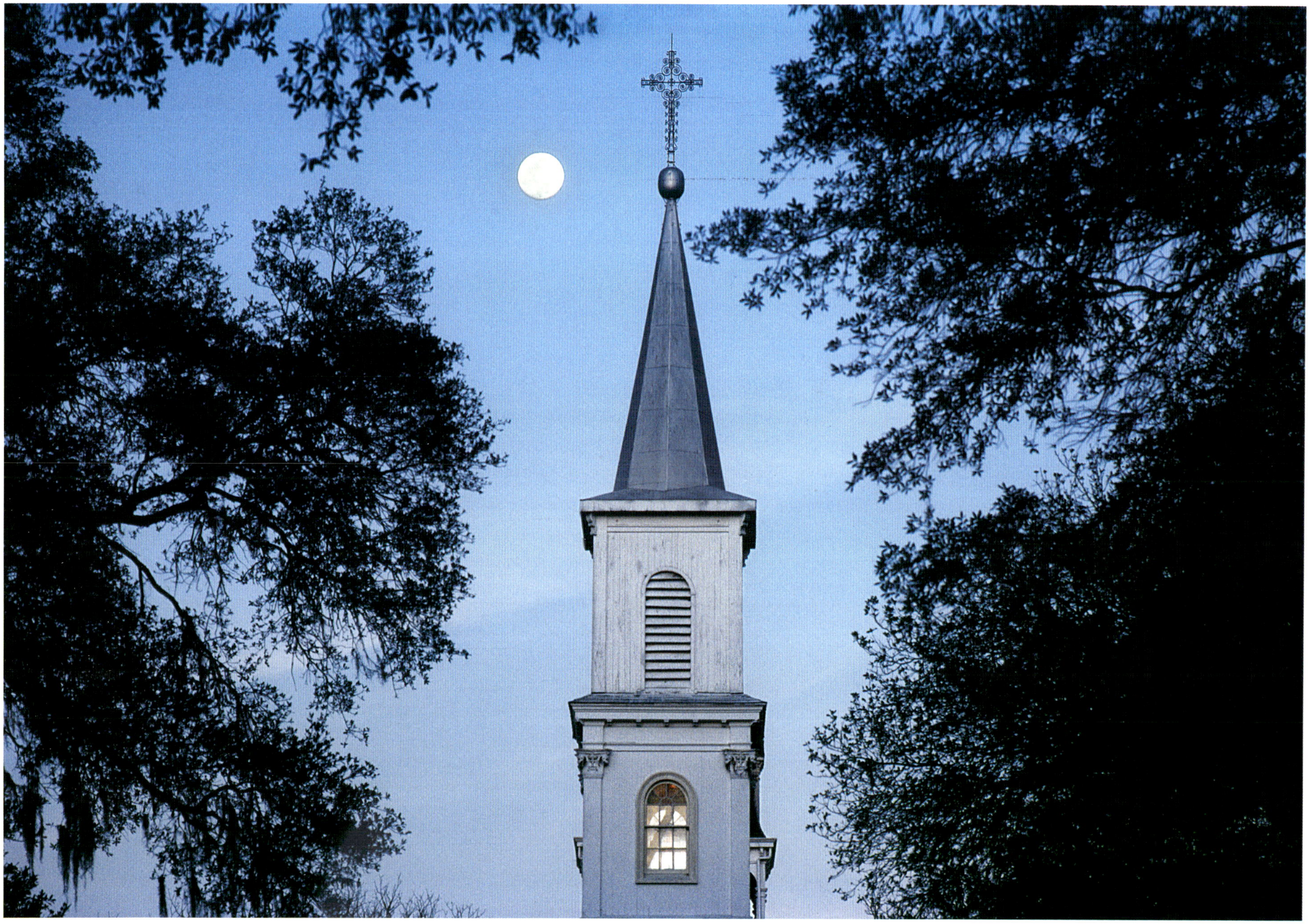

The Kitchen Shop
1984

Hilary Slaughter puts the finishing touches on the The Kitchen Shop sign.

This structure is essentially two buildings wedded together. The front features a false façade and original French doors and was probably built around 1900 using two-by-four stud walls similar to contemporary construction. The rear, with its exposed beam ceilings, predates the Civil War and employs mortise and tenon pegged construction common during that era. The chamfered front posts extending over the sidewalk were protected when the street was redone because the building is one of the many structures in Grand Coteau on the National Register of Historic Places.

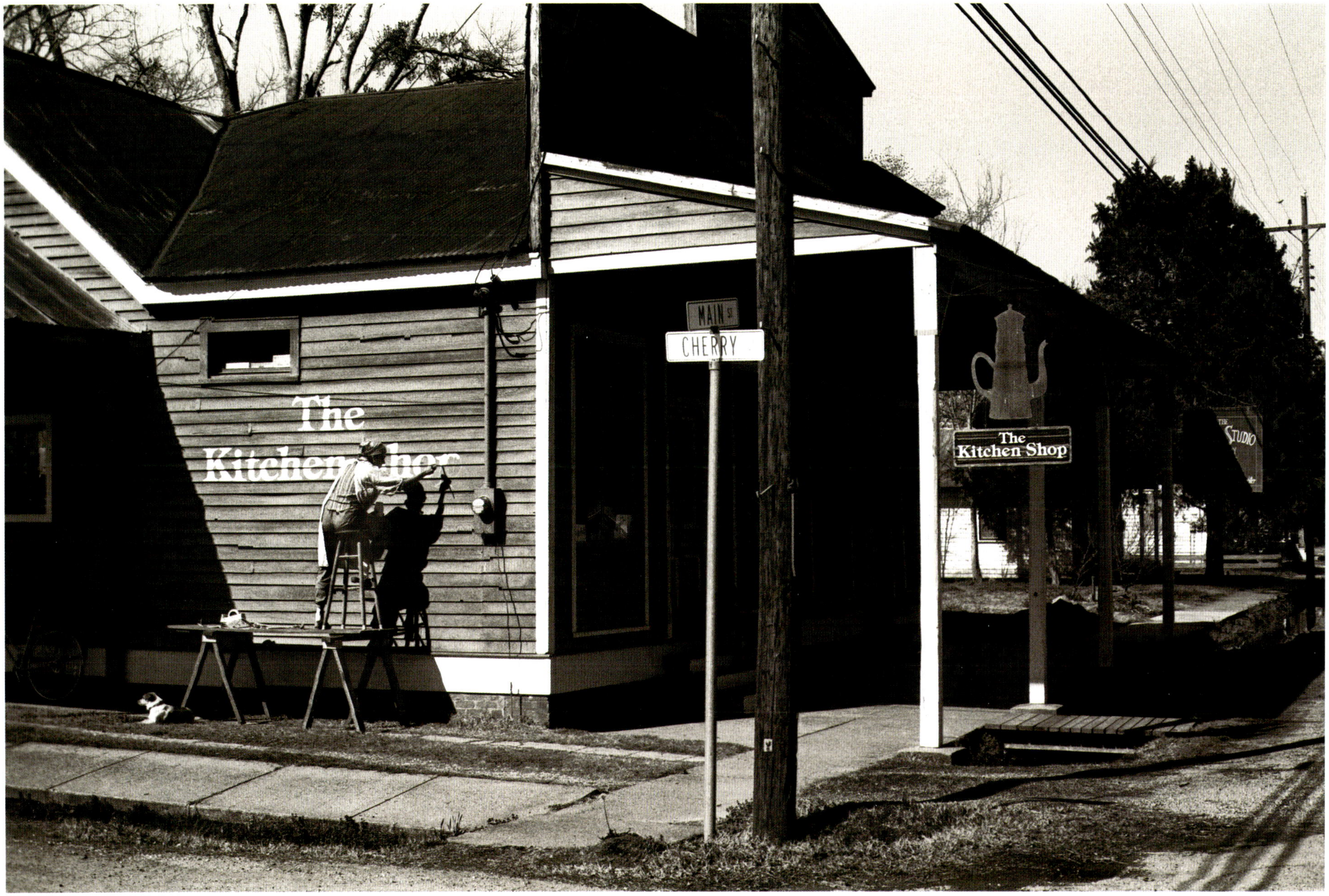
The
MAIN ST
CHERRY
The
Kitchen Shop
STUDIO

Rodriguez Walk
1985

The tranquil, azalea-lined Rodriguez Walk leads from St. Charles College to Our Lady of the Oaks Retreat House. Though faded now, the bricks were originally green, red and natural. At one time, Jesuit novices were required to silently read from the spiritual writings of Alphonsus Rodriguez, SJ (1532–1617) every afternoon as they paced along the walkway.

Polish refugee Thomas Malczewski, a bridge engineer, laid the concrete blocks of the walkway. During World War II, he had served in the Polish army but was captured and held in a concentration camp for his Catholicism. He emigrated to the United States and came to work for St. Charles College, assisting with construction and book binding. He lived in Grand Coteau for the rest of his life.

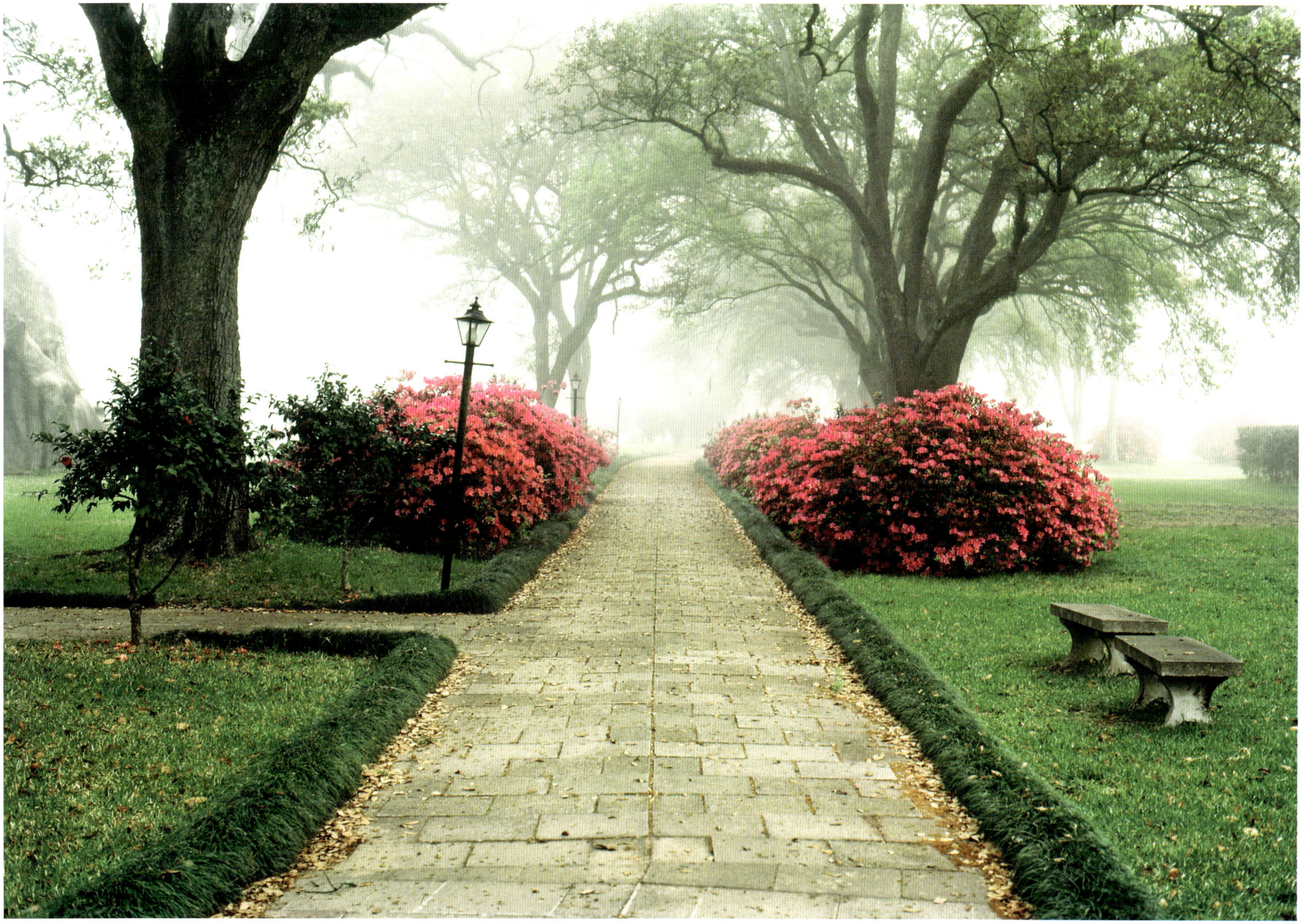

David Alpha – Chimney Repair

1985

Take a good look at this chimney atop Grand Coteau's singularly impressive Queen Anne structure, directly opposite Our Lady of the Oaks Retreat House. This house was built in 1885 for Dr. Edward M. Millard's widow. The hard part wasn't laying the bricks; the hard part was hauling everything up there: the lumber, the mortar, the bricks, the tools, the water, and of course one's self. David Alpha, when not restoring the past or building the future, is known for his paintings of Louisiana landscapes.

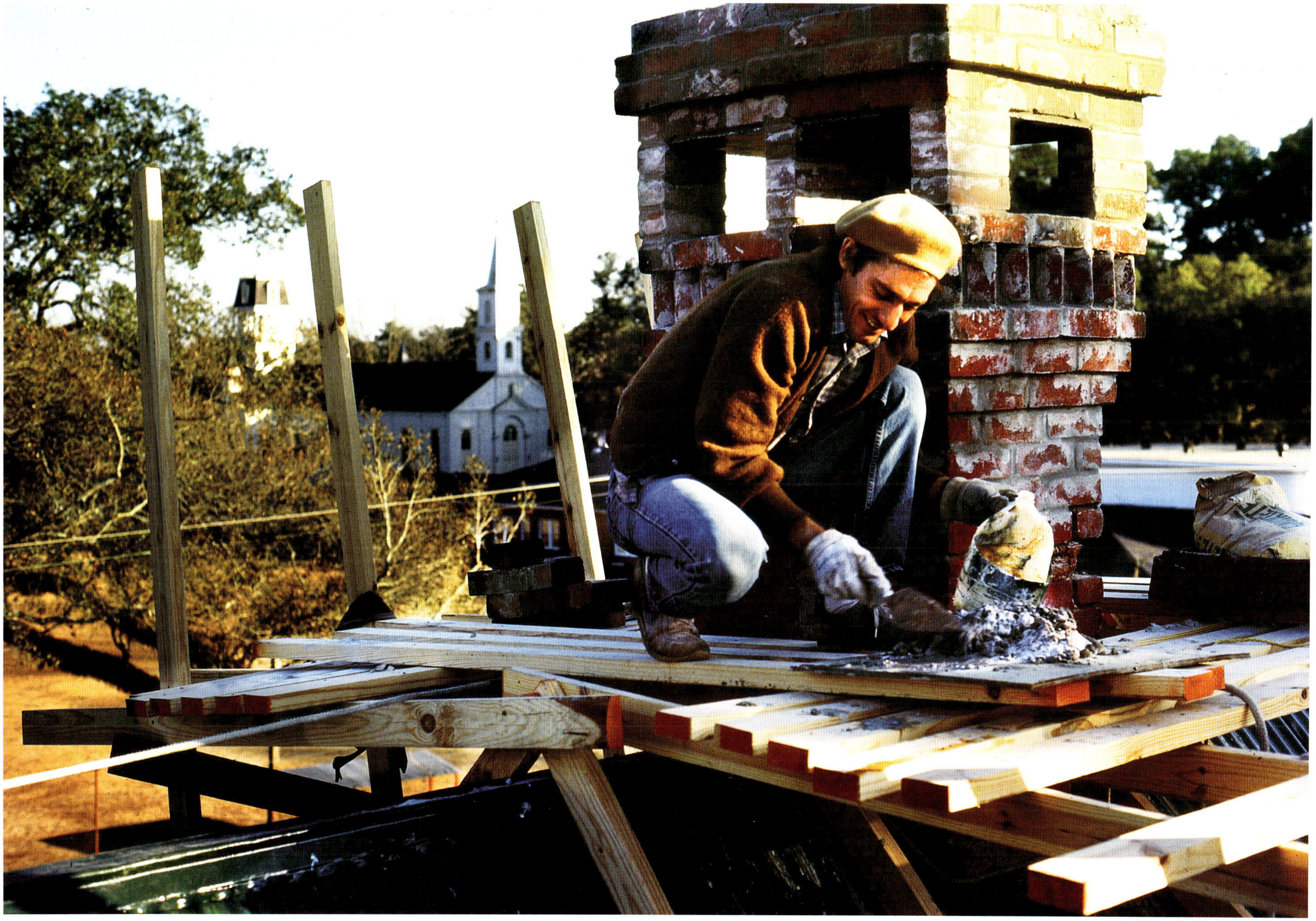

Azaleas in Bloom

1985

Magenta azalea bushes frame the view of St. Charles Church's east bell tower. Most were planted in the 1960s by Brother Walter Eckler and groundskeeper John Tate (page 58), who received them at no cost from a nursery that was going out of business. Each spring, hundreds of azaleas and camellias bloom along the walkways and grounds of St. Charles Borromeo Church and St. Charles College.

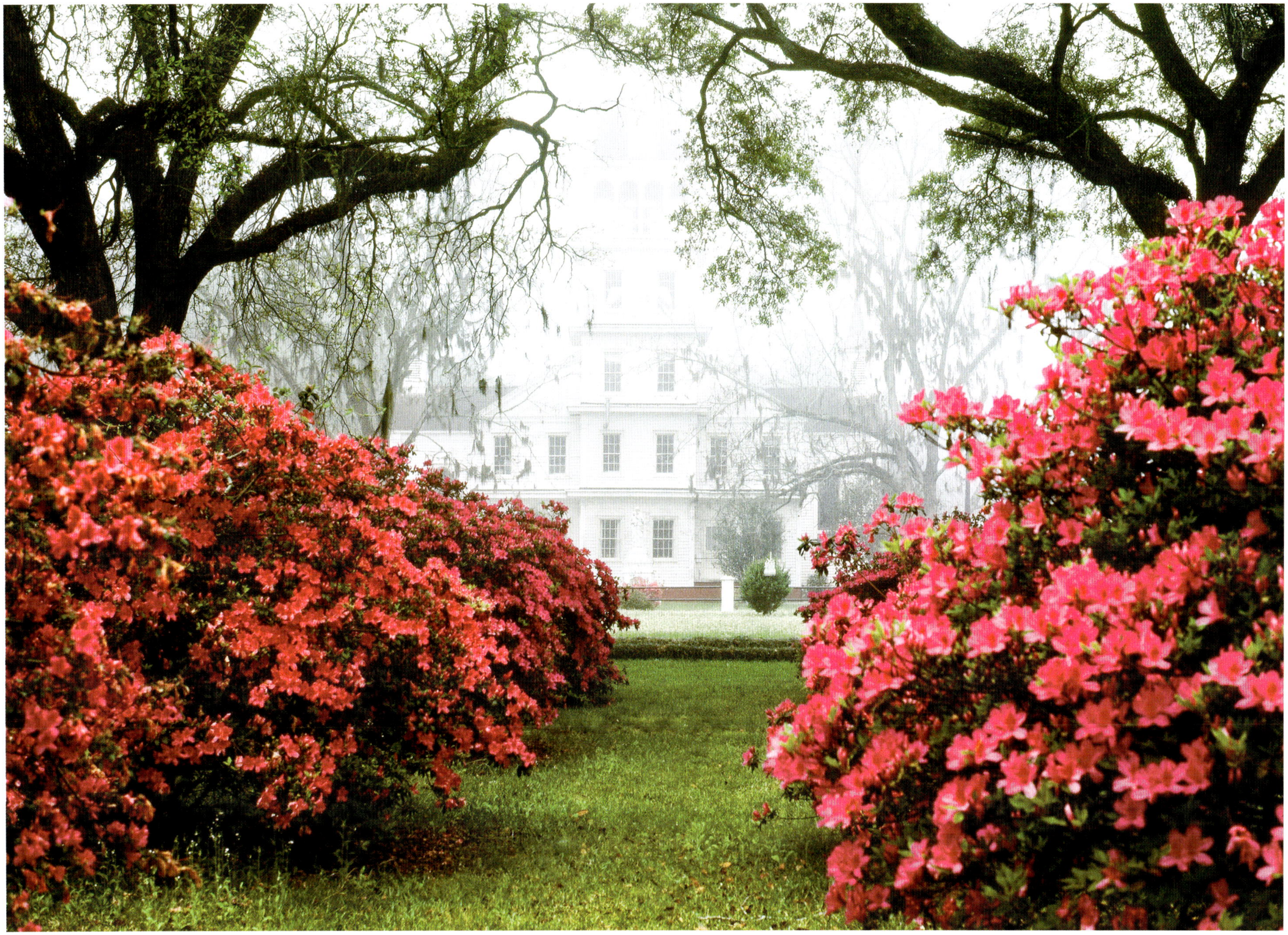

Chretien Pointe
1985

Chretien Point, located four miles southwest of Grand Coteau, is included in this book for two reasons. First, it is a nearby existing significant structure that was contemporary with antebellum Grand Coteau. Second, Hypolite Chretien II, who died from yellow fever shortly after the home's completion in 1835, is buried in the Grand Coteau cemetery amongst other Chretien relatives. There is significant lore surrounding the Chretiens including their friendship with the pirates Jean and Pierre Lafitte, and the exploits of Hypolite's wife Felicite.

Photographer's Note: The large columns and deep porches make Chretien Point seem quite immense. Actually it is just three rooms across and one and a half rooms deep. The stairs leading to the second floor take up a good amount of space as well. My favorite spot is the second floor veranda that no doubt was used more before the era of air conditioning. The arched doors and windows with accompanying shudders add a delicate touch. Louis Cornay, the owner when this photograph was taken, commented that if you traveled west in 1830s, the next significant structure would be the Alamo!

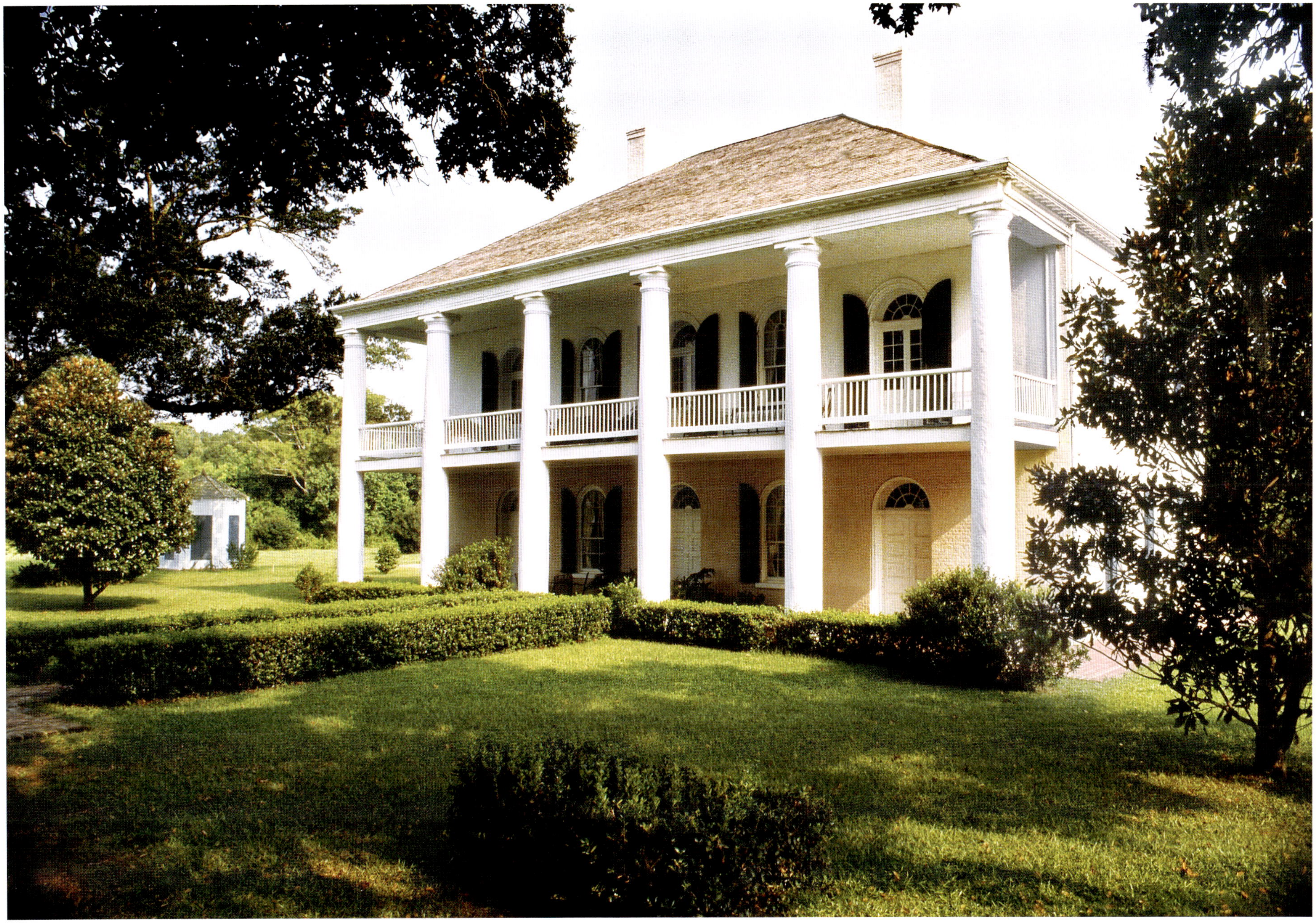

Watermelon Greens
1985

PHOTOGRAPHER'S NOTE: This photo was taken from my backyard looking over the fence where Jimmy Stelly ran his watermelon business. Jimmy, often referred to as the "Watermelon King," had melons delivered from as far away as Florida and Mexico. One summer he received and distributed fifty-nine semi loads of melons.

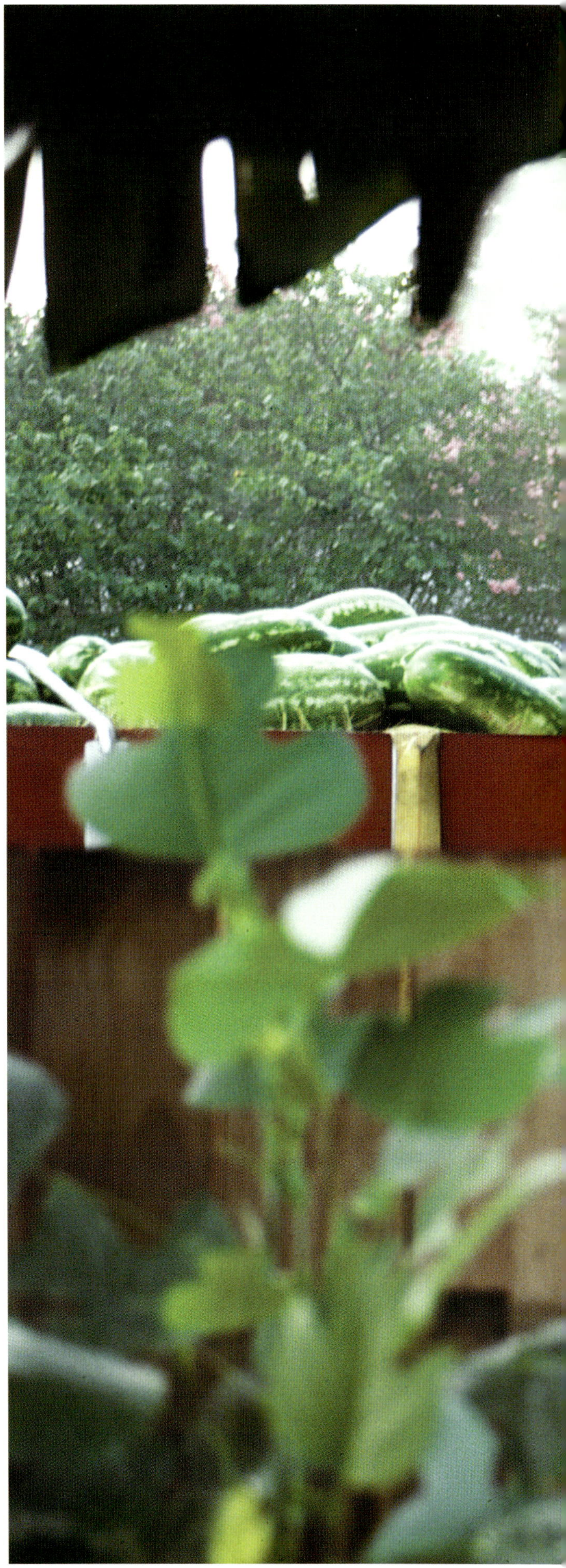

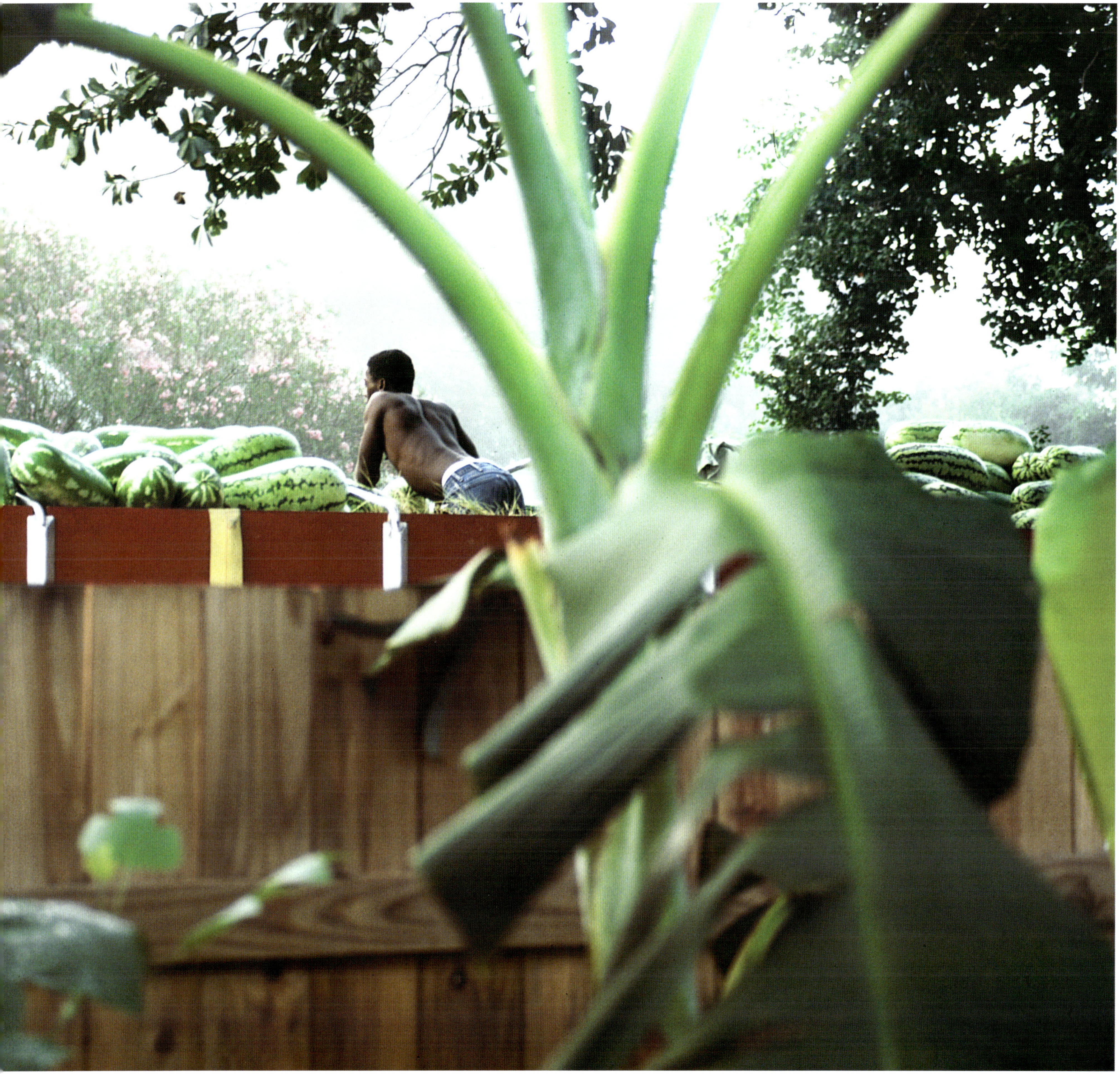

Grave of Mary Wilson – Academy of the Sacred Heart Cemetery

1985

In 1866 Mary Wilson, a young novice, was studying to become a member of the Society of the Sacred Heart when she became deathly ill. The sisters of the order prayed a Novena to John Berchmans for nine days, from December 6 to December 14, beseeching God to send Berchmans to cure Mary Wilson. Finally, Berchmans appeared to Mary Wilson, and she was healed. Dr. Edward M. Millard examined her and declared that there was no medical explanation of her quick recovery. On December 17, she received the habit of the Society of the Sacred Heart. A month later, as Wilson wrote a letter to the archbishop to be forwarded to Rome, John Berchmans appeared to her again. This time he told her that she had done well writing her letter. He also told her to be faithful to the Sisters of the Sacred Heart, and that she would die before her noviceship ended. Wilson died on August 14, 1867. This miracle eventually led to the canonization of St. John Berchmans. A small chapel on the Sacred Heart campus honors St. John Berchmans, and a museum displays academy life in the time of Mary Wilson.

The original metal crosses in the cemetery have been removed and replaced with marble headstones for easier maintenance.

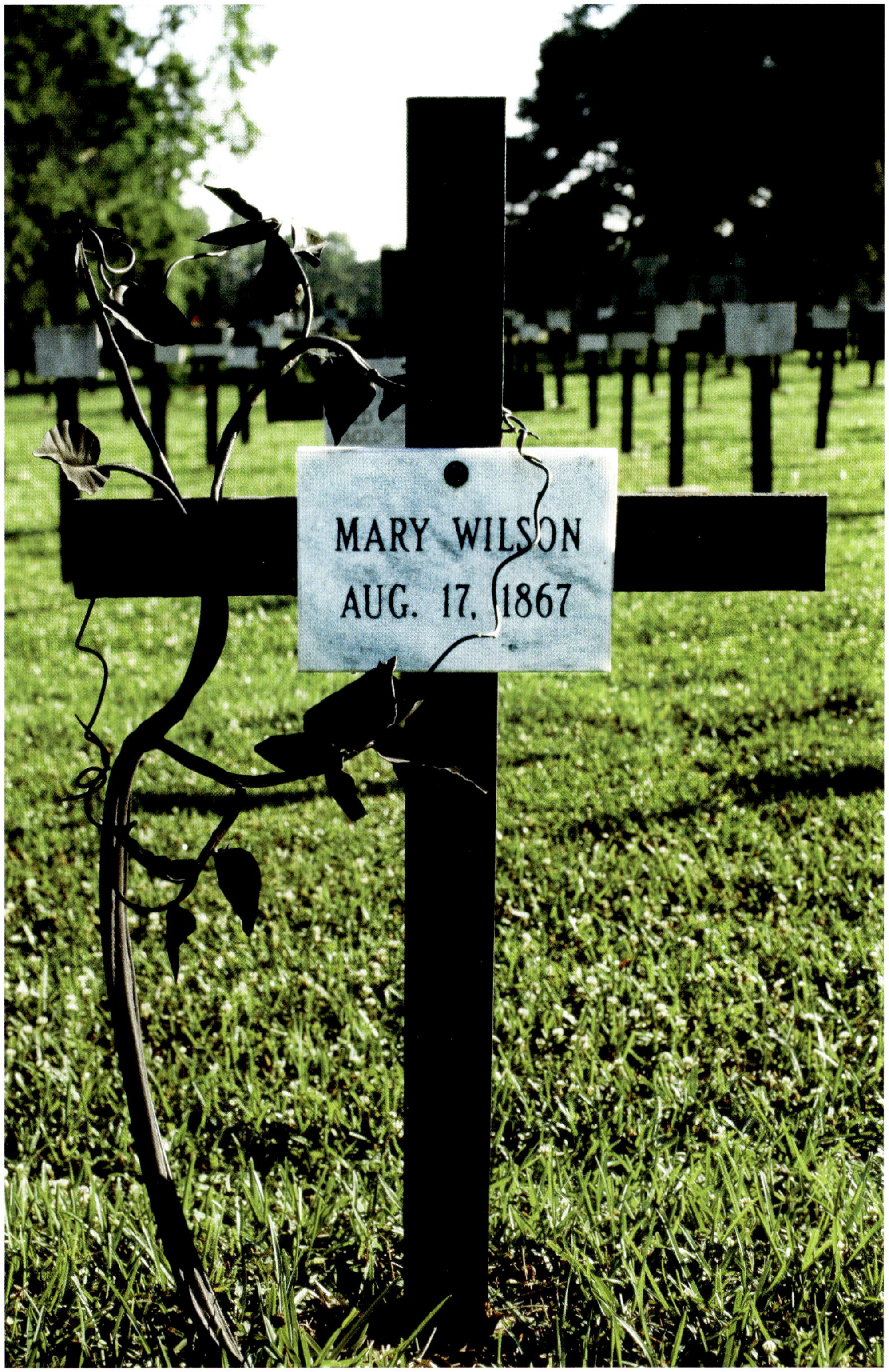
MARY WILSON
AUG. 17, 1867

CHOIR PRACTICE – ACADEMY OF THE SACRED HEART

1987

The choir practices for a Christmas program in the Academy of the Sacred Heart chapel. Previously, the chapel was more ornate, but when renovated in the 1970s, ornamentation was stripped in favor of a more simplistic decor. These changes occurred partly in response to Vatican II's call for a more modern and approachable Catholic Church. The Christ figure behind the altar seemed of another era, and the school replaced it, opting for a more contemporary one. Many statues were removed and the original altar rests in St. Martinville.

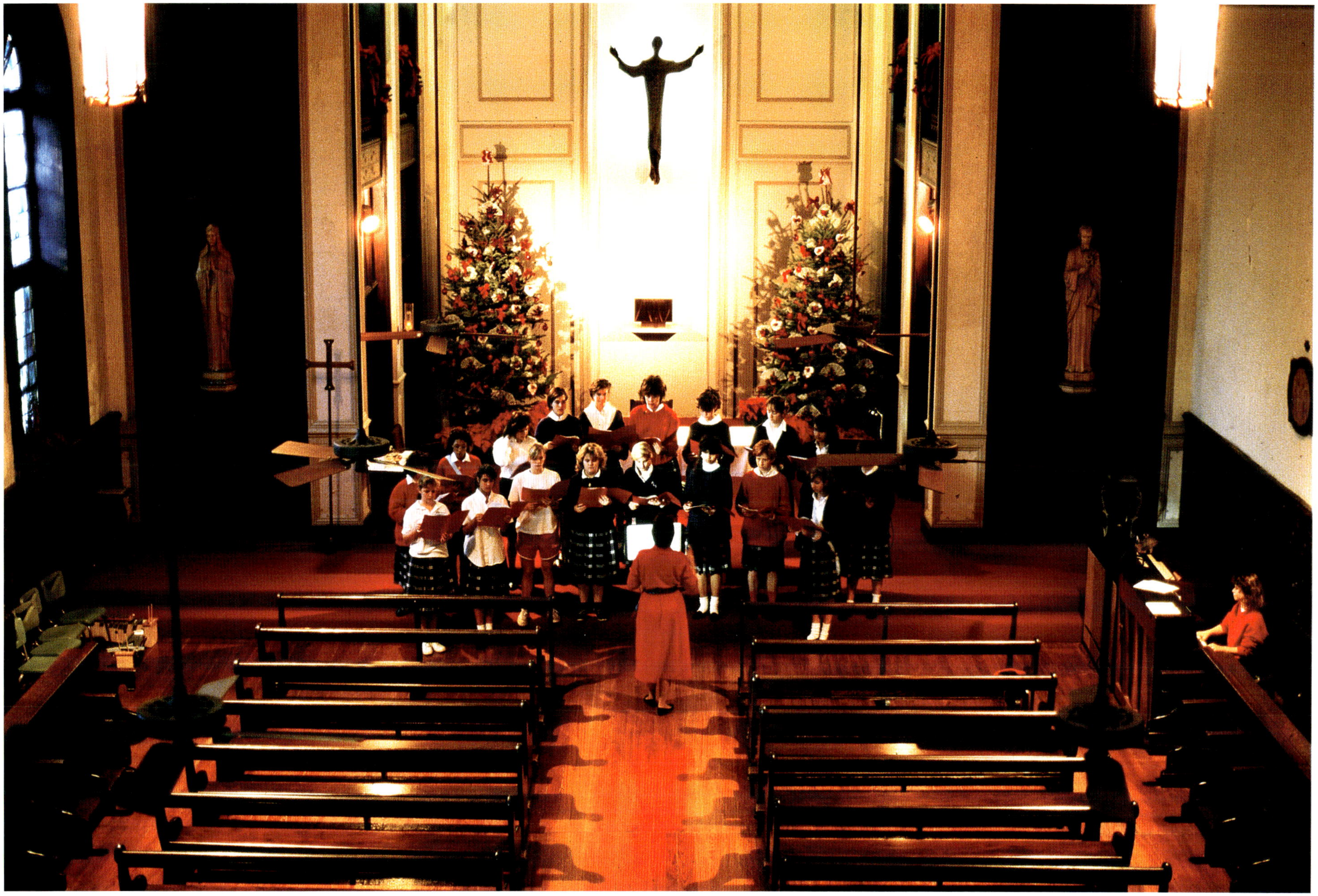

St. Charles College

1987

A cross stands silhouetted against the evening sky over the castle-like roofline parapet of St. Charles College.

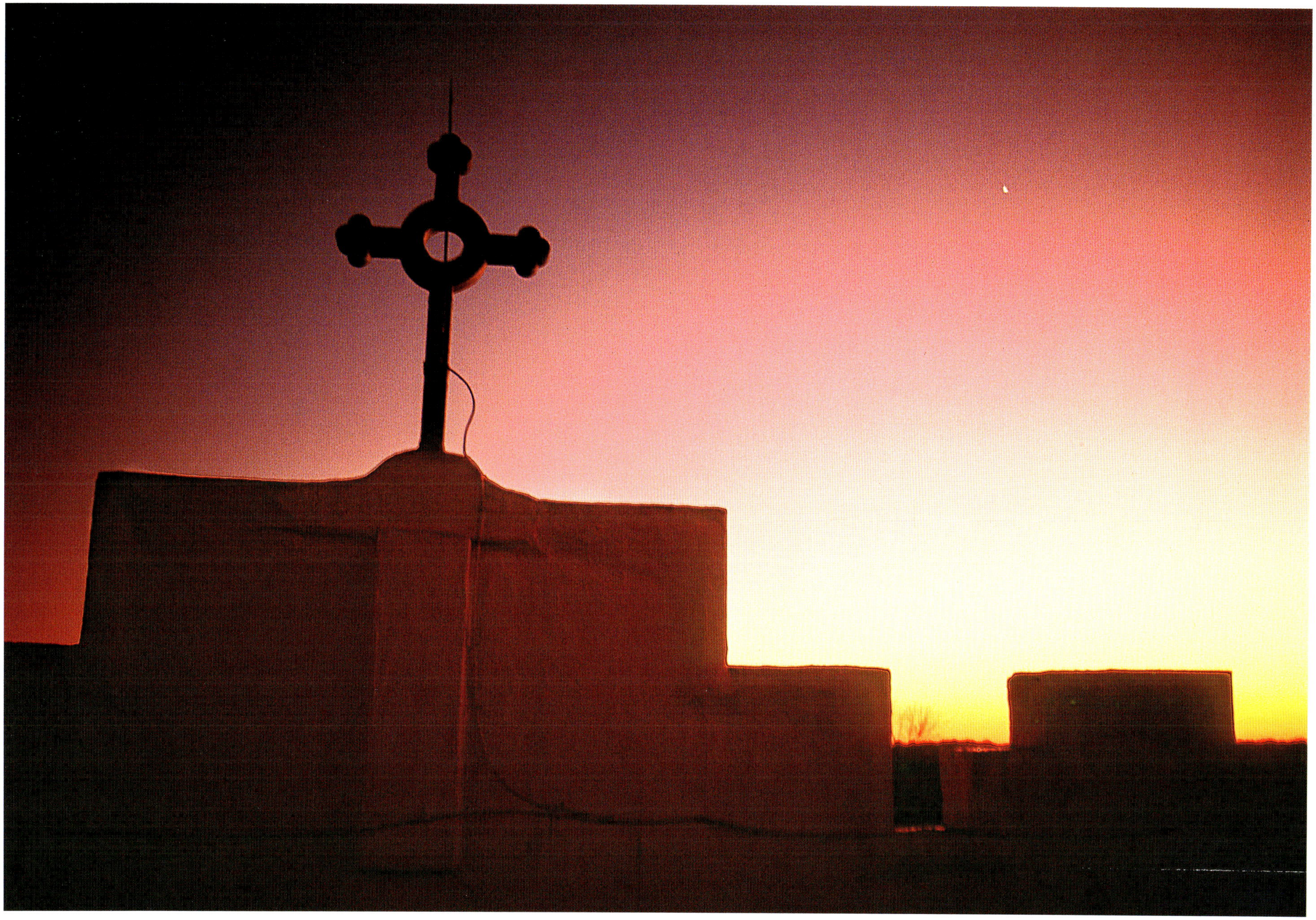

Aloysius "Luch" Ivy
1987

Aloysius Ivy (1923-2007), commonly known as "Luch," was a muleskinner in the U.S. Army and saw action in Europe during World War II. With his wife, Joyce, he owned Ivy's (presently Catahoula's), a general store that supplied groceries, gas, fireworks, and boots, among other things.

Photographer's Note: He was an independent sort who spoke his mind. He referred to most everyone as "hoss." Bits of wisdom came forth in the guise of clever observations. His bluntness could be offensive and his toughness aggravating. However, there was a charitable side to his personality that he managed quietly—I only heard about it after he died. Saying he had charm would be a little overboard, but there was just something about him that couldn't be denied. A self-made, wealthy man, he was buried in a blue denim work shirt, just as he requested.

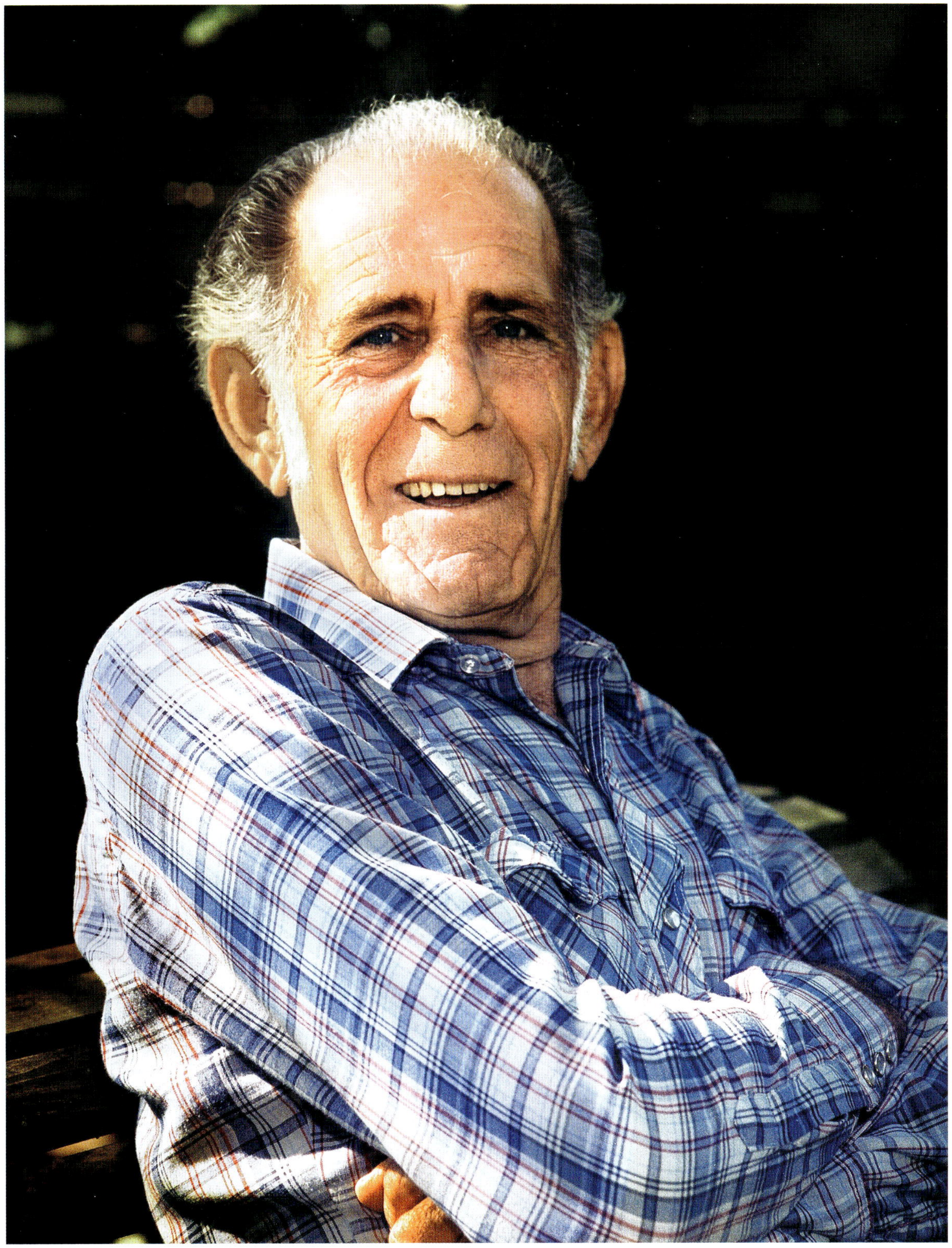

Wrought Iron Cross – Academy of the Sacred Heart

1987

A wrought-iron cross crests the chapel of the Academy of the Sacred Heart. The cross, which was a gift from Mother Digby, originated in France, as did the original crosses in the Academy's cemetery.

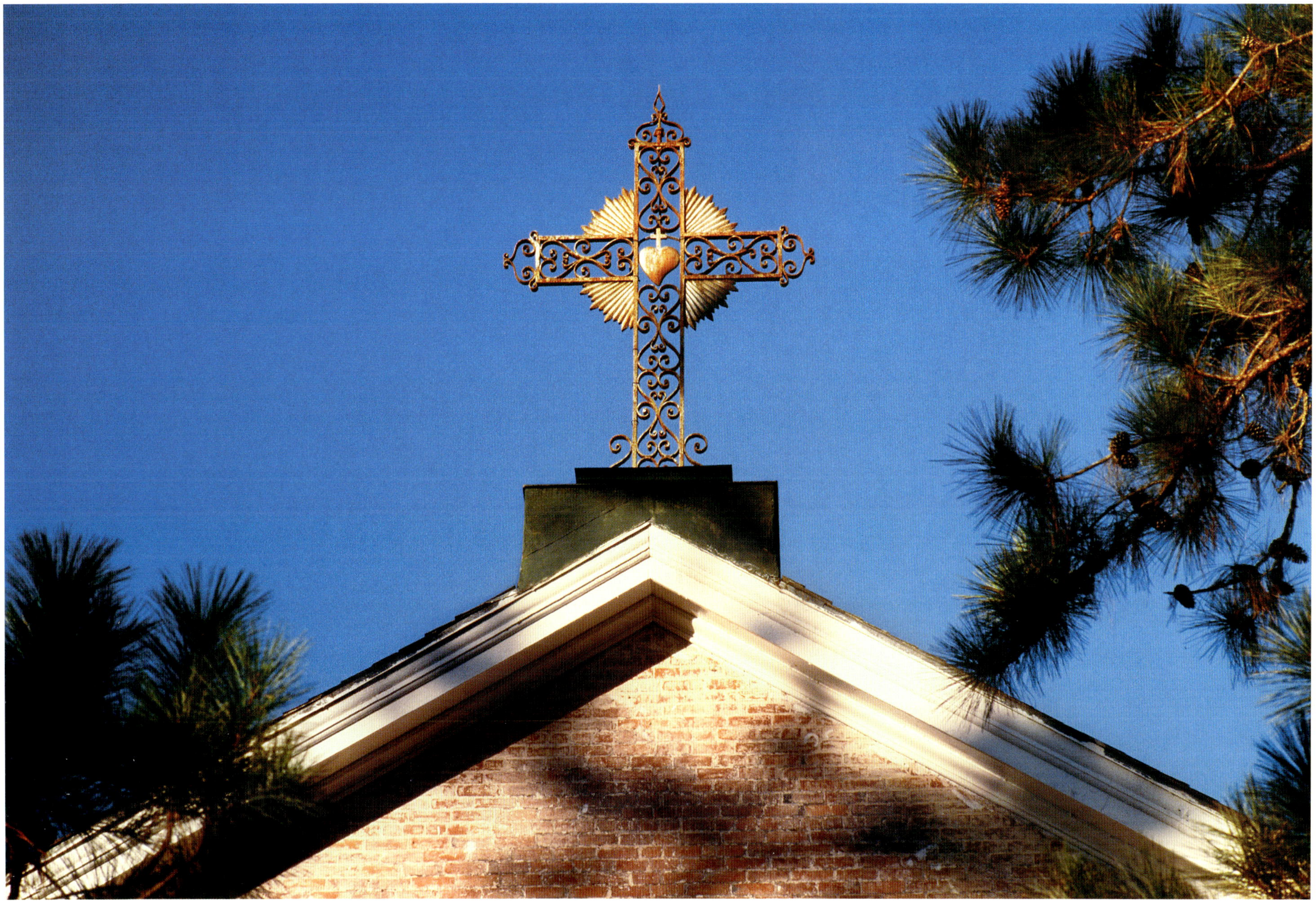

MAYOR MARY MURRAY
1988

Mary Murray poses in her first car—a prized possession for someone who previously walked to work. One of twelve children, she attended the Colored School for Girls, which was later named St. Peter Claver. At the time, the school only went to the seventh grade. With the encouragement of the nuns, Murray traveled to Lafayette to attend Holy Rosary High School, then went to Xavier University in New Orleans. To help pay for college, she lived with a French family, caring for their children and teaching them English. After graduating, Murray returned to Grand Coteau, where at the request of Father Thensted, she taught at St. Peter Claver School for thirty-one years.

Murray gave back, to the Grand Coteau community by serving as alderwoman for fifteen years, eventually becoming the first female mayor of Grand Coteau. In 2012, Murray received the Martin Luther King Jr. Award from Lafayette Diocese's Office of Black Catholic Ministries for outstanding community service.

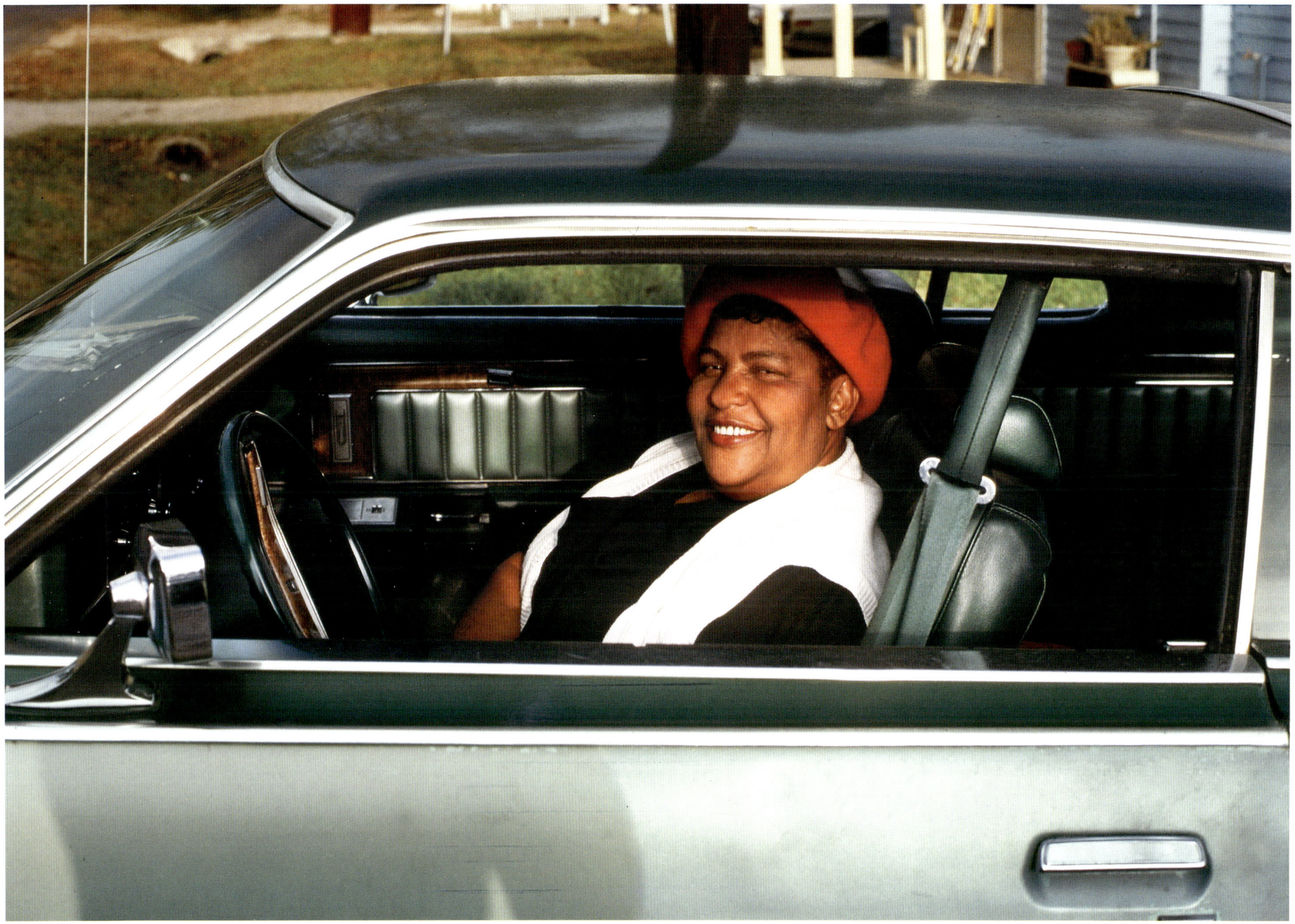

Alcide Charles

1988

Alcide Charles (1906–2007), brother of Mary Louise Charles (page 98), stands in the side yard of Madame Chatrian's home. Charles was a sharecropper on Chatrian's land, growing potatoes, corn, and cotton, as well as keeping a garden of vegetables for his family. His first language was Creole French. The second oldest in a family of eight children, Charles's schooling was interrupted by the obligation to harvest crops alongside his father. Later Charles and his wife raised eleven children in a two-bedroom house, always making certain that they attended school—though they too could not begin until after the late October harvest.

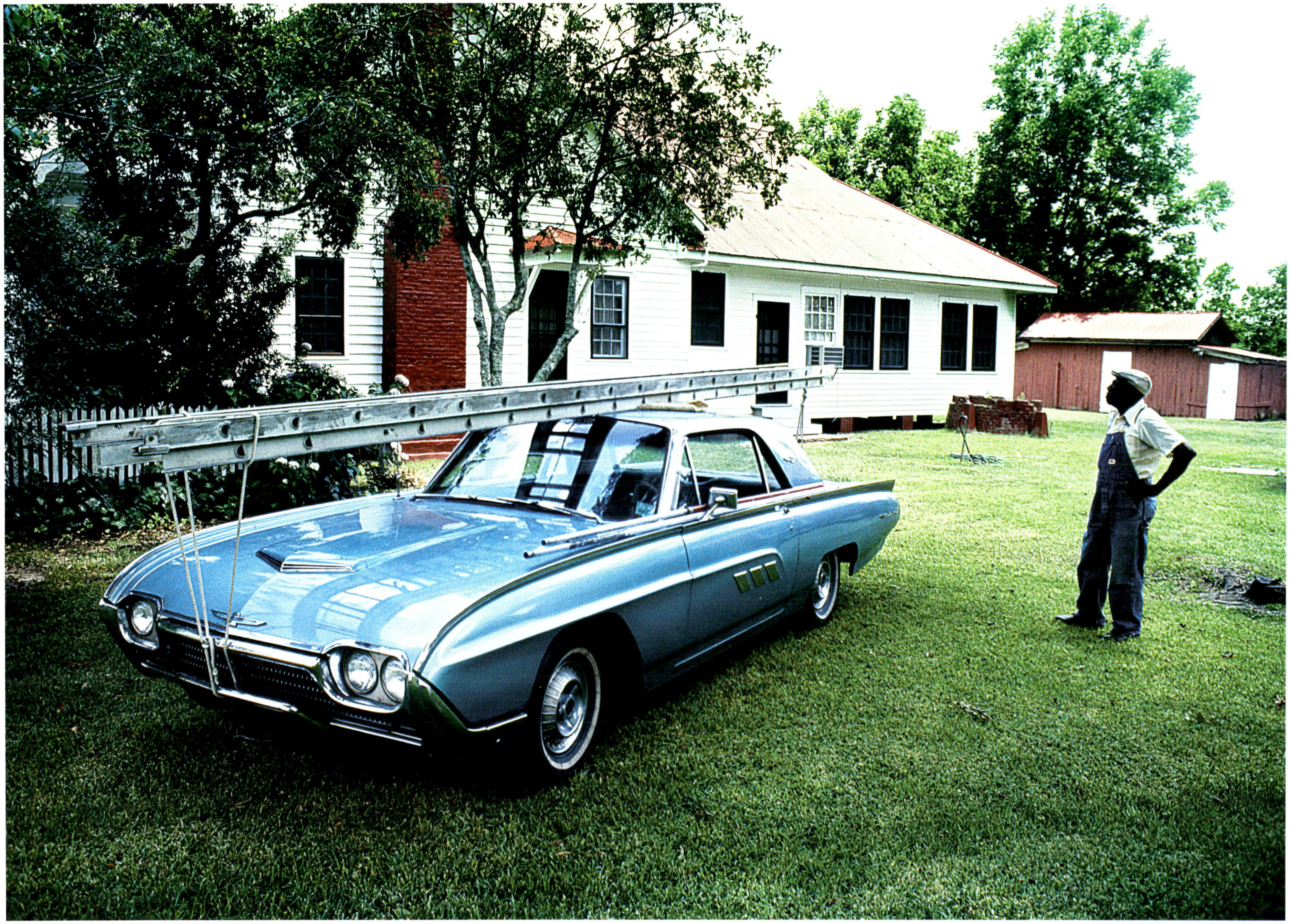

Snowfall – Academy of the Sacred Heart
1988

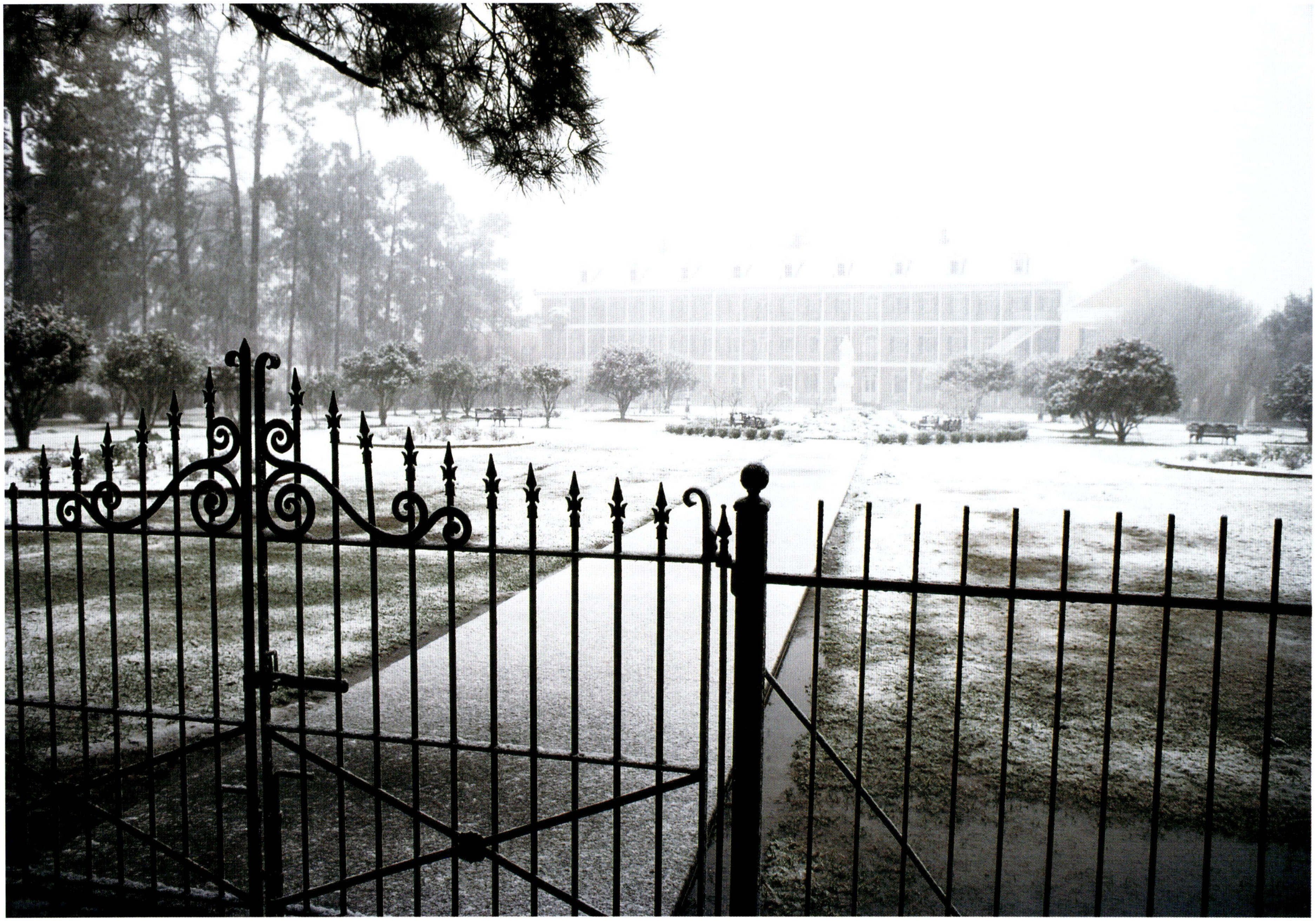

Winter Wheat

1989

Jesuit priests once drove horse-drawn carriages over this path from St. Charles College to the Academy of the Sacred Heart to conduct mass.

The fields of St. Charles College are currently populated by cattle, but over the years they have supported crops like corn and sweet potatoes. At times, as seen here, winter wheat was planted, resulting in a glorious green tableau.

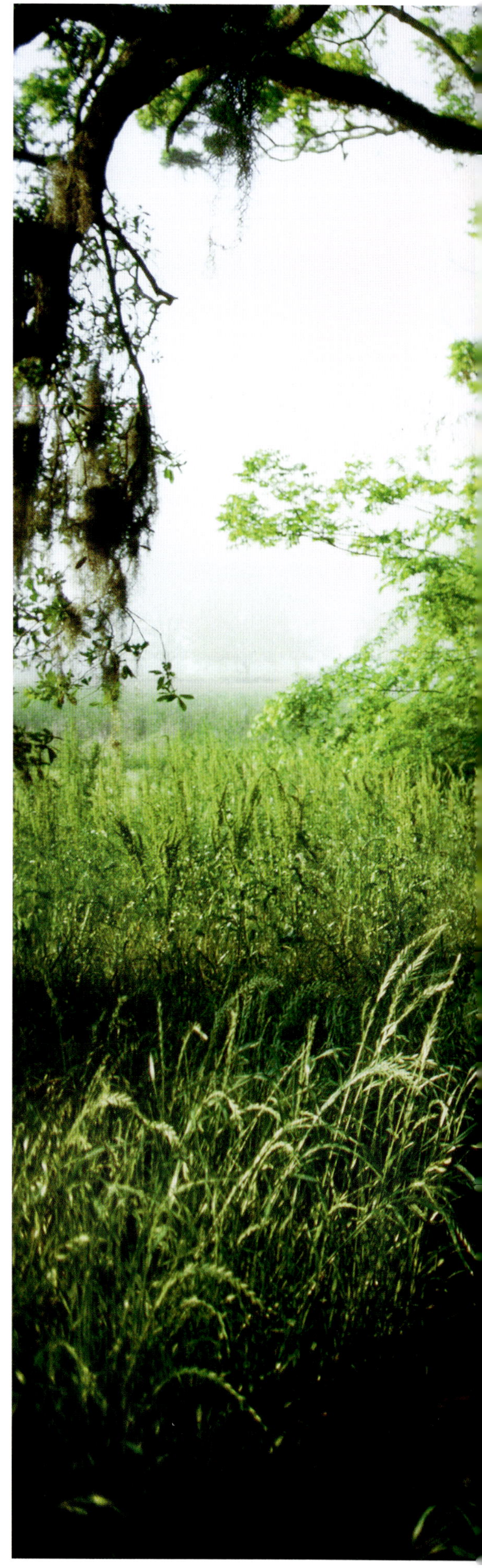

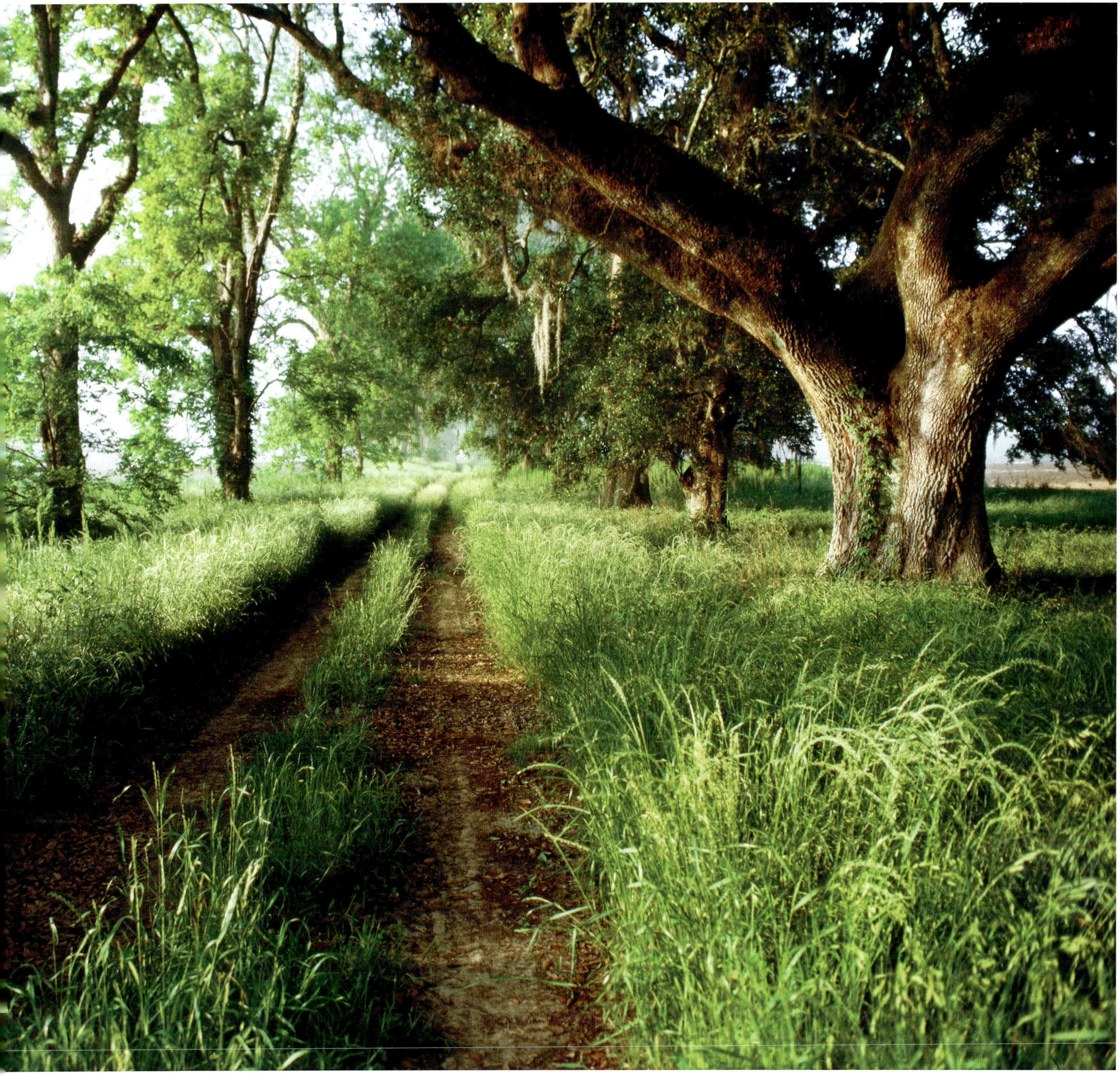

Contemplation
1989

A nun meditates on the green lawn of St. Charles College. Originally retreats were available only for priests and nuns. St. Charles College became one of the few places in the country offering directed retreats to the public during the 1970s. Retreats at St. Charles College differ from the group programs offered at Our Lady of the Oaks Retreat House in that most are one-on-one. The exercises are often based on the teachings of St. Ignatius Loyola. Solitude and silence are usually core aspects of these retreats, which can range from three days to a month. Including weekend spiritual workshops, the college averages nearly one-thousand annual retreat participants.

In addition to retreats, Jesuit novices begin their training at St. Charles College, studying to become priests under the vows of poverty, chastity, and obedience. An average of ten to fifteen men enter the novitiate annually. The two-year term begins with a thirty-day silent retreat. Over the course of the term, the entrants undergo extensive studies in theology and spirituality. While in Grand Coteau, they do apolistic work, such as working with youth at the Thensted Center and visiting the elderly.

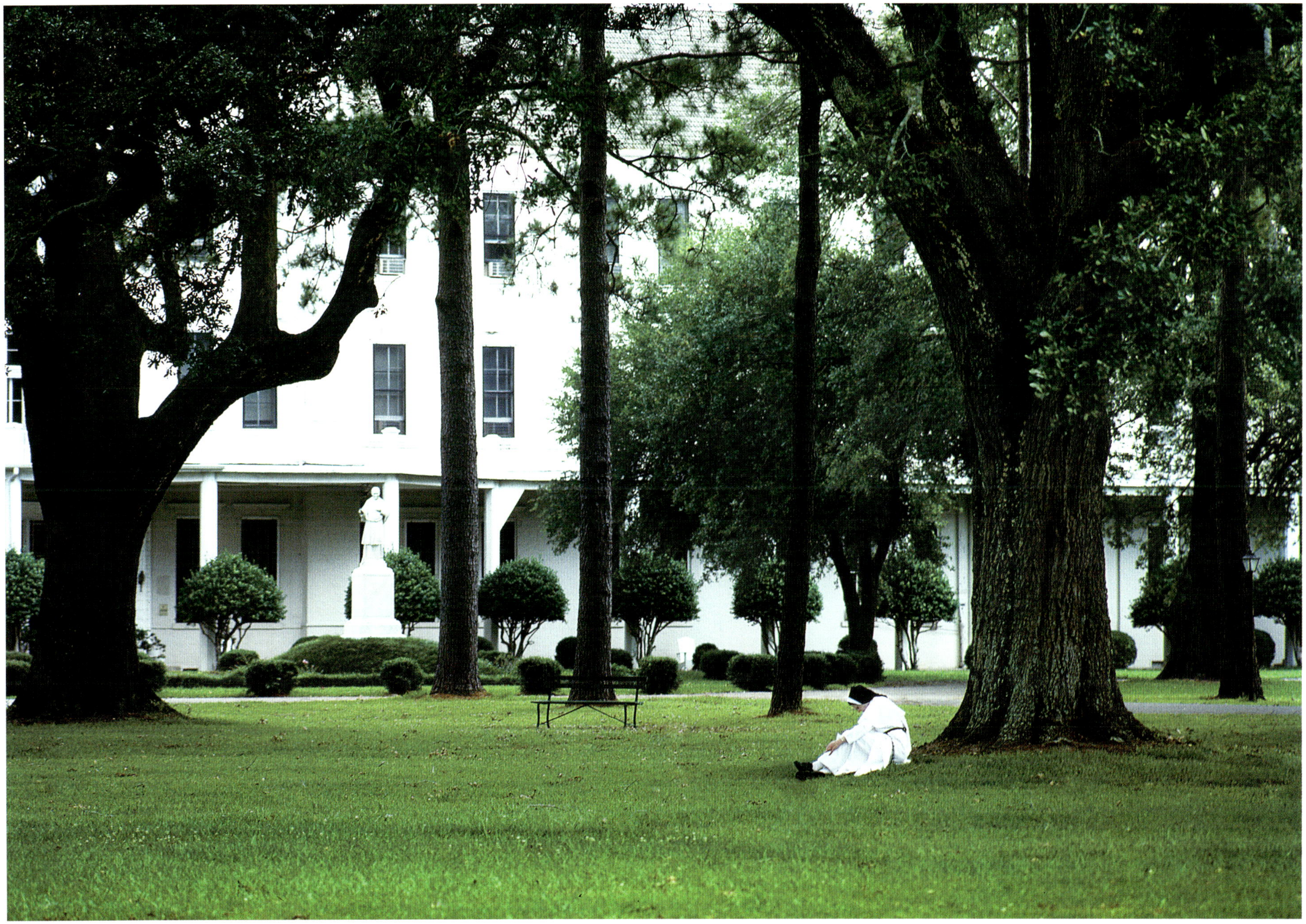

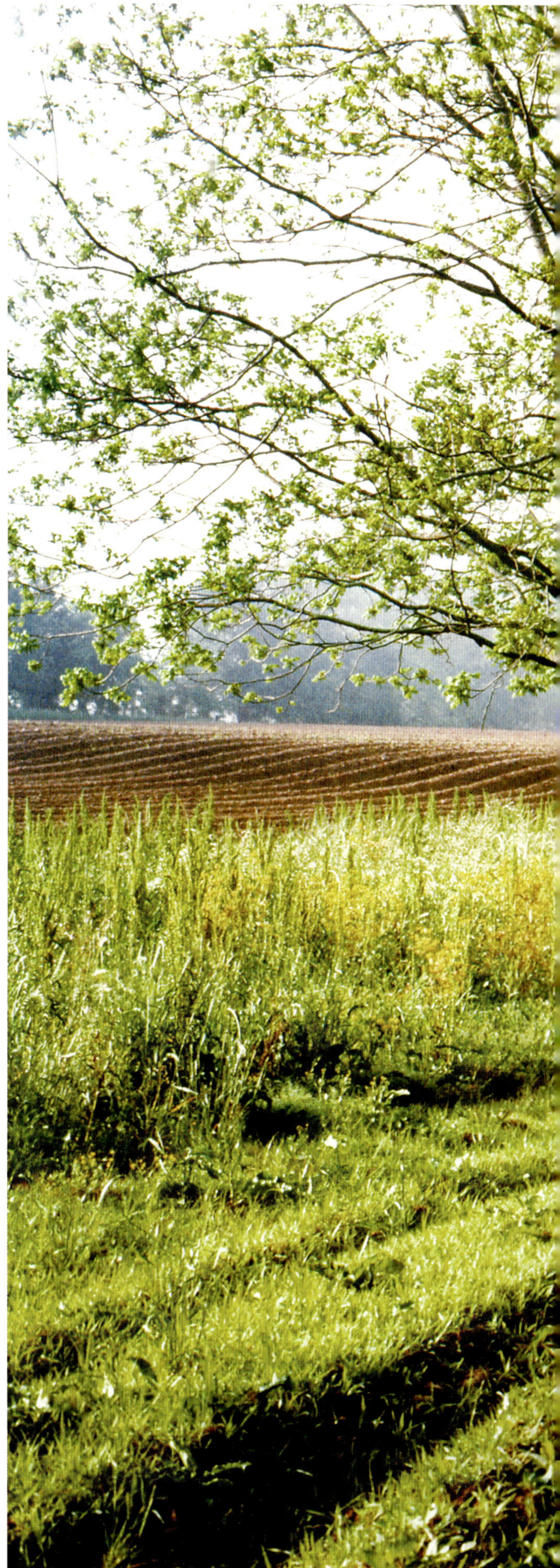

PLOWED FIELD
1989

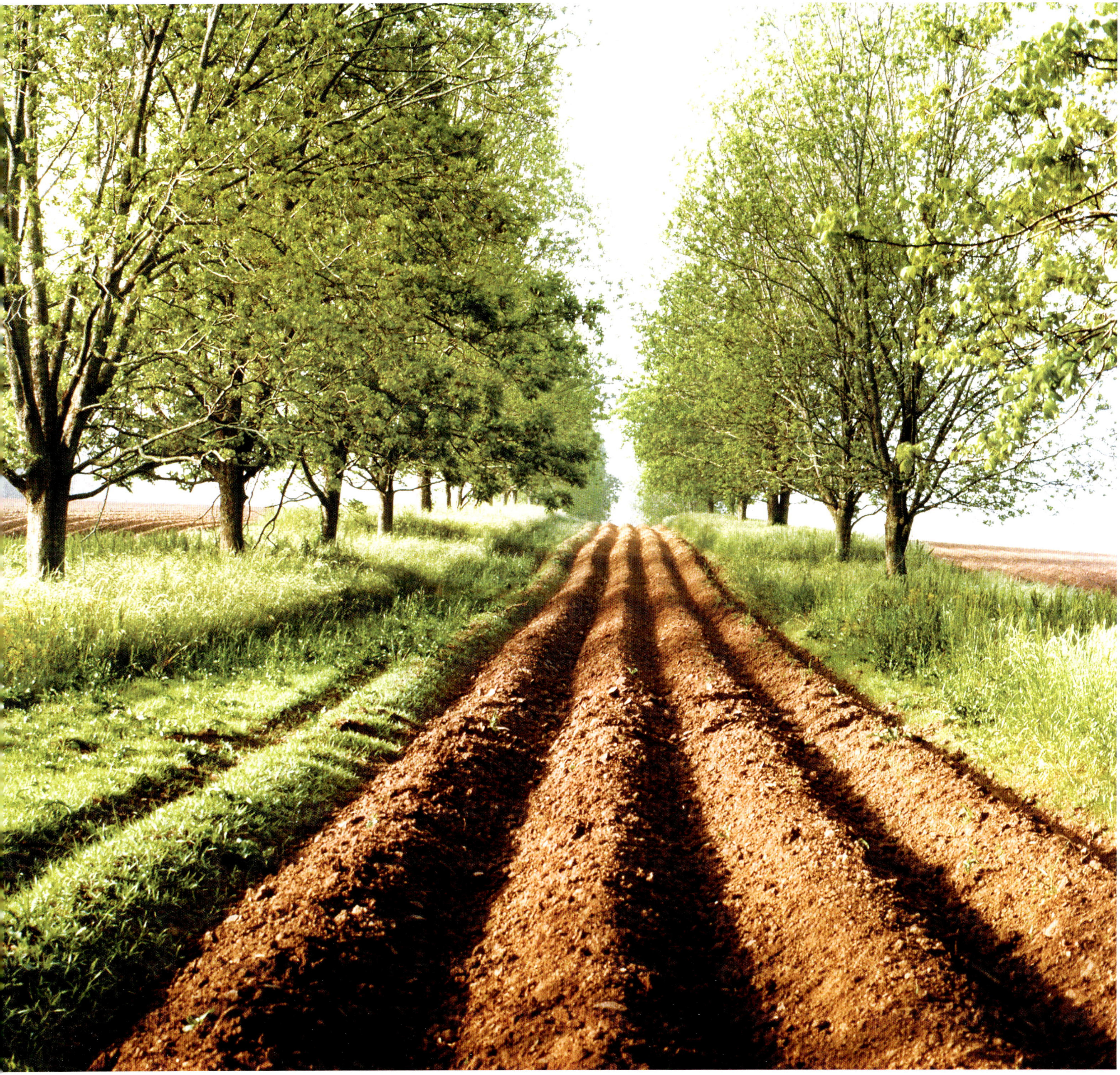

Ben Wren

1990

Father Ben Wren leads a meditation during a Zen retreat in a space that had been converted into a Zendo on the third floor of St. Charles College.

Wren entered the Novitiate at age eighteen in 1949. His mother was born in Hong Kong, his father was an American Marine, and he was raised in Georgia. He used Zen as a form of non-directed meditation, believing it opened the practitioner to the experience of God. Father Wren earned advanced degrees in Asian studies from the University of Arizona, before teaching high school in Texas. In 1970, Wren joined the faculty of the history department at Loyola University in New Orleans where he taught popular Asian and world history courses. He initiated the Zen retreats at St. Charles College and many lay people participated, some returning every year for more than ten years. Sometimes he sat cross-legged, even in Mass, in a back pew.

PHOTOGRAPHER'S NOTE: Ben Wren was a big man, powerful both physically and philosophically. His face clearly reflected his Asian lineage. The Zen retreat day began at 6:00 a.m. with folk dancing followed by two successive twenty-five minute "zazen" meditations. There were three more of these zazen segments during the day interspersed with tai chi, ikebana, spiritual instruction, and meals. Ben Wren was witty, charming, enlightening, irreverent, and when it came to zazen, very strict.

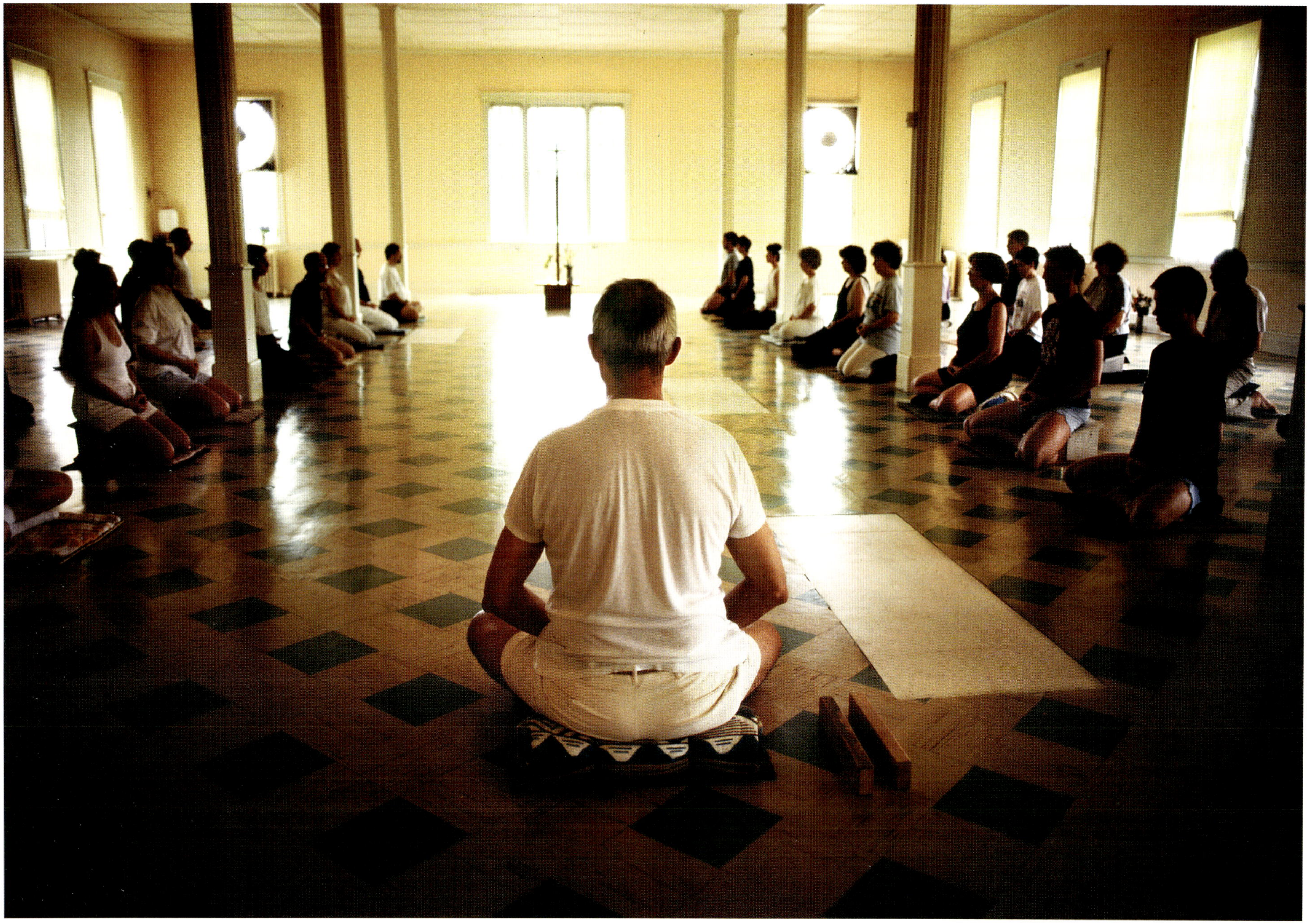

Mary Louise Charles

1990

Mary Louise Charles (1908–2010) wears a sunbonnet as she ponders her past. During the Great Mississippi River Flood of 1927, when she was a young girl, her family fled the rising waters of their home in Prairie Basse, located five miles east of Grand Coteau. Alongside scores of others, Mary Louise's parents and seven siblings traveled by mule-drawn wagon to the higher ground of Grand Coteau. Weeks later, after the waters receded and the family prepared to return, Mary Louise was invited by Madame Theresa Chatrian to stay as a live-in domestic for the family—an offer she gladly accepted.

Charles received little formal education in her life, except for a few years of schooling when she was a child. She never married and spent most of her life working and caring for the Chatrians. Over the years, she became a close companion of Madame Chatrian, especially after Madame was widowed in 1942. When Chatrian passed away in 1978, in accordance with the will, Mary Louise Charles inherited the Chatrian home (circa 1845) and eleven acres of land. Mary Louise Charles lived to be 101 years old.

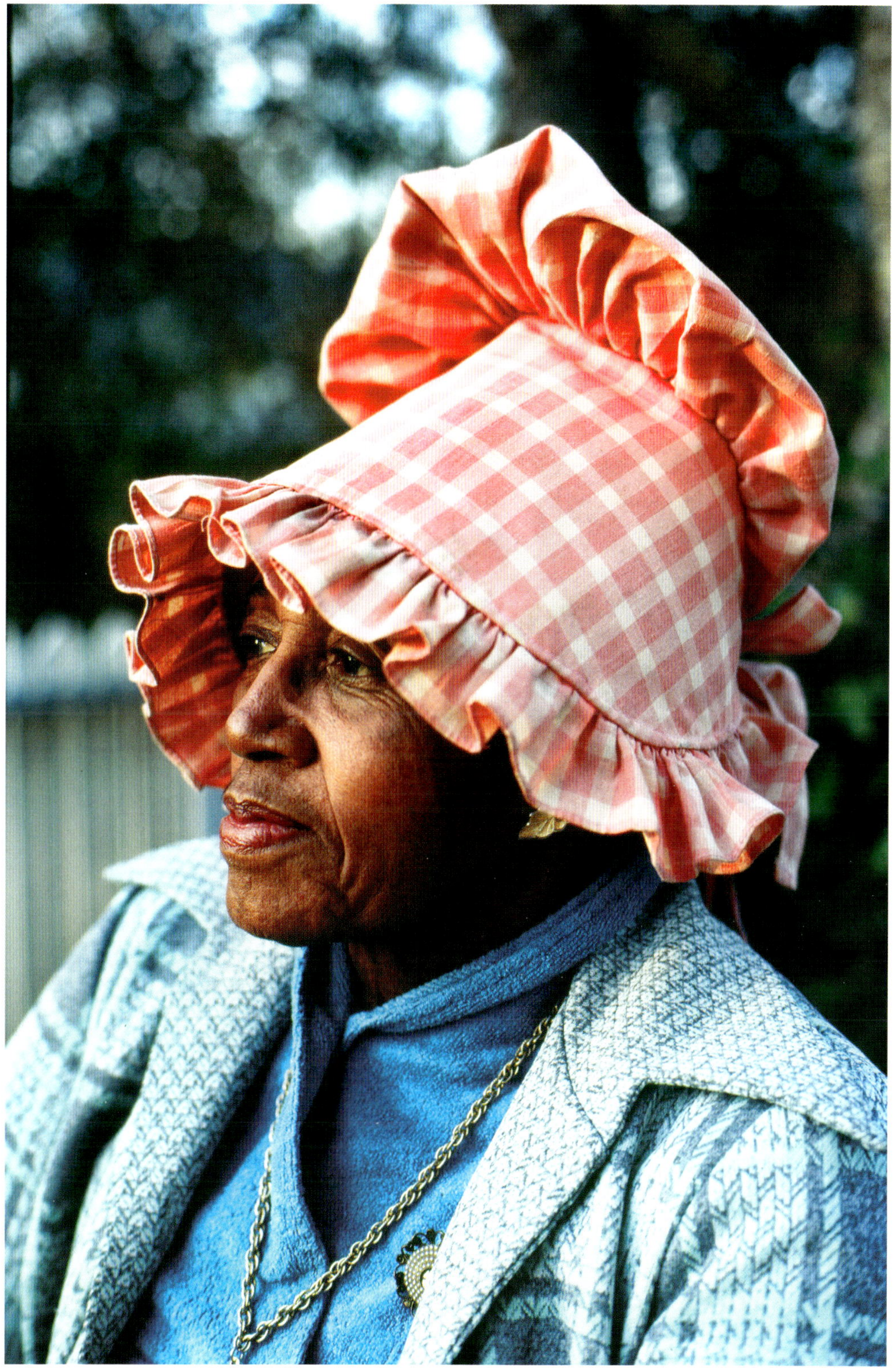

Chatrian Street Barn

1990

Following a storm, sunlight illuminates a weather-worn barn on Chatrian Street. The building once held stores of sweet potatoes, corn, and other crops from Madame Chatrian's farm. Local lore suggest that the Pony Express once utilized the barn as a horse exchange point. Currently Cowbird Farms uses it as a chicken brooder for their pastured poultry business.

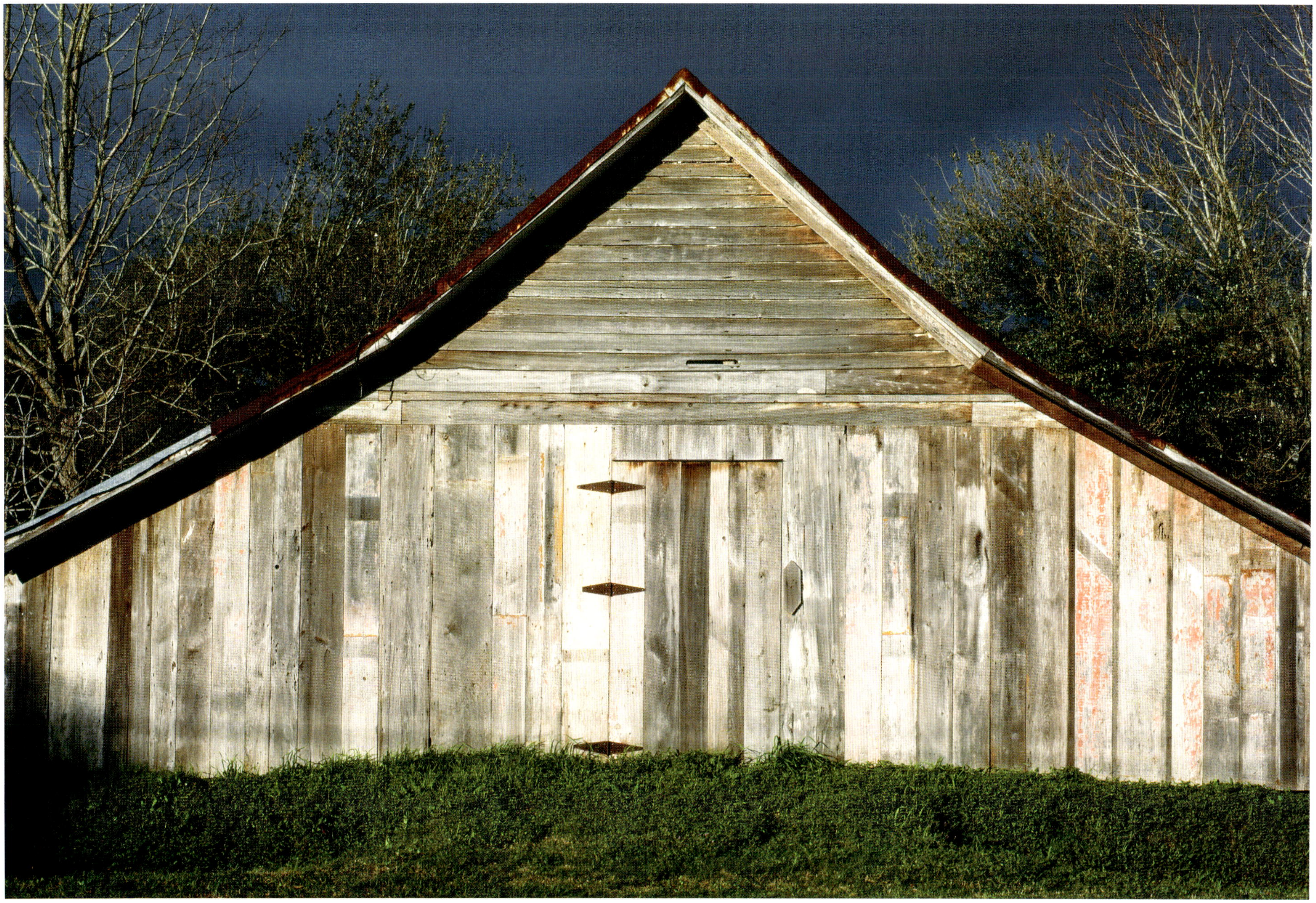

Walking Shadow
1990

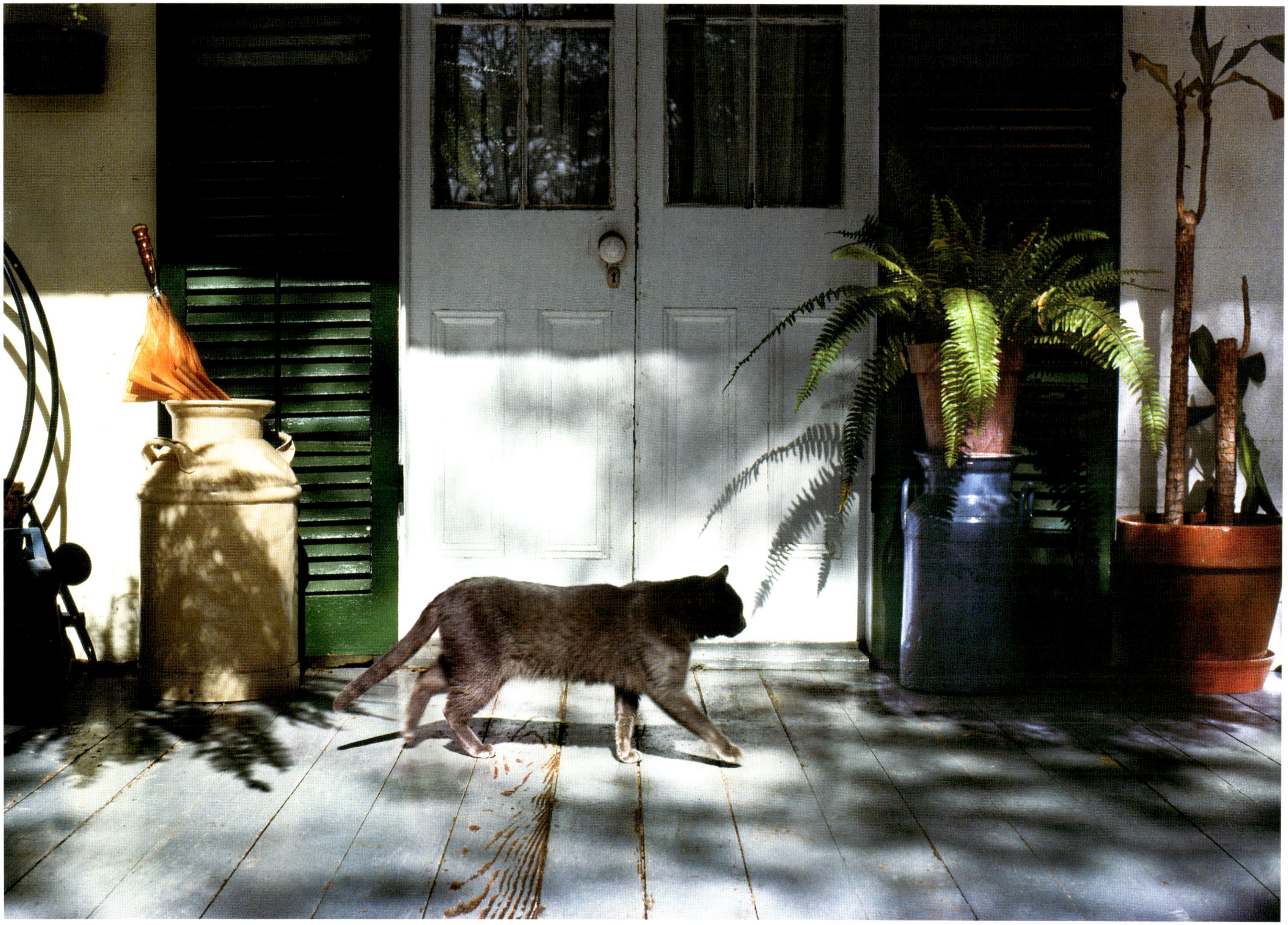

Live Oaks and Butterweed (senecio glabellus)
1993

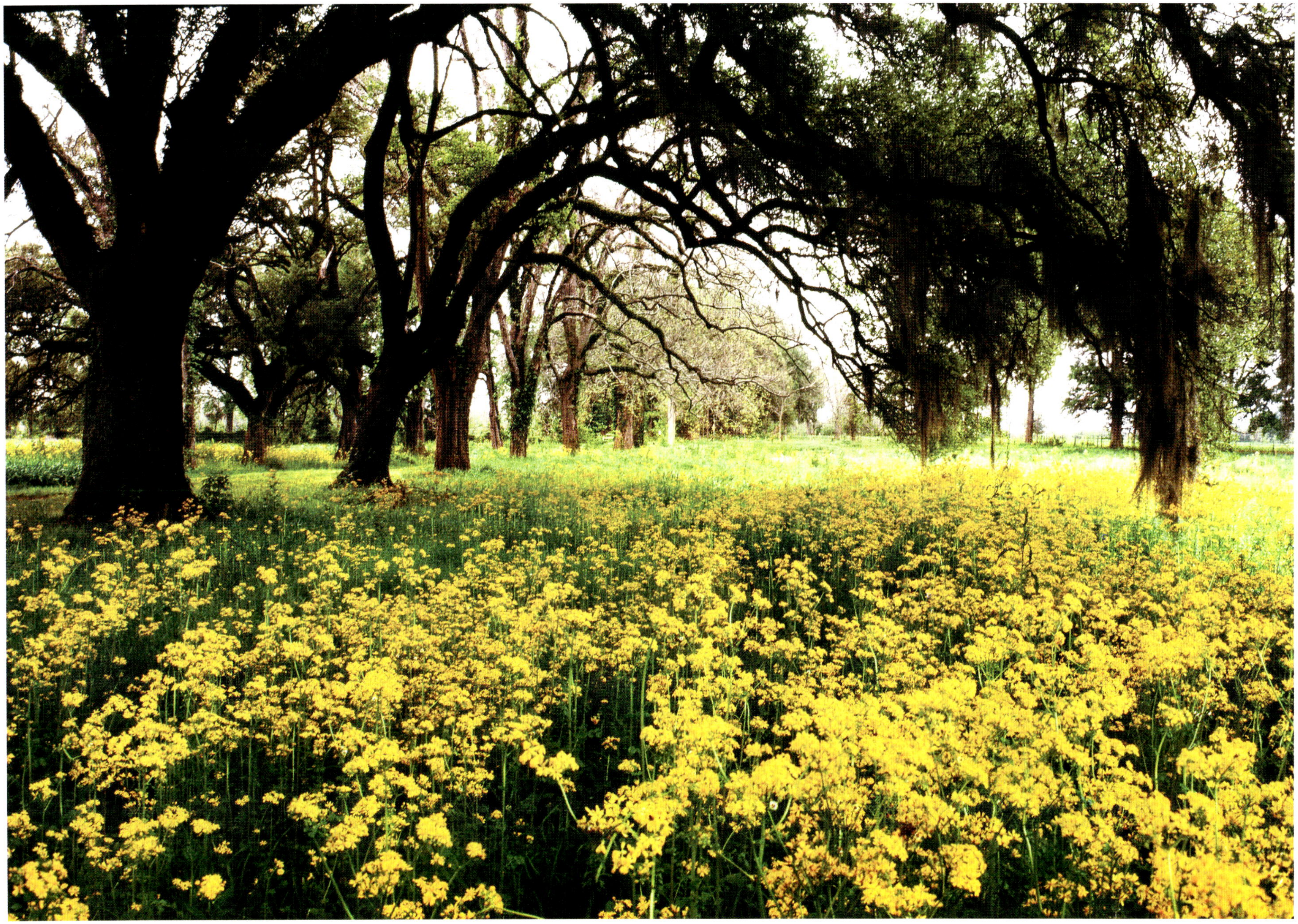

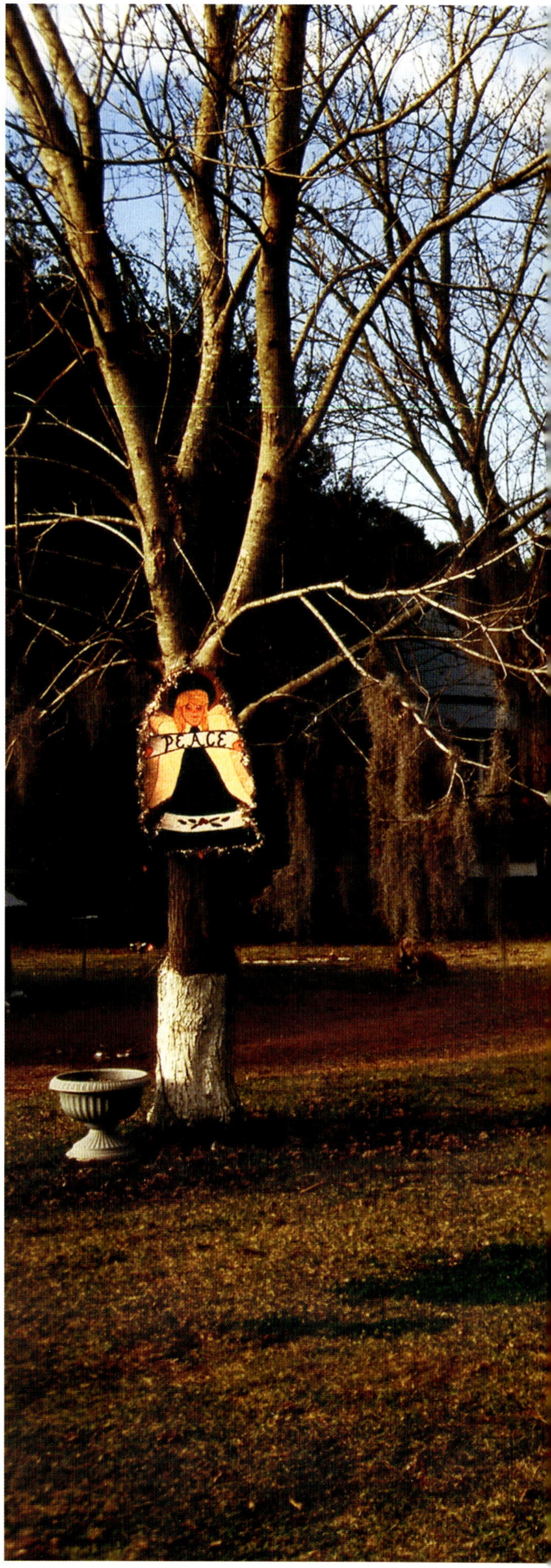

Cottage Manger Scene
1993

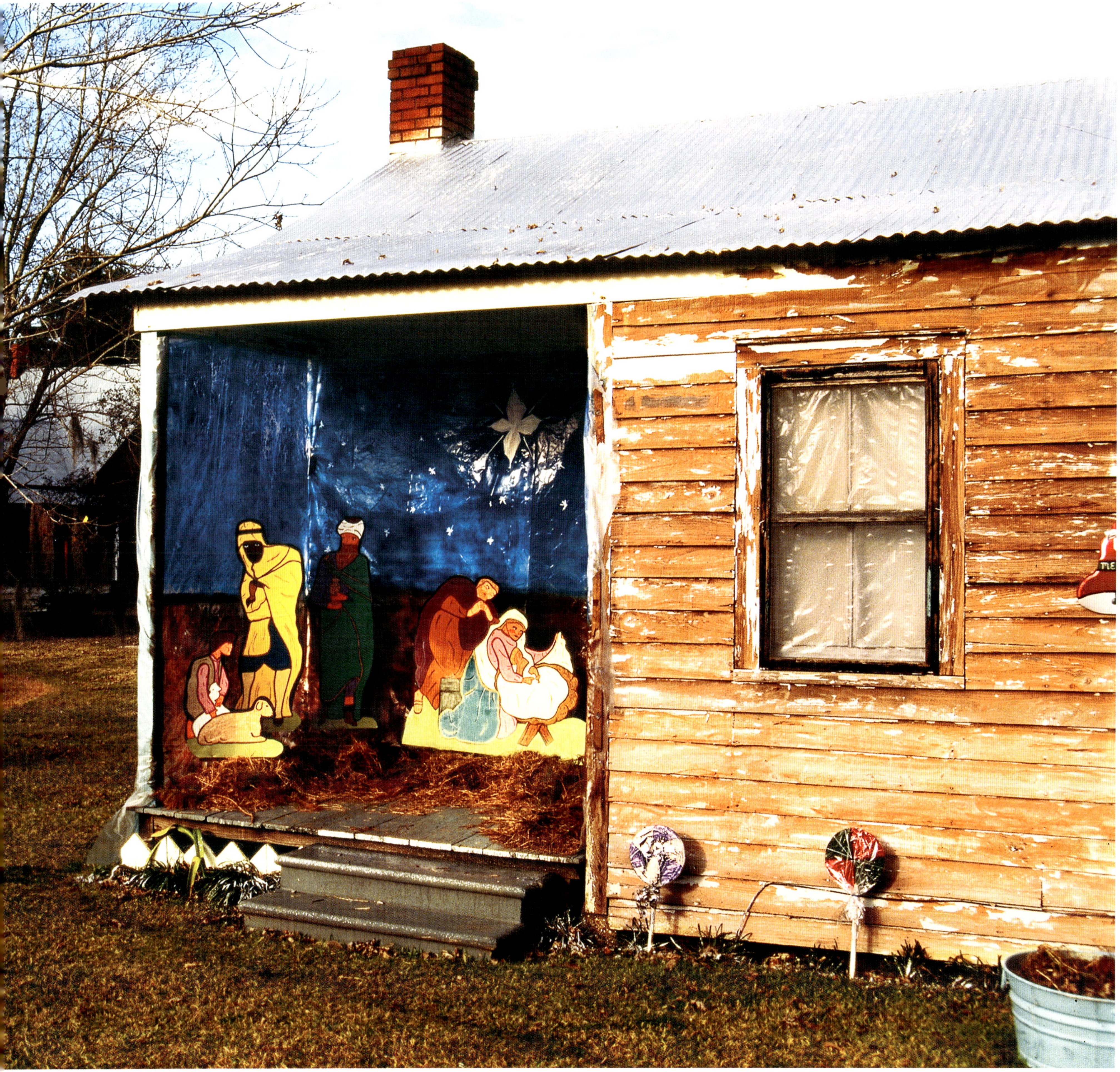

Fresh Tomatoes

1995

For about five years in the 1990s, Mike Ryan grew organic herbs, vegetables, flowers, persimmons, and figs in the backyard of his home. The house, a pre-1840s raised cottage, is presently owned by the Brinkhaus family.

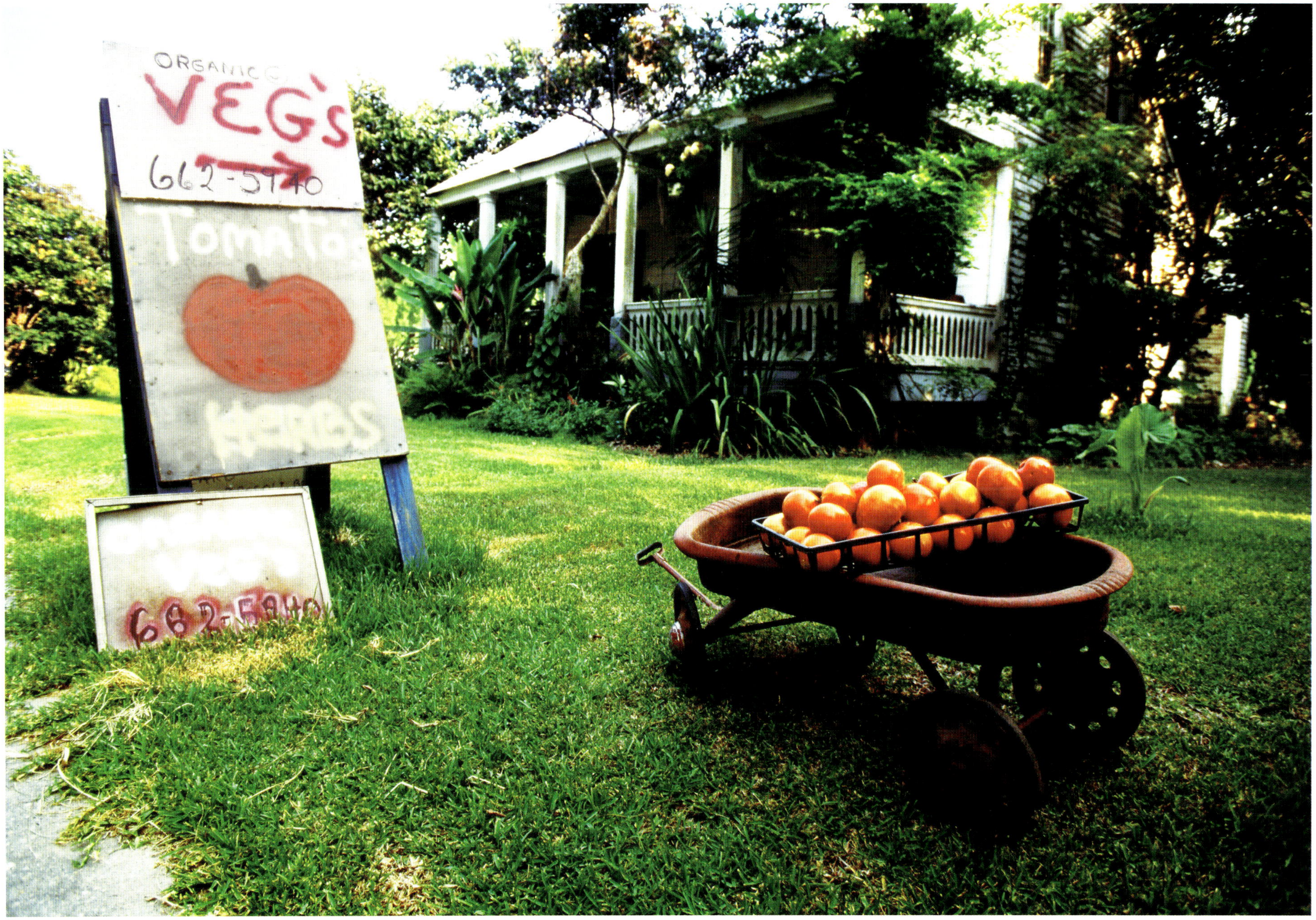
ORGANIC
VEG's
662-5940
Tomato's

The Red House
1995

"The Red House" is a landmark on the main street of Grand Coteau. This Acadian cottage has a floor plan typical of its architectural style with no halls and two front doors that open into the house. Mortise and tenon construction was used in constructing the building. The steps or stairway on the front porch lead up to the garçonnière, the second floor where the boys slept. Unlike the girls, the boys enjoyed the freedom to come and go as they pleased in the evenings. As living space was limited, having the stairs on the outside of the house also allowed for more room inside. This may be half a house, part of an estate settlement that resulted in the home being divided in two—not an uncommon way to settle an estate in the 1800s. Currently, the structure houses Petit Rouge Antiques. (Also see page 10.)

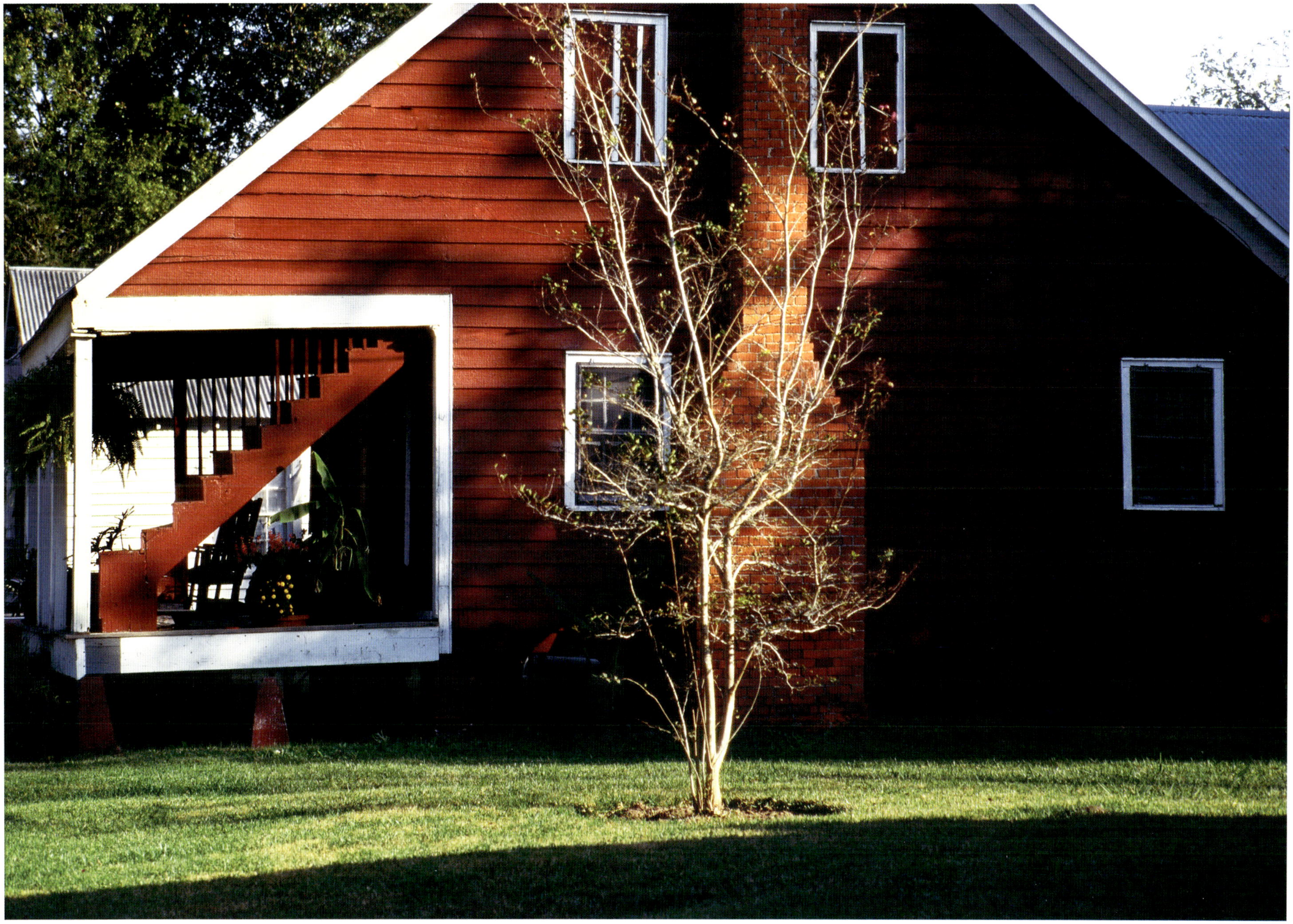

Spanish Moss Hangs from Sunlit Live Oaks

1995

Grand Coteau is noted for an abundance of spectacular trees. Certainly one can attribute this to the foresight of arborists from centuries past. And then there is another factor: the soil. Grand Coteau sits on the edge of the ridge that borders the land where the Teche-Mississippi River system once meandered. This edge is often referred to as the Coteau Ridge. Driving north from town on the interstate one can view the ridge's drop-off just before the next exit. This ancient un-leveed river periodically overflowed, depositing a rich layer of alluvium. A soil map published by the United States Department of Agriculture places Grand Coteau completely within this narrow band of soil.

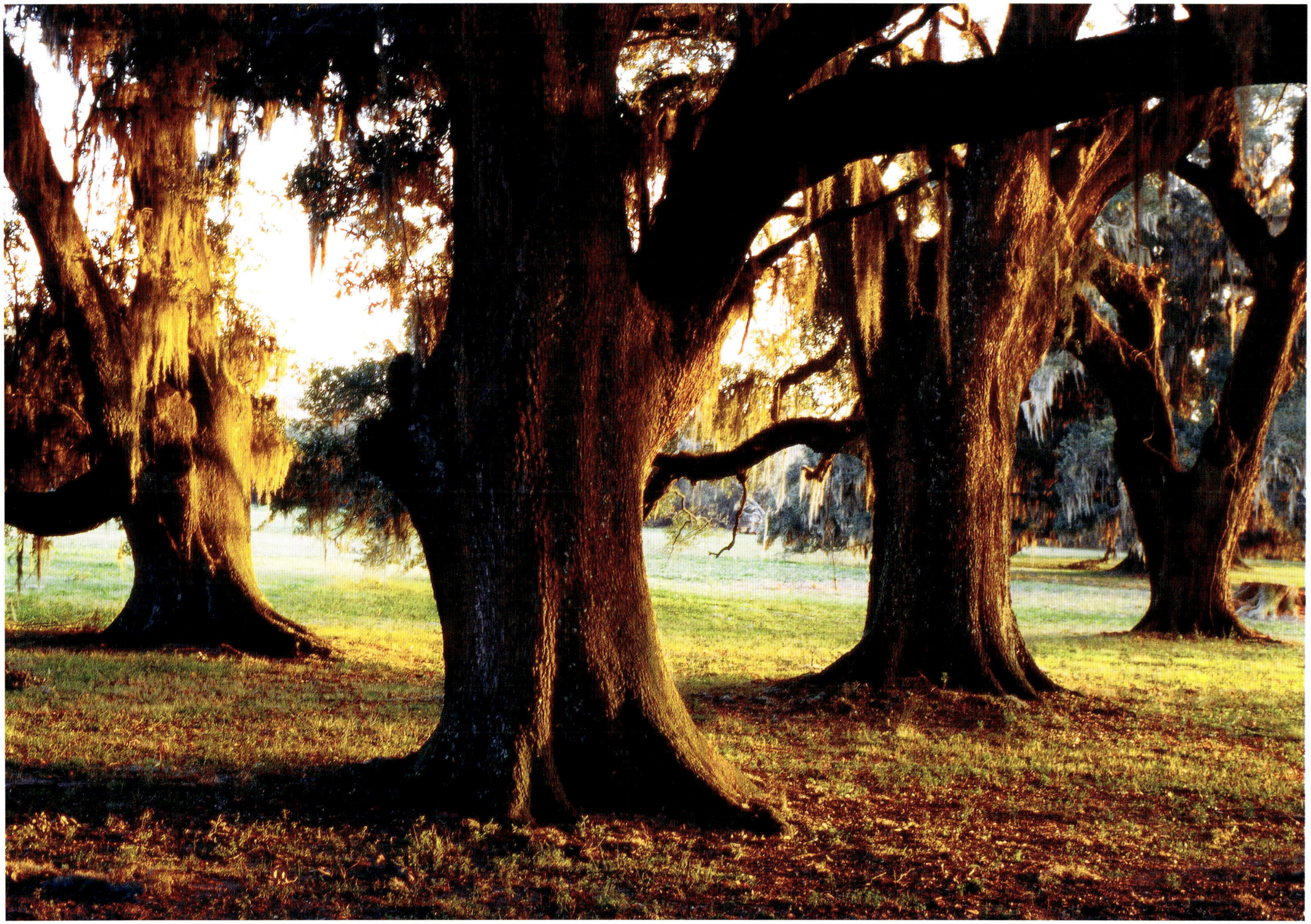

Gallery Renovations – Academy of the Sacred Heart

1995

Foreshadowing the development of Grand Coteau, the Academy of the Sacred Heart was founded in 1821. Construction of the main building was begun in 1830. Consisting of four sections, the three-story brick building features attenuated Federal and Greek Revival details and was built with bricks formed from clay dug on the property. The Academy of the Sacred Heart was individually placed on the National Register for Historic Places in 1975, five years before its inclusion within the historic district.

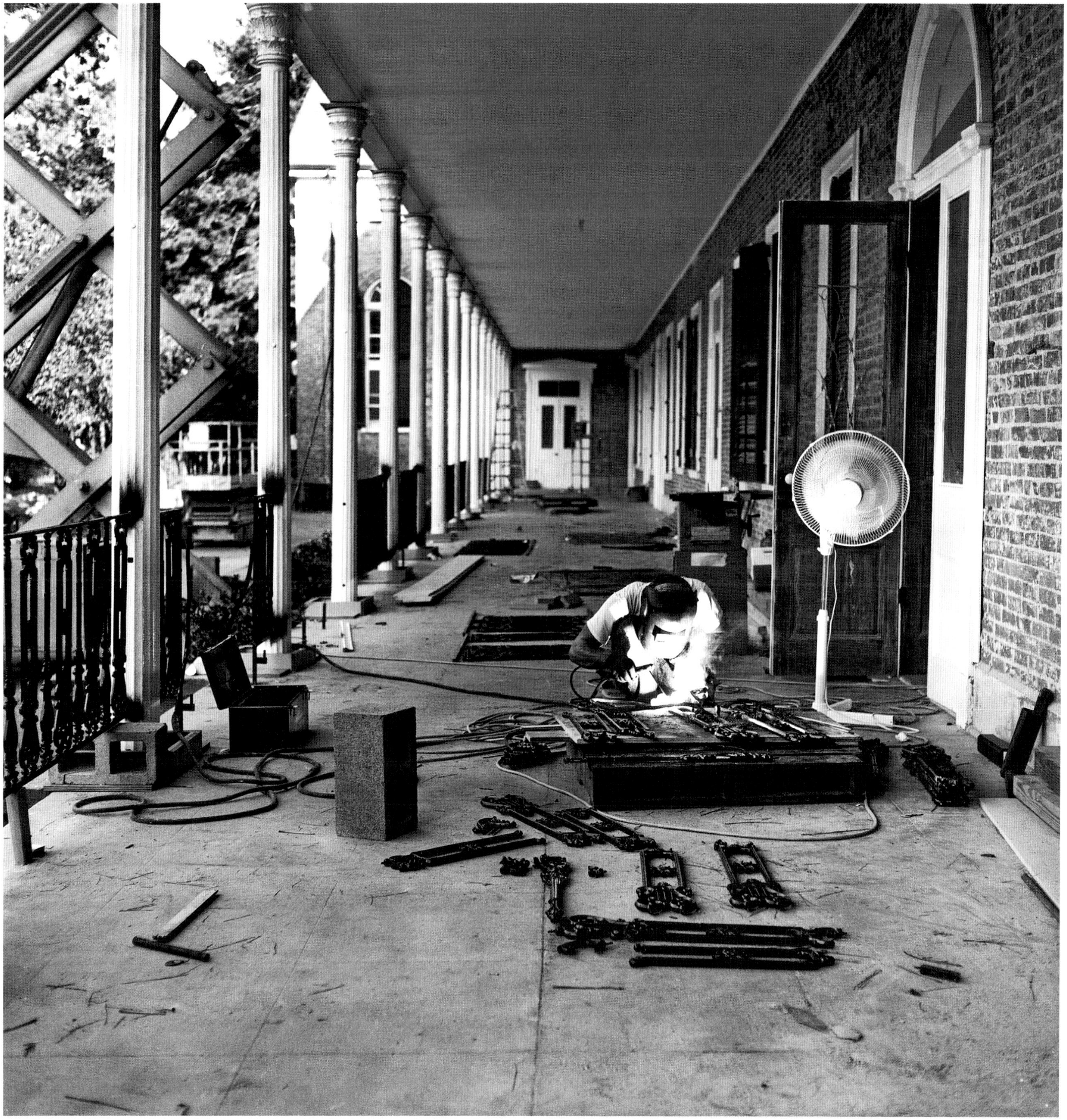

Front Gate – Academy of the Sacred Heart
2000

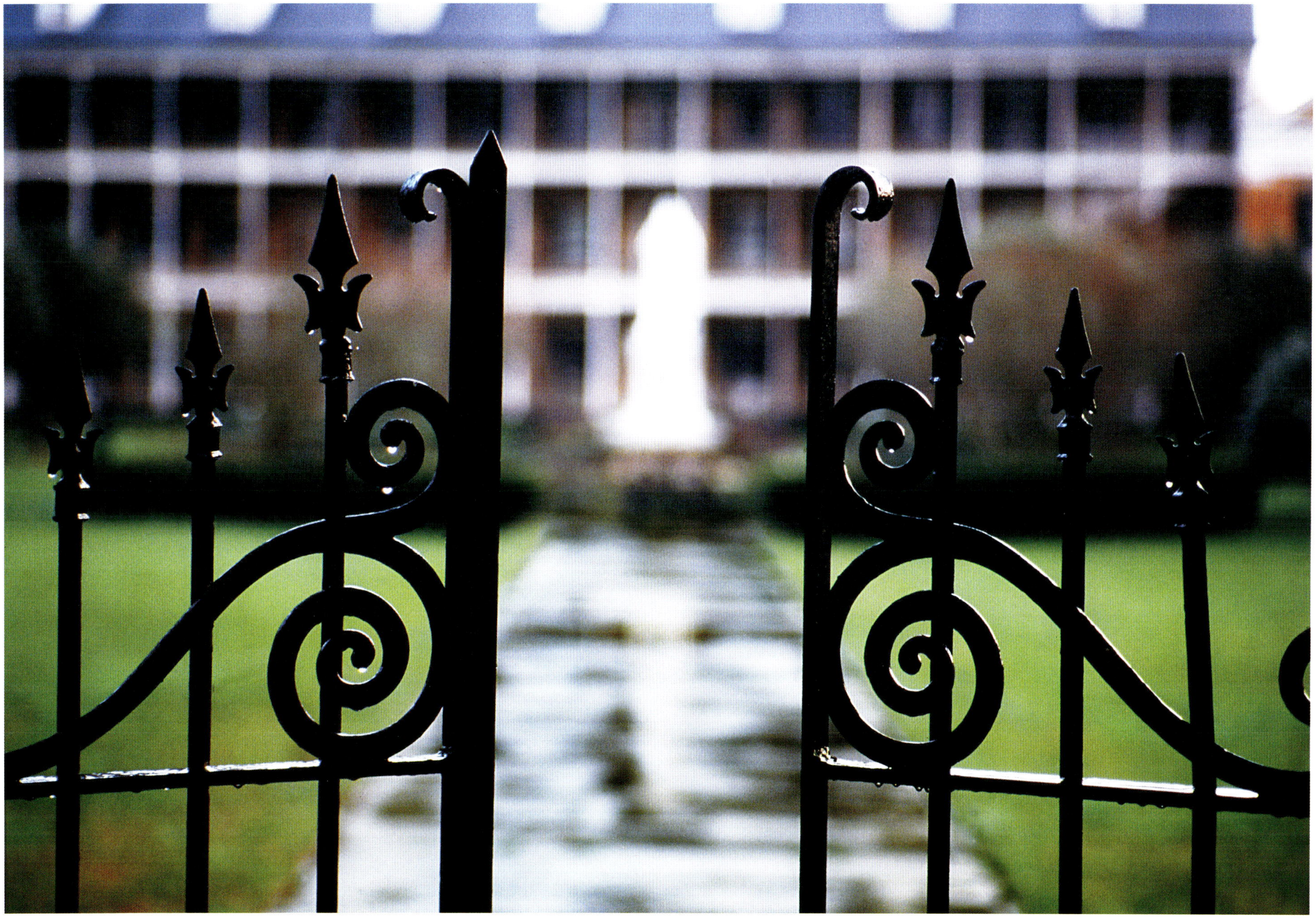

Hurricane Gustav Aftermath

2008

The multitudes of photographs taken of this alley across from the Academy of the Sacred Heart usually show beautifully manicured grounds, but hurricanes disperse damage with disregard for such care. However, these giants withstood Gustav's wrath with grace—no serious damage, just a big mess.

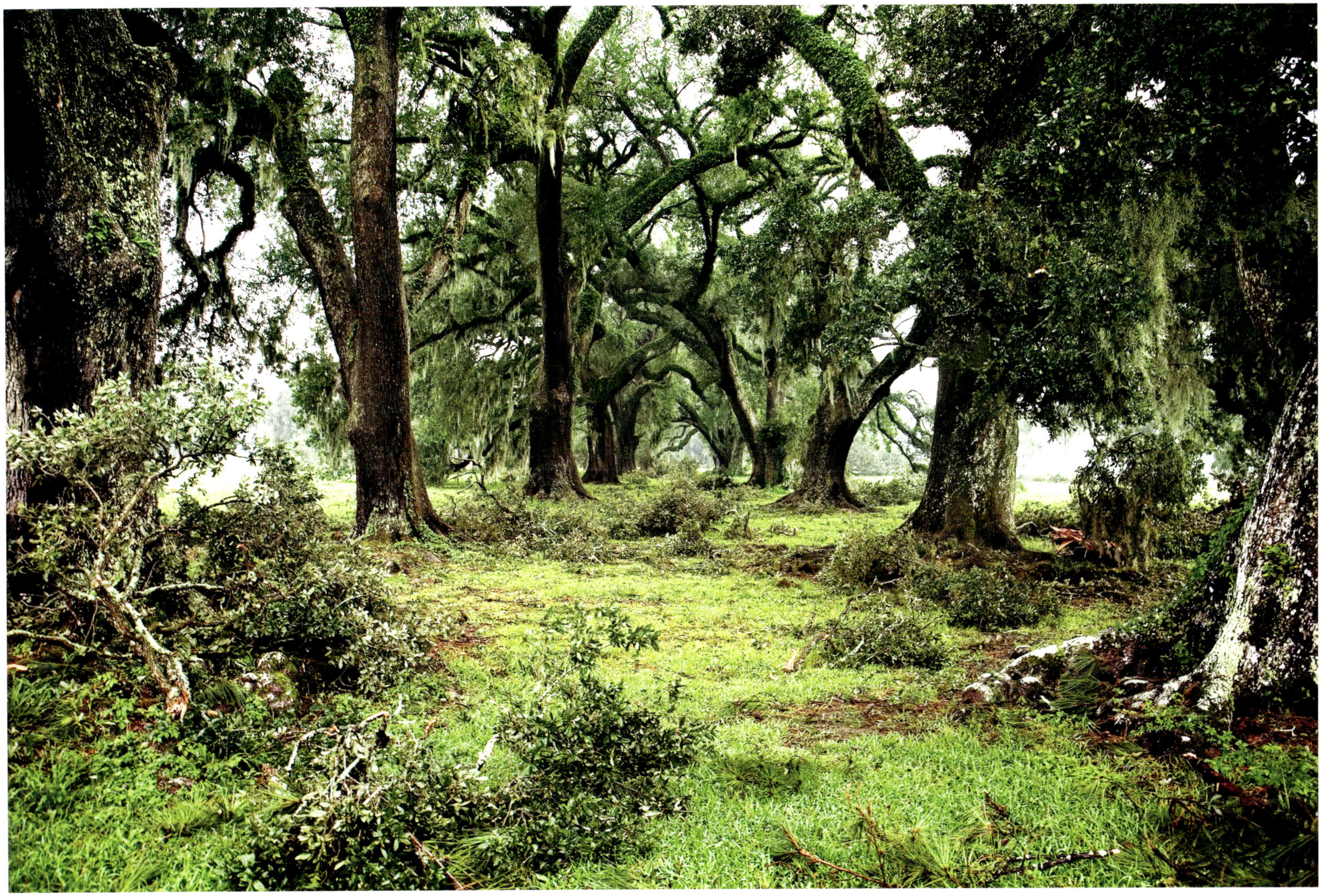

Casa Azul and Catahoula's
2008

Casa Azul gift shop shimmers with activity on the night of a poetry reading. This mid-nineteenth century building with front facçade was originally Maurice Polange's general store. In the early 1900s, the building became Rena Smith's general store. Elders still lean over the counter to share childhood memories about Miss Rena and her sisters or to reminisce about the coconut candy they enjoyed.

After serving as a general store, the building is now home to Casa Azul, which sells eclectic gifts. Is also serves as a venue for the Festival of Words, a nonprofit organization that hosts literary, musical, and other cultural events on a weekly basis.

Opened in 1996, Catahoula's Restaurant introduced Grand Coteau to a new audience of food lovers. Housed in the old Ivy's general store and named after the Louisiana state dog, Catahoula's, with its expansive wood floors and windows overlooking a panorama of oak trees, exudes sophisticated country charm.

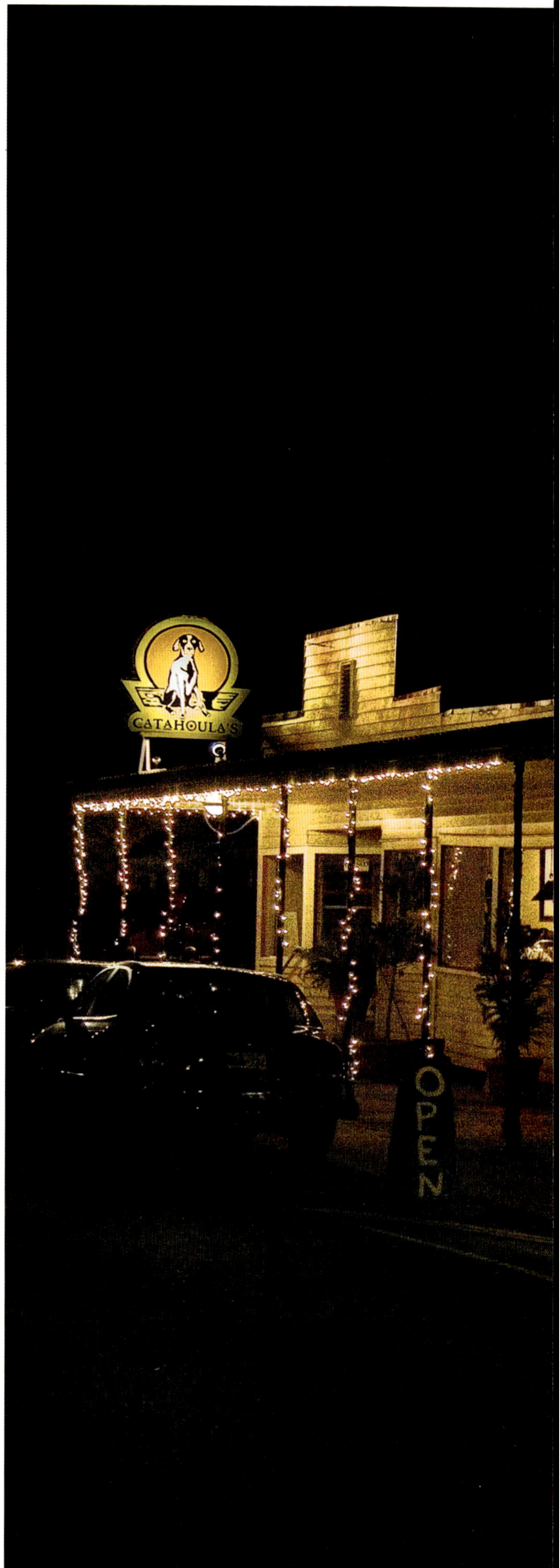

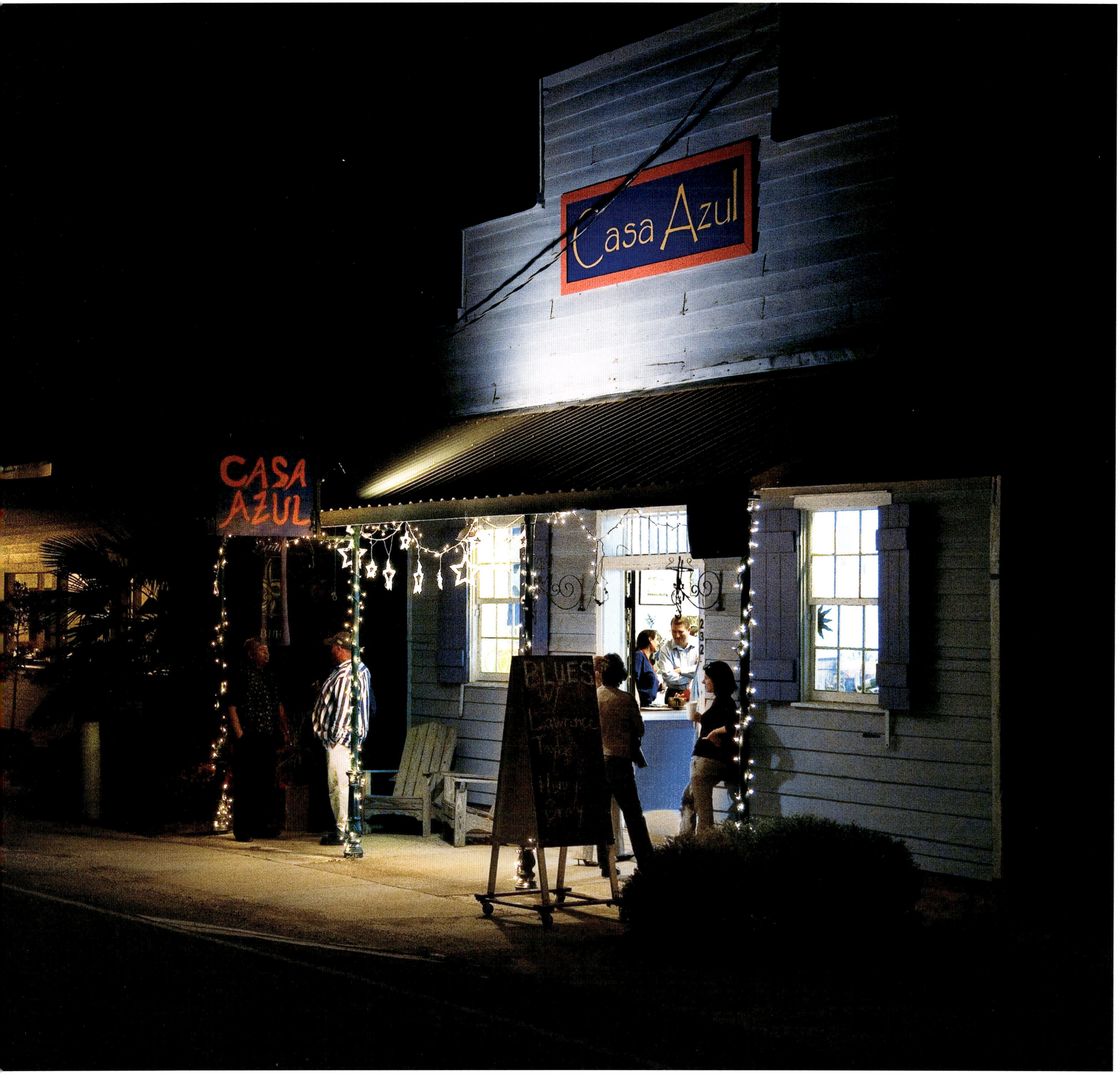
Casa Azul
CASA
AZUL
BLUES

Cottage Fire on Chatrian Street

2009

Between the first responder with a garden hose and the high tech follow-up crew, the fire, which was started by a malfunctioning dryer, was quickly controlled. This is one of six similar cottages on Chatrian Street, each emitting a simple charm. They were once part of the Chatrian estate and most likely housed employees. (Also see page 36.)

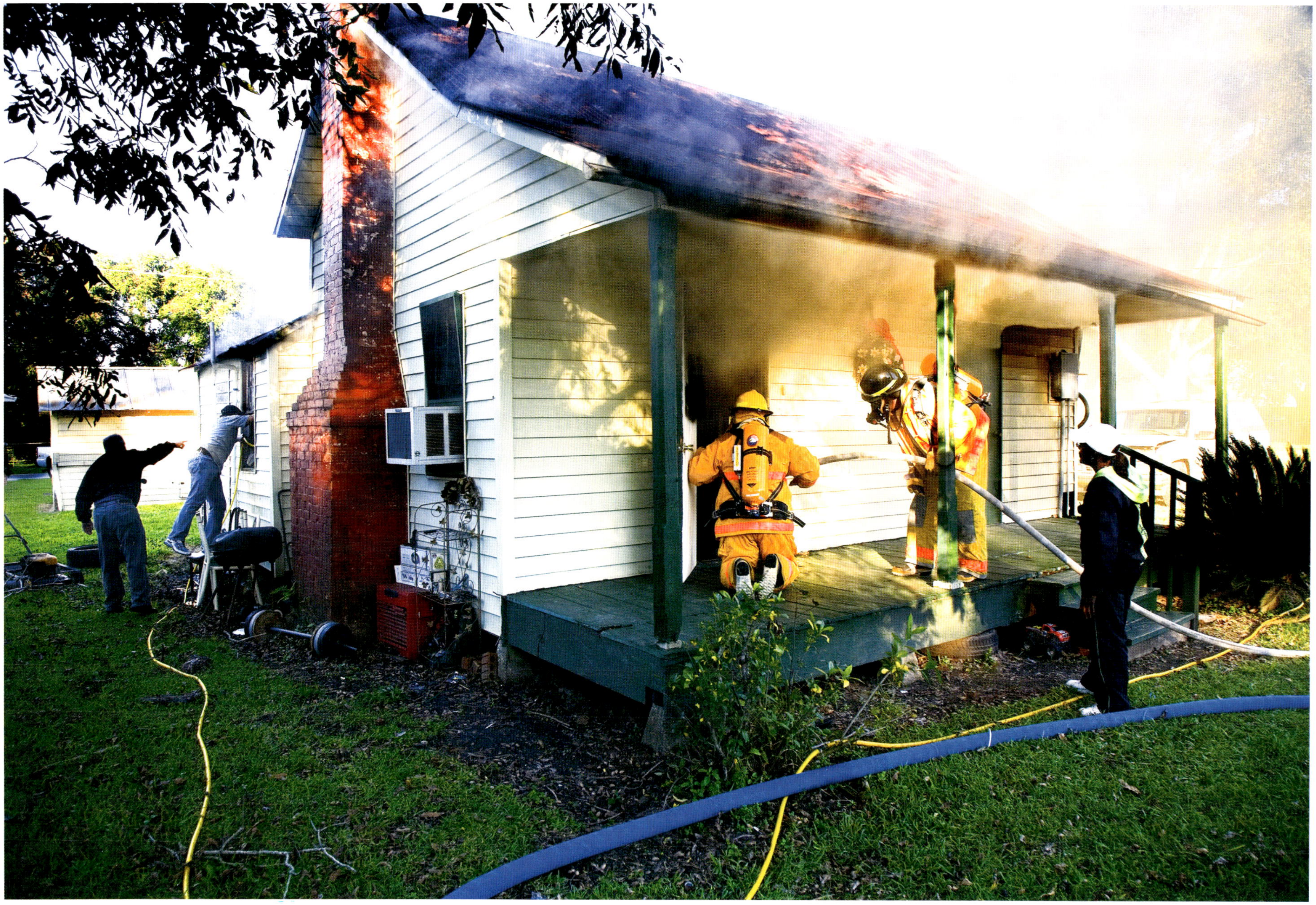

Funeral Procession
2009

A horse-drawn hearse leads a procession in this New Orleans-style funeral for Paul James (1942–2009).

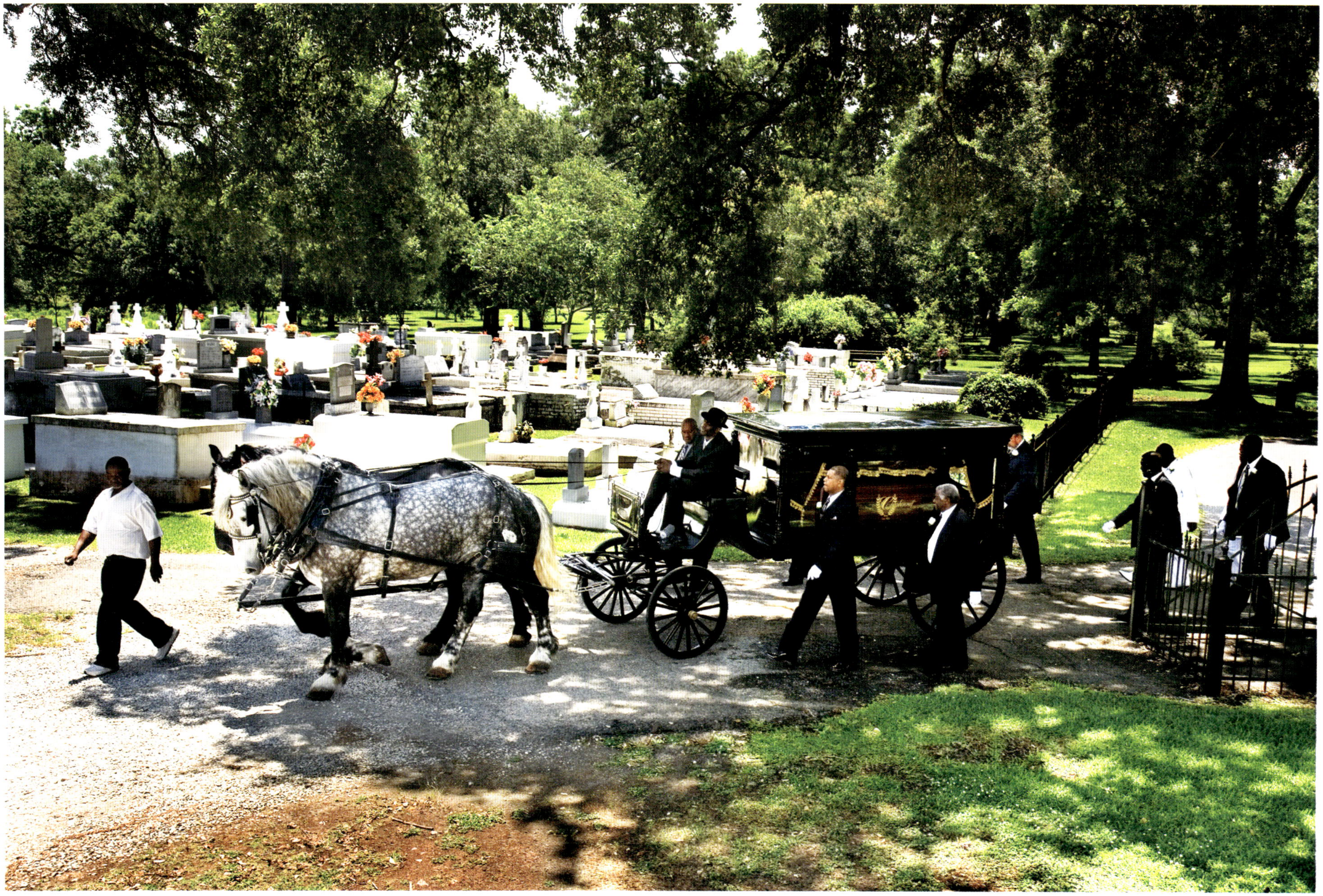

SELF-PORTRAIT
2009

PHOTOGRAPHER'S NOTE: Two things about this Church Street cottage renovation stood out for me. First the longleaf pine floors, which were incredibly hard and never showed any damage despite all the things I dropped on them. Second was the attic where the craftsmanship of nineteenth century carpenters was on full display—exquisitely precise construction using only hand tools.

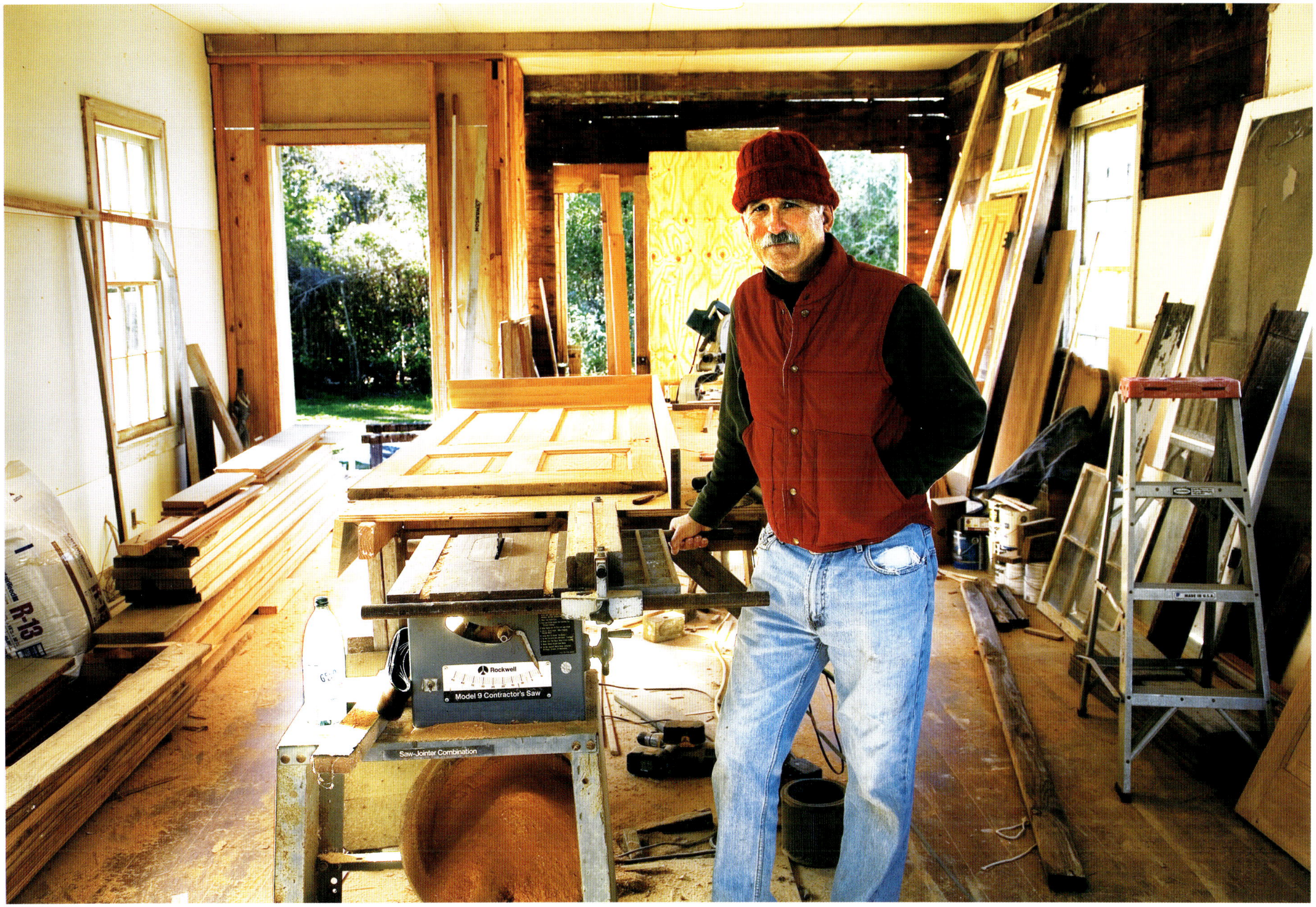
R-13
Rockwell
Model 9 Contractor's Saw
Saw-Jointer Combination

Belfry – St. Charles Church

2011

The rear tower of St. Charles Church was built in 1886 to house this massive bronze bell. Weighing 3,104 pounds—a thousand pounds more than the Liberty Bell—and measuring forty inches high by fifty-four inches across, it was donated by Eleanora Millard in honor of her late husband, Dr. Edward Millard, who died in 1882. Named "Eleanor" after Mrs. Millard's favorite niece, the bell was originally forged at the Meneely Bell Foundry in Troy, New York. For years, church manager Darrell Burleigh tolled it manually with a rope until an electrical drive was installed in 2002. Eleanor, following an old local custom, rings twice daily: at noon and at 6 p.m.

Photographer's Note: I don't usually get acrophobia, but this location is a little unnerving. All four sides are open and the rail is rather short. It may have something to do with the bell and all the supporting apparatus. It just fills the space. I wonder what it's like to be there when it's ringing.

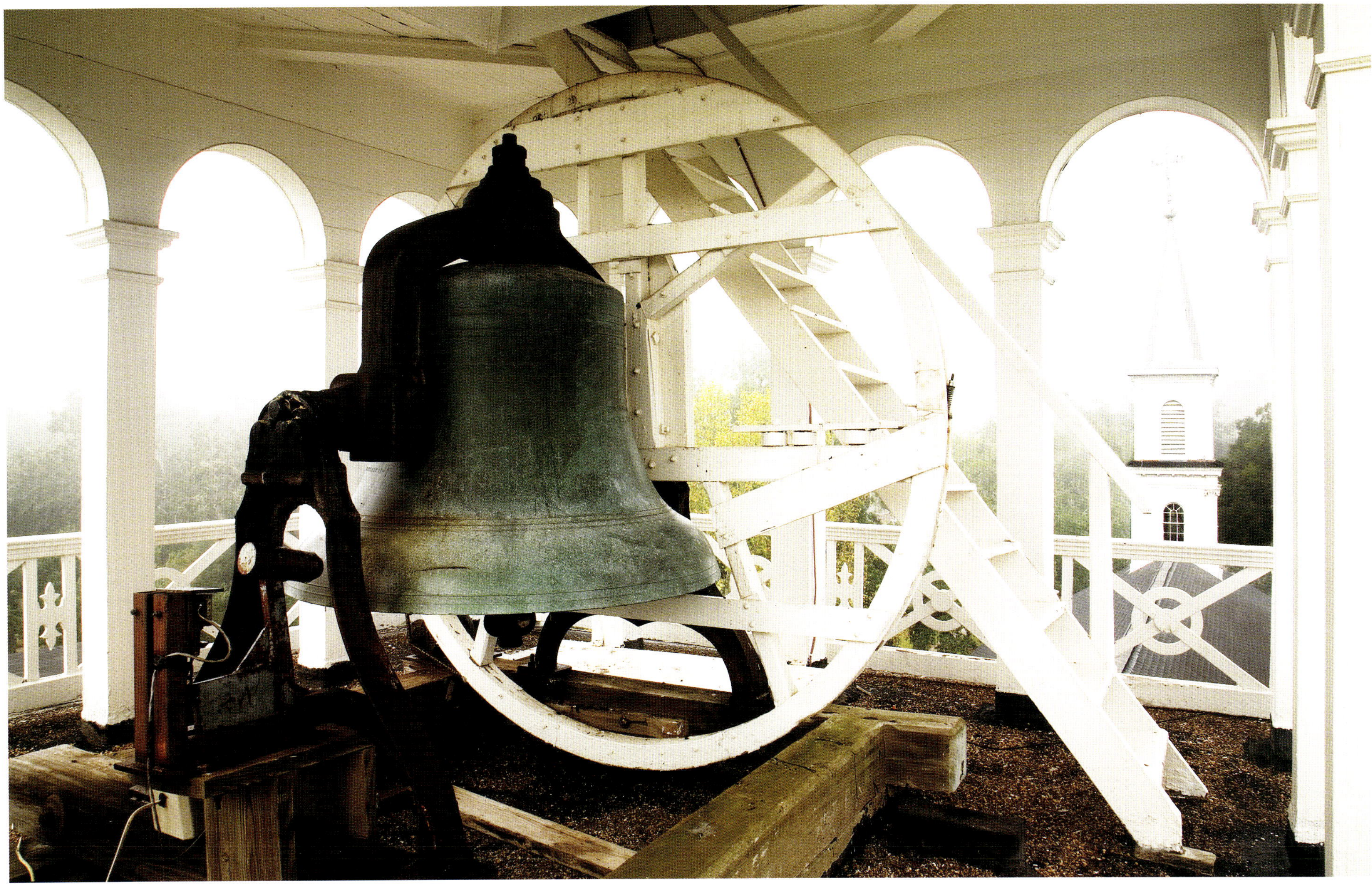

Toby Rodriguez with Daughter Josephine

2011

Visual artist Toby Rodriguez holds his two-year old daughter Josephine in front of the historical Brinkhaus shop, where Rodriguez currently lives. Rodriguez has held a lifelong dream to live in Grand Coteau. He feels that this historical town's peaceful environment inspires his art.

Once a cobbler shop and millenary, the building was owned by Frank Brinkhaus, who made shoes and repaired old ones while his wife, Cora Richard Brinkhaus, known as "Memère," created hats. The projecting showcases once displayed shoes, hats, formal party dresses, ribbons, and veils. The original hand-wrought iron bars and hinges still secure the battened doors and shutters.

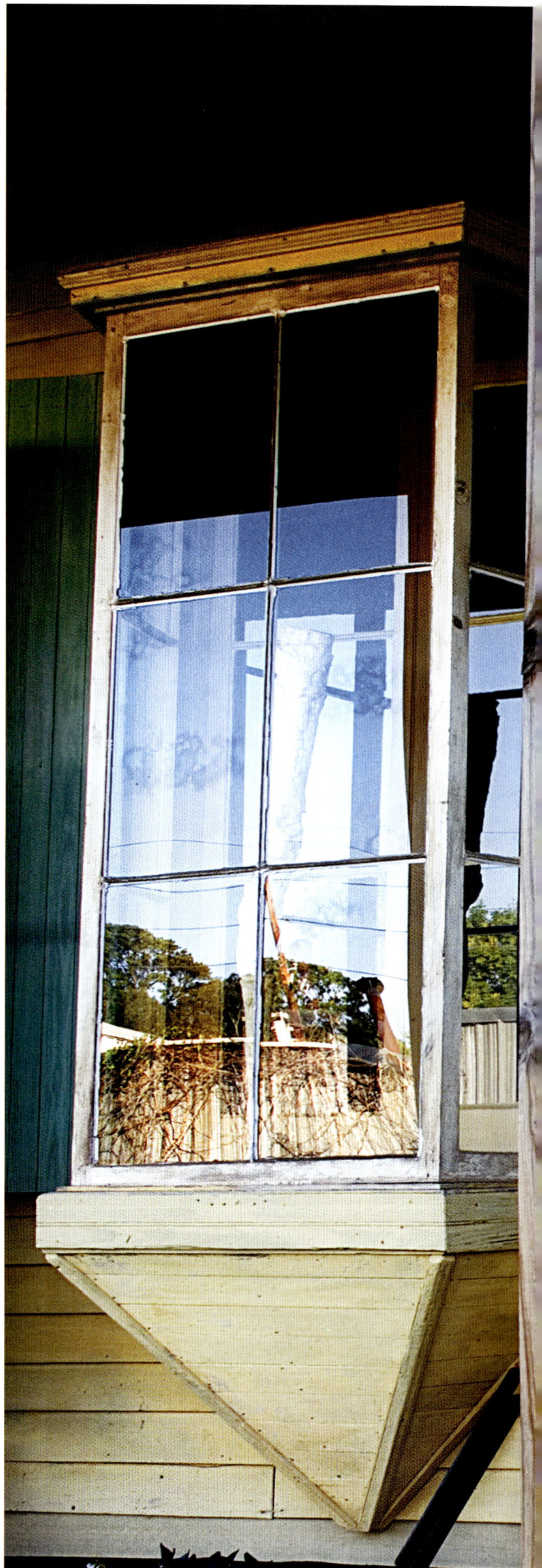

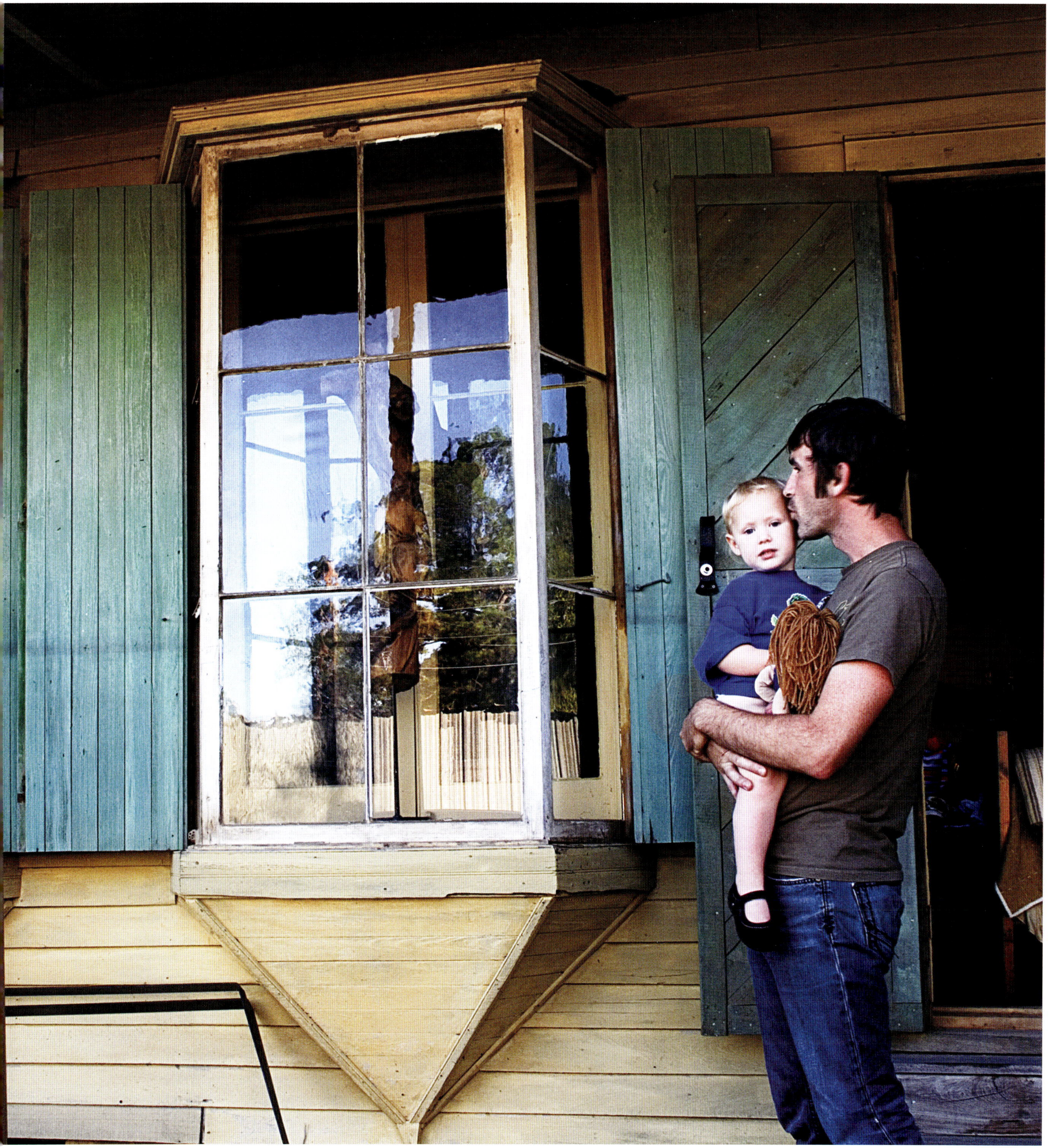

François Simon Cross – St. Charles Cemetery

2012

The similarly intricate scrollwork suggests that this cross, the one on Joseph Colomb's grave, and the one on the St. Charles church steeple (page 60) were all made by the same blacksmith, François Foraz.

Photographer's Note: It is important to keep in mind that this is a thoroughly French grave and you must pronounce Simon accordingly: See-mon. My favorite name in the cemetery is Napoleon Robin, and once again to feel the beauty you must give Robin the French pronunciation: Roe-banh. "Hi, my name is Napoleon Robin." Wow!

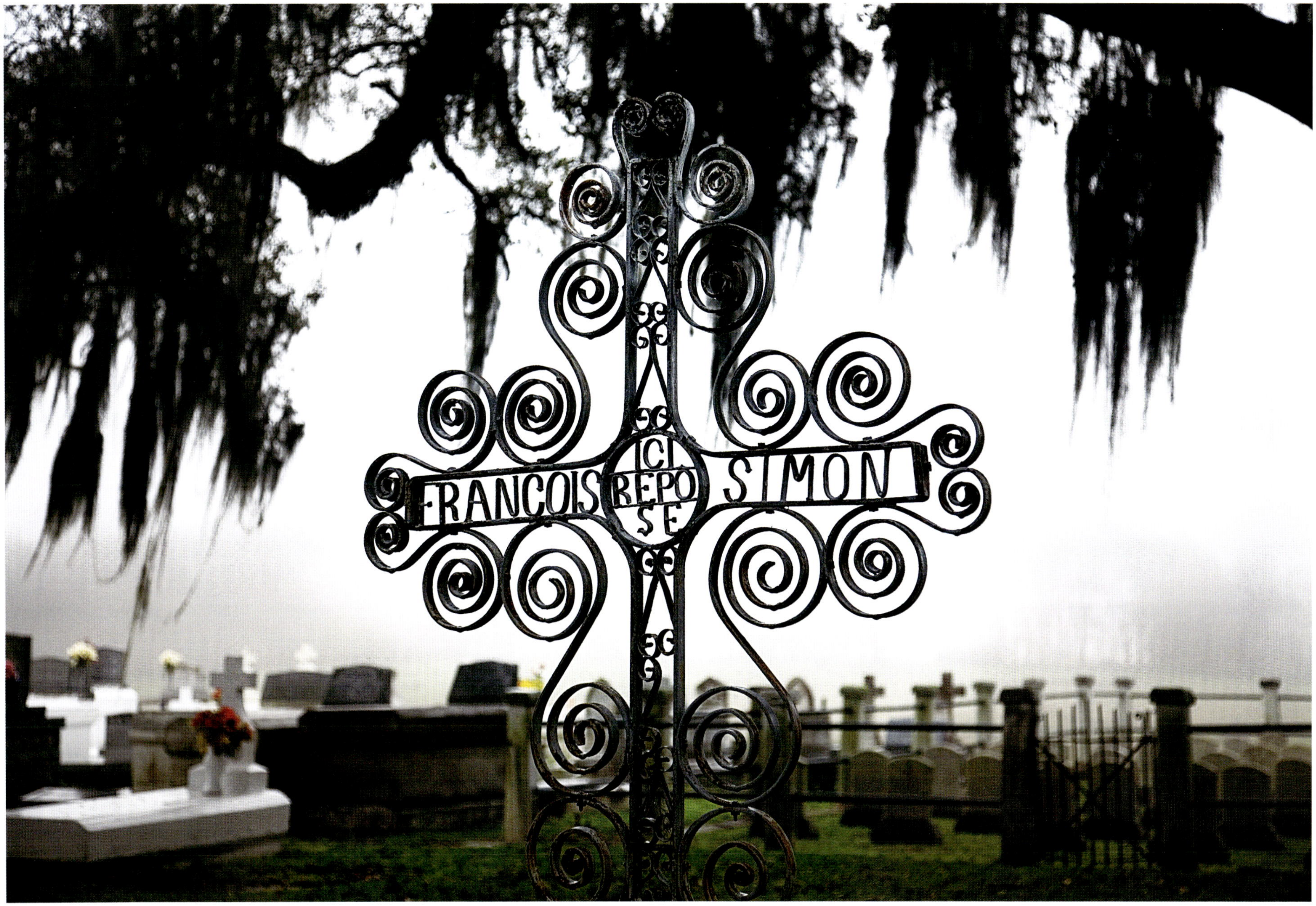
FRANCOIS
ICI
REPO
SE
SIMON

Nancy Brewer in The Kitchen Shop

2012

Nancy puts the finishing touches on a batch of *gâteau na na* destined for the oven. This desert, made with pecans, honey, and sweet dough, is a Kitchen Shop favorite. Nancy estimates that she has baked over twenty-thousand. The Kitchen Shop was once the Quality Bakery, run by the Chatrian's. Cardboard tokens inscribed with "Good For One Five Cent Loaf" have been found from the early 1900s.

Photographer's Note: Hilary and I opened The Kitchen Shop in 1983. Nancy Brewer and her husband, artist Jesse Poimboeuf, returned in 1993 from an eight-year hiatus in New York City. While there, Nancy attended the New York Cooking School. Asked in a class to state her dream, she wrote that she wanted to take over The Kitchen Shop in Grand Coteau. And so it came to pass.

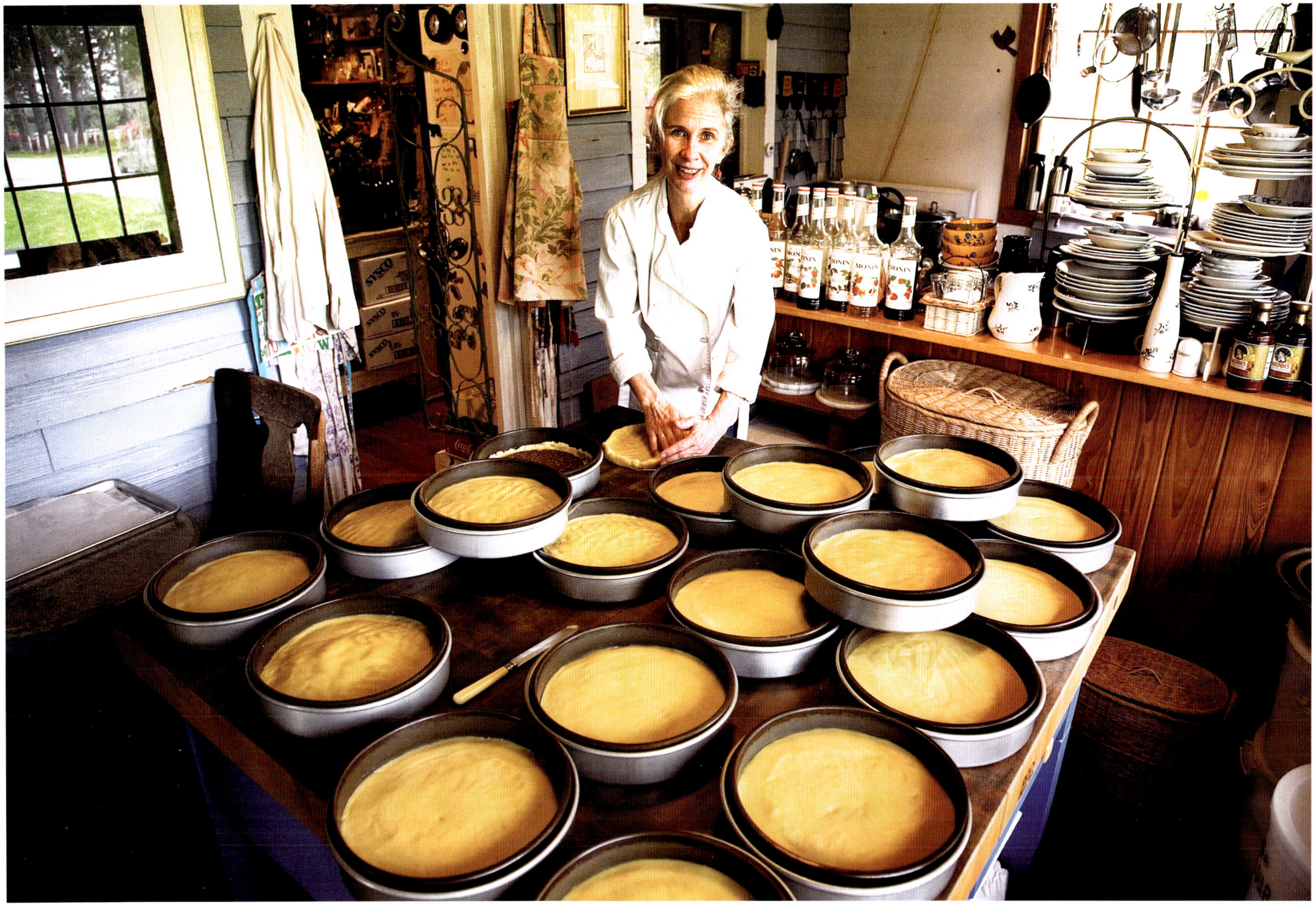
SYSCO
MONIN

Flooded Alley
2012

Rapidly rising floodwaters form a lake around the trunks of the oaks. On March 12, 2012, overnight storms brought twelve to fifteen inches of rain that inundated the area. Although floodwaters closed down Interstate 49 from Lafayette to Opelousas, including the Grand Coteau exit, the town received little damage, as it is on high ground. However, in surrounding communities such as Carencro, hundreds of homes were flooded. This was the worst flash-flood in recent memory.

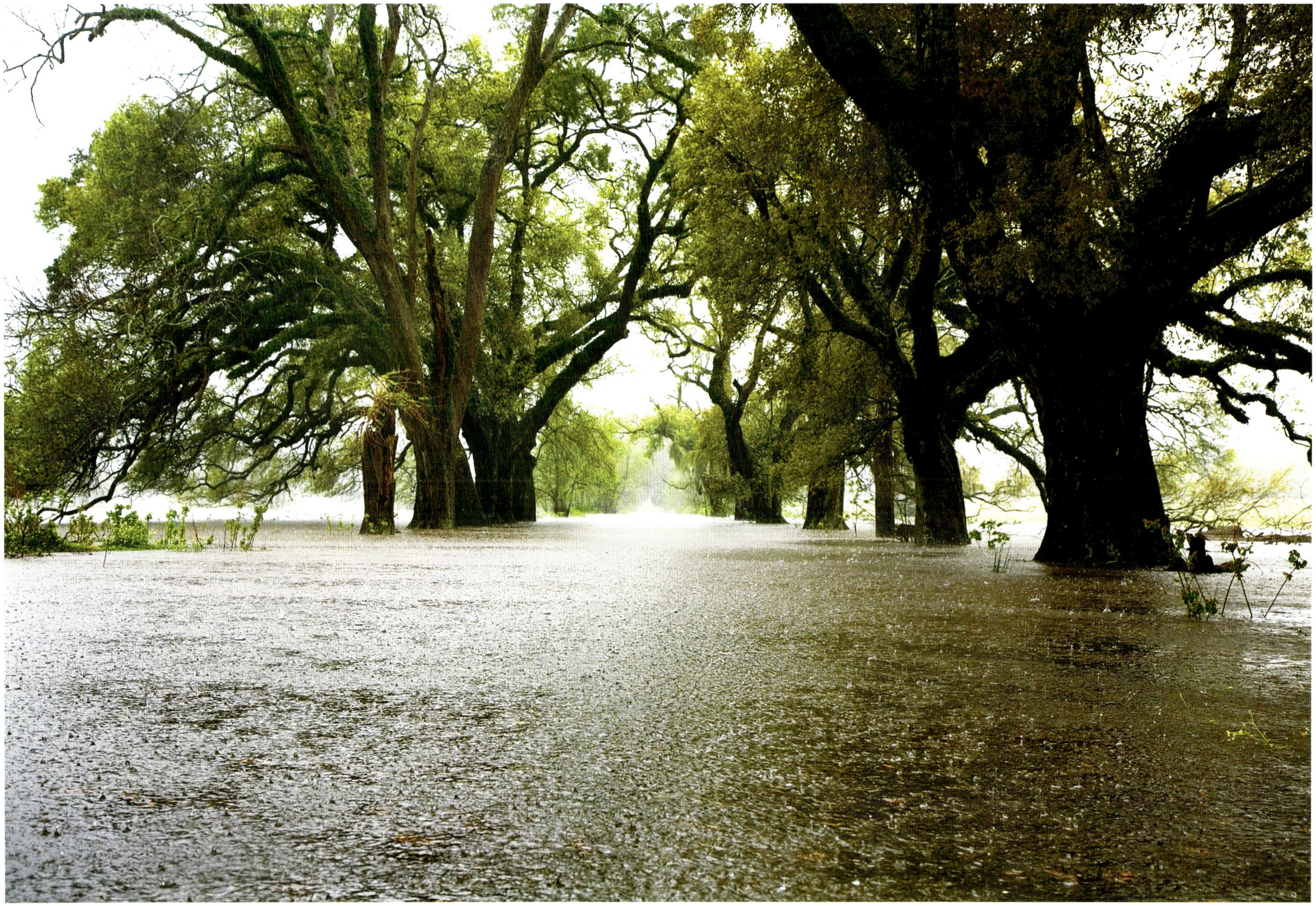

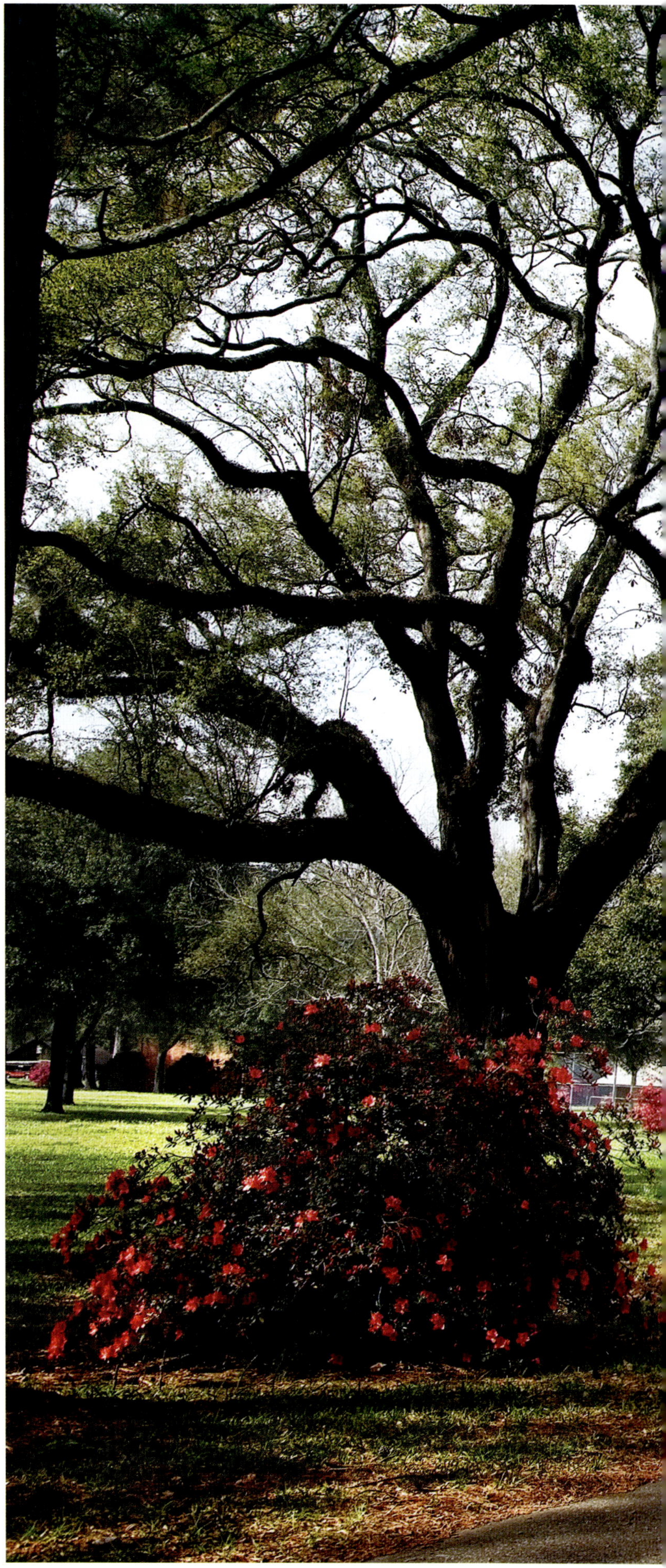

ENTRANCE – ST. CHARLES COLLEGE
2012

Tall, swaying pine trees line the entrance to St. Charles College. The present building, a three-story Gothic Revival design, was constructed in 1909, after the original structure burned in 1900. The five-part building is constructed of red bricks painted white. It has a strong reference to English late-medieval architecture, a nationwide fashion for educational institutions at turn of the century. The interior has been remodeled several times since the 1930s. The college is currently undergoing construction to update retreatant facilities and to create an assisted living home for Jesuits. Great care was taken to preserve the architectural integrity of this handsome, historical structure.

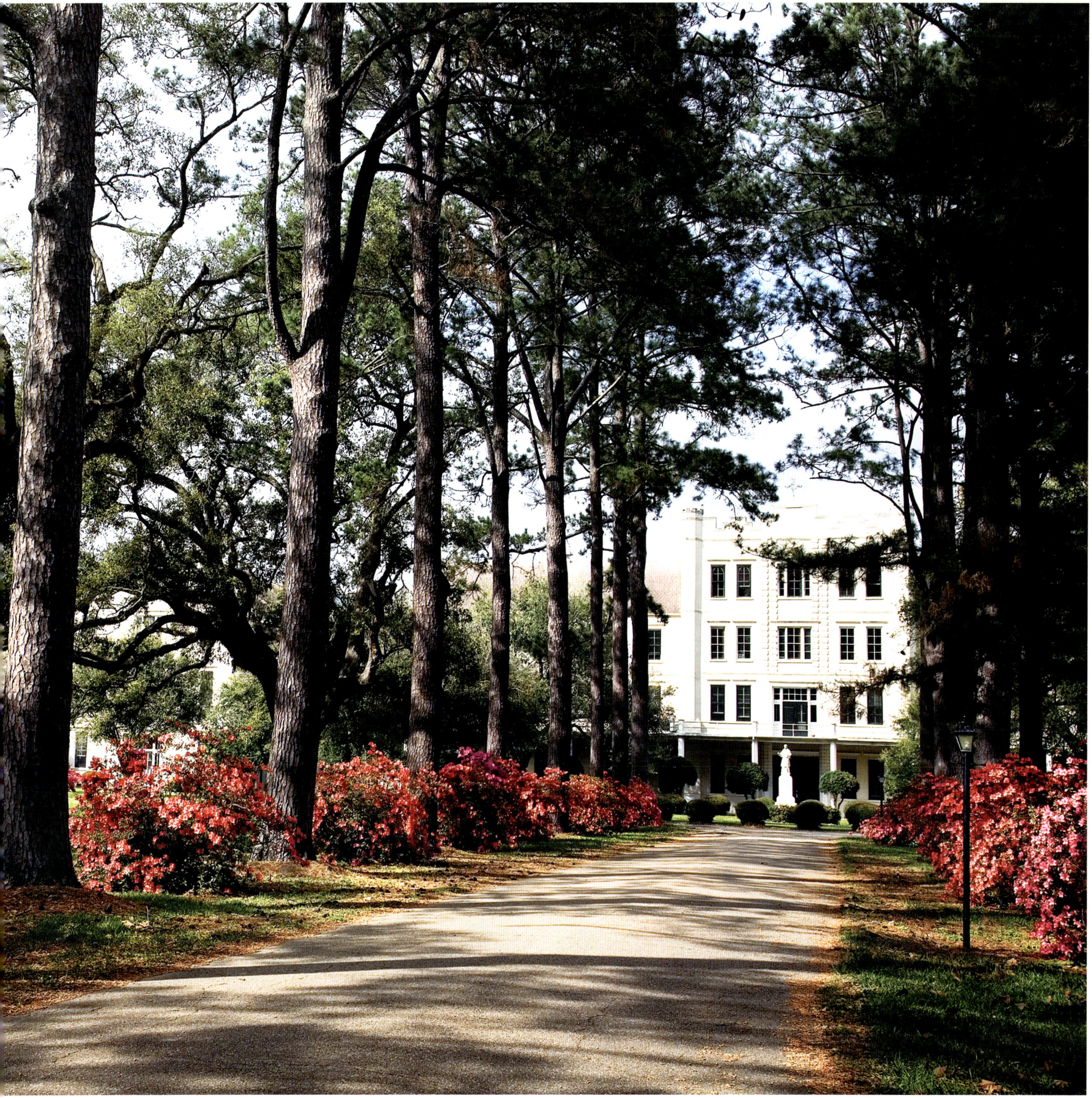

Statue of St. Charles Borromeo

2012

A statue of St. Charles Borromeo welcomes visitors to St. Charles College. The college stands on land set aside for Catholic education by Mrs. Charles Smith, the widow of a wealthy planter. Both St. Charles Church and St. Charles College were named in honor of Smith's patron saint—Saint Charles Borromeo.

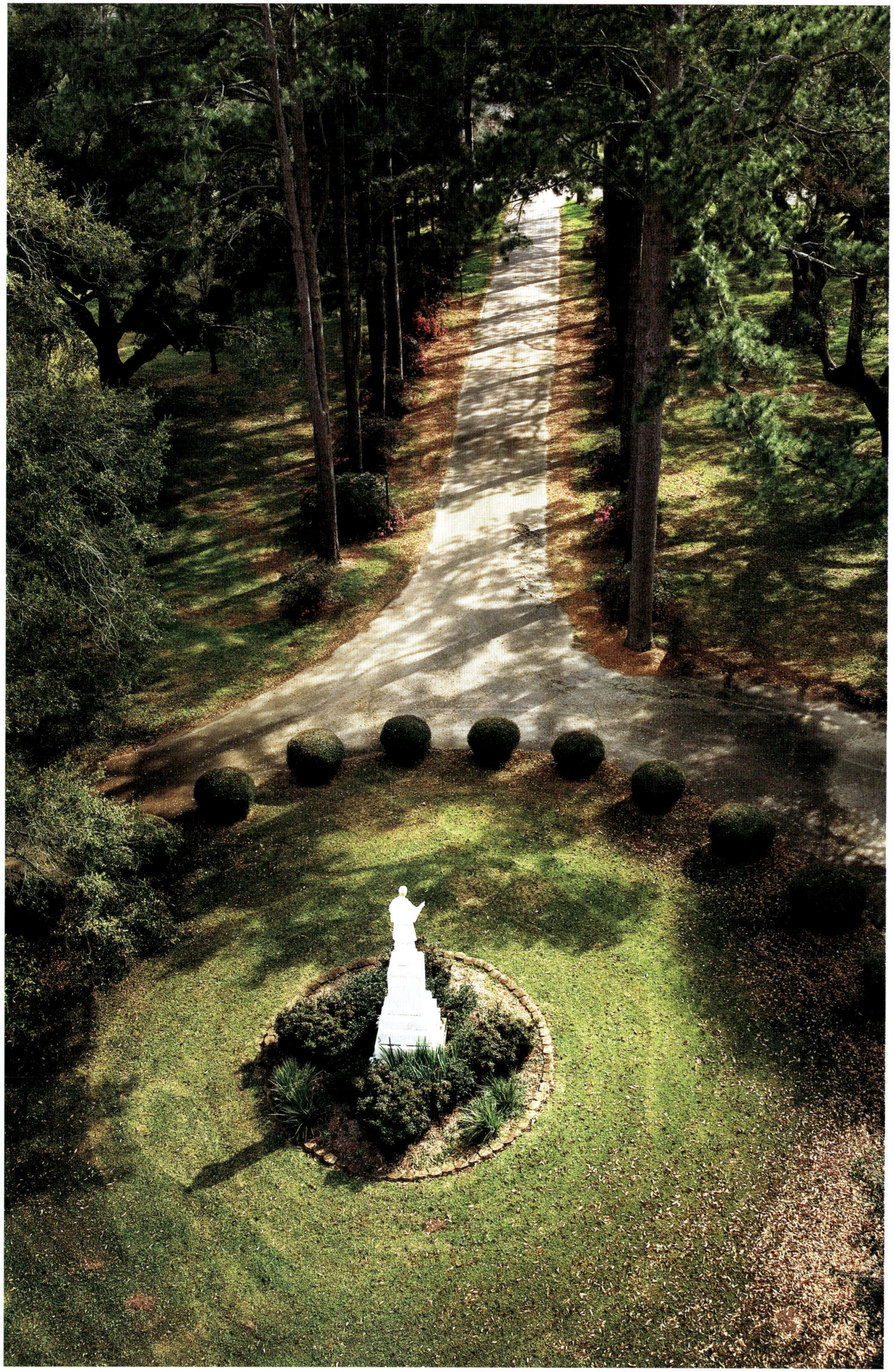

Our Lady of the Oaks Retreat House

2012

Built in 1938 by the Bishop of Lafayette, the Spanish-styled Our Lady of the Oaks Retreat House is located where the original St. Charles Church stood.

Unlike the individually-directed retreats offered at St. Charles College, Our Lady of the Oaks specializes in group retreats. Most are facilitated by a trained lay person and sessions are based on the teachings of Jesuit founder Saint Ignatius Loyola.

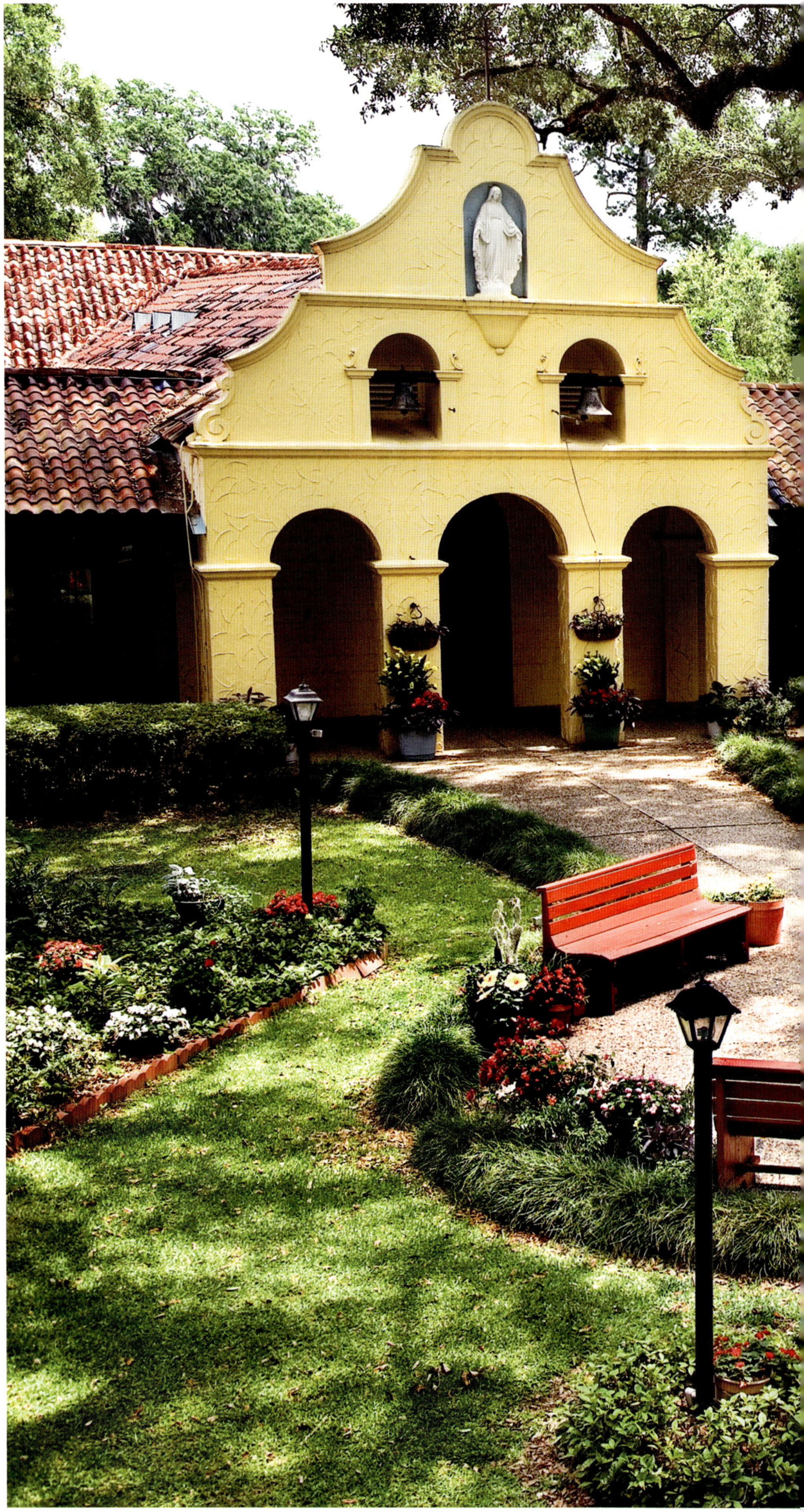

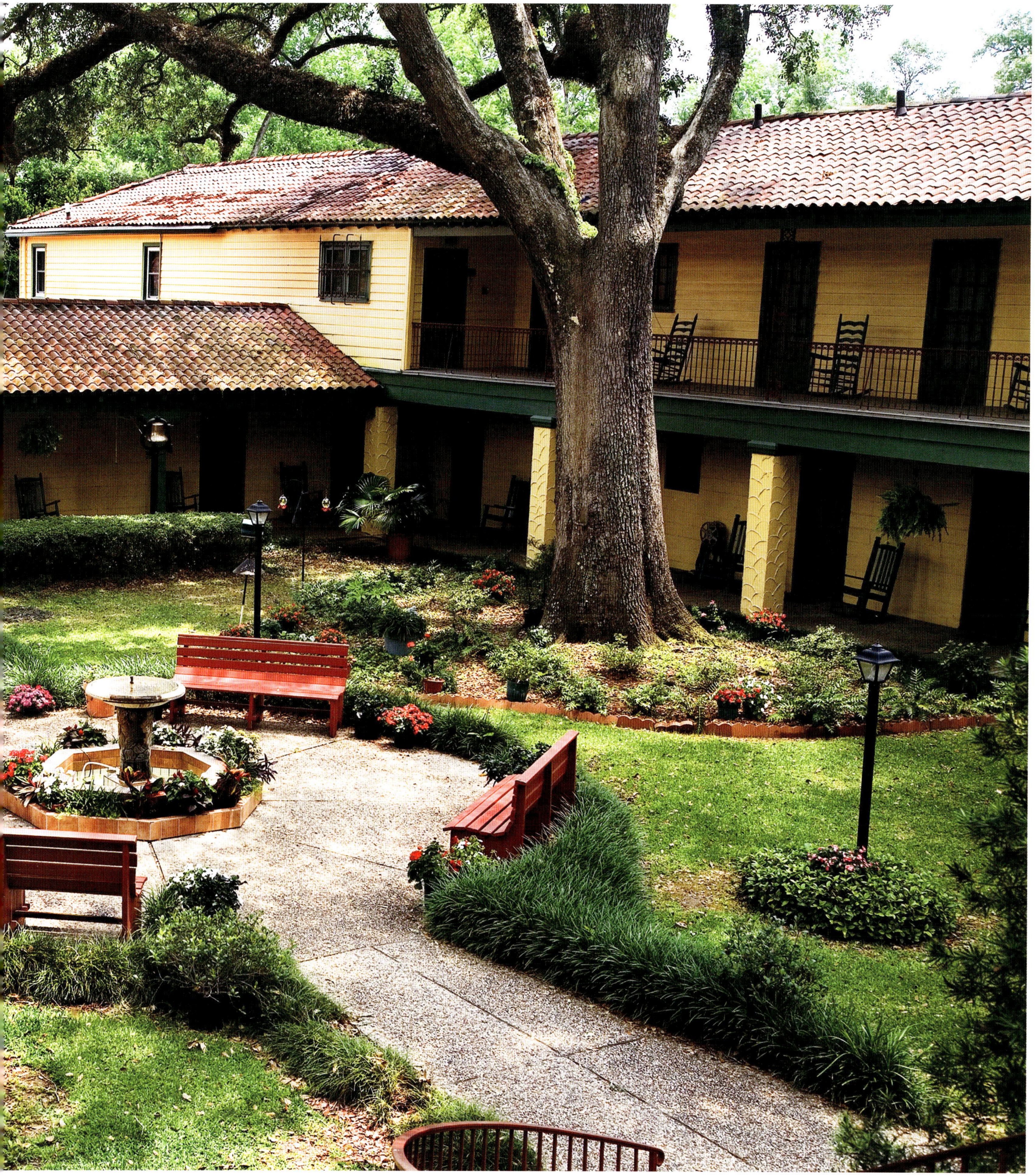

Way of the Cross – Our Lady of the Oaks Retreat House

2012

Retreatants from New Iberia, Coteau, and Loreauville participate in the Way of the Cross which consists of scripture and prayer at fifteen stations along the oak-lined entrance. Our Lady of the Oaks offers two and three day retreats to men, women, and couples. The Retreat House hosts approximately fifty retreats annually.

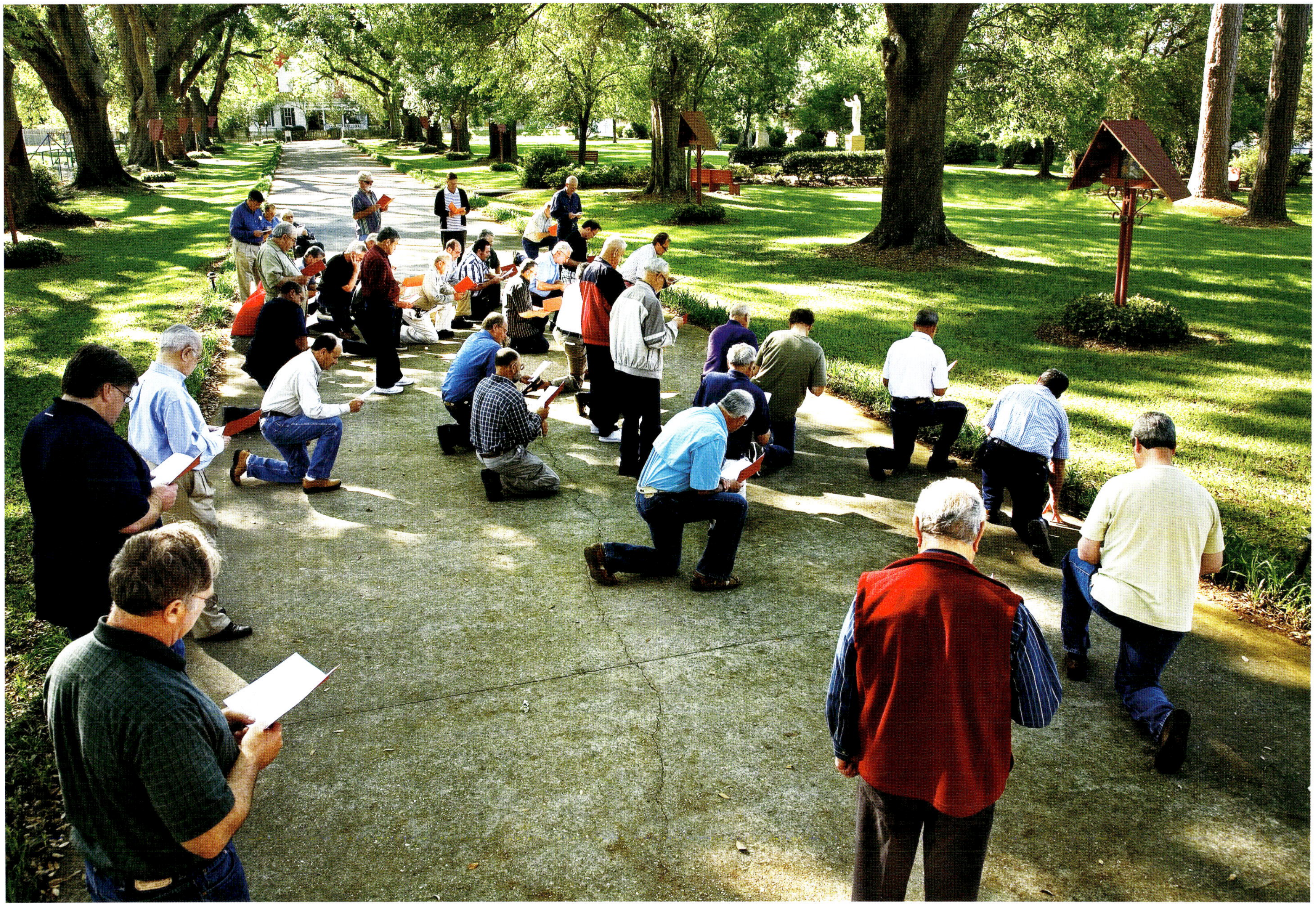

Xavier Henry
2012

One of sixteen children, Xavier Henry is a skilled cowboy, diligent steward of the land, and respected citizen. His fields are tidy, his fences stay mended, and his herds are healthy. More than fifty-five years of ranching knowledge are brought to the care of more than 380 “momma” (his term) cows and their accompanying bulls.

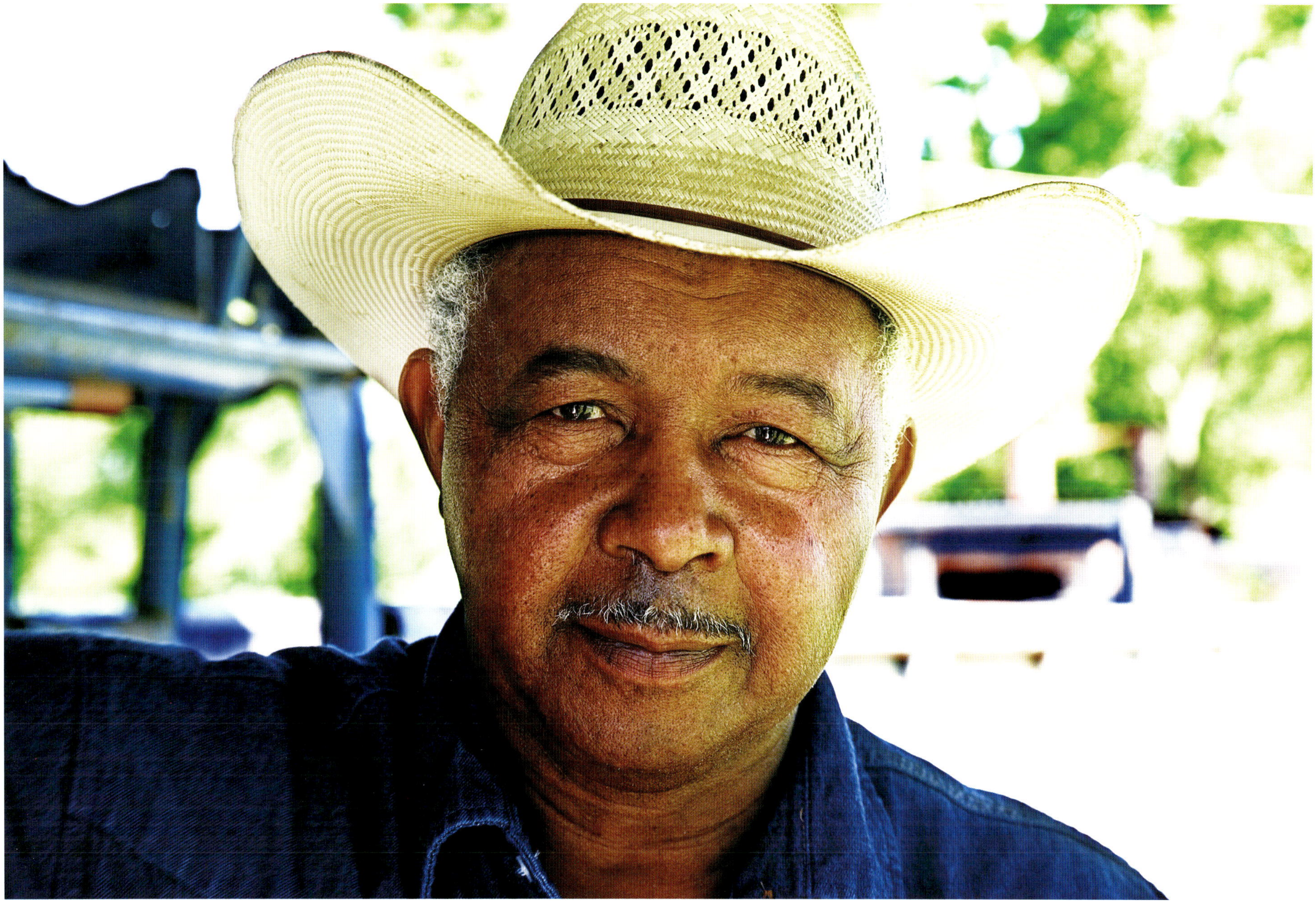

Tanya Nehrbass Schulze

2012

Tanya, a graduate of Sacred Heart (class of 1977) and currently an art teacher there, has thrown and decorated a lot of "pots" (her term) and other items in her studio built by husband Rudy. Her colorful glazes and joyful renditions of local flora and fauna are her signature style.

Photographer's Note: We lived next door to Tanya for ten years. Our houses were accessed by a common gravel lane. Her three girls, our two boys, and other neighborhood children grew up in a village atmosphere. If the kids were at Tanya's, you could bet they were hanging around the kitchen table drawing, painting, pasting, and surely playing with clay.

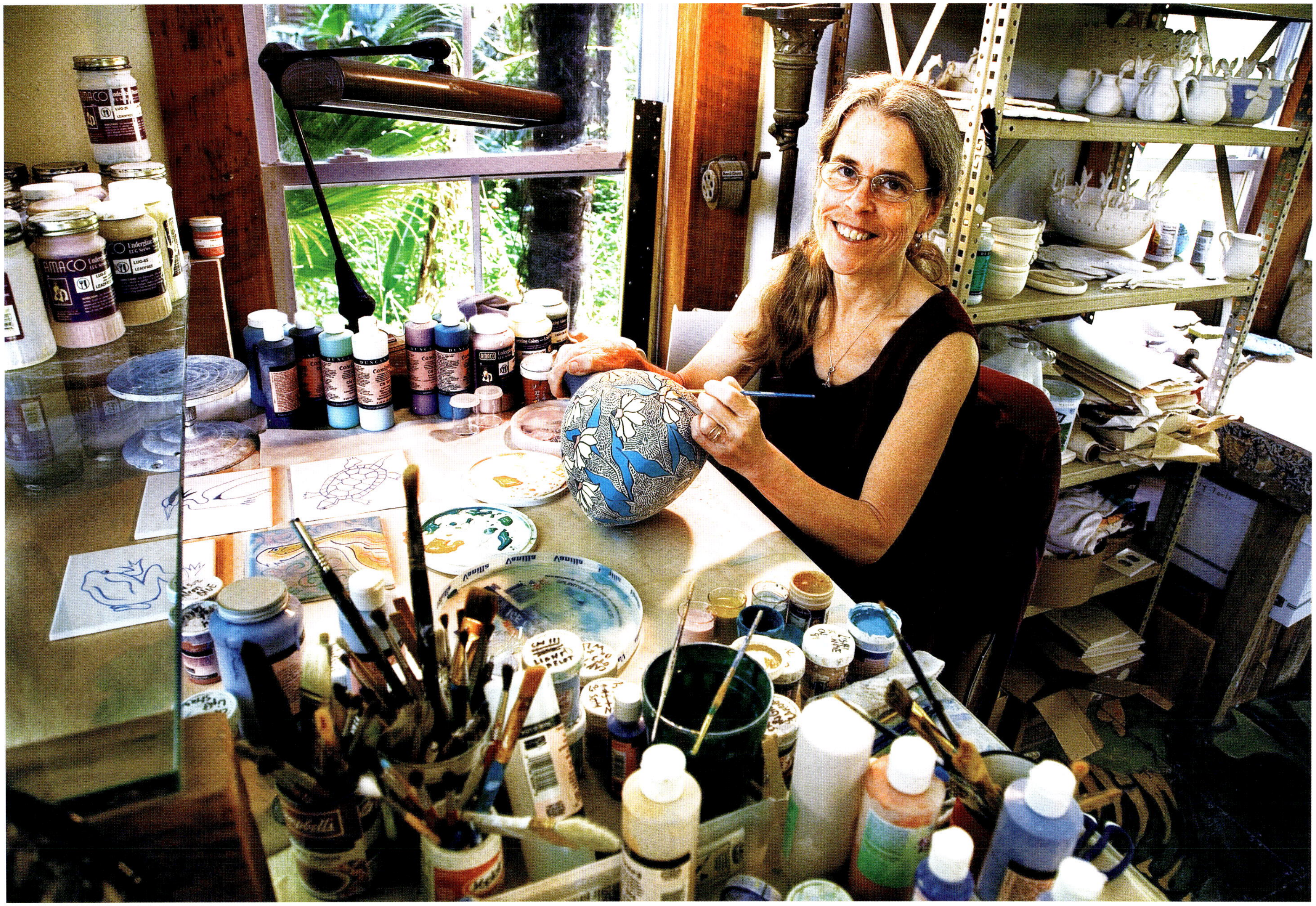
AMACO

Gardens – Academy of the Sacred Heart

2012

The Gardens at the Academy of the Sacred Heart were created in 1836, modeled on the Gardens of Versailles.

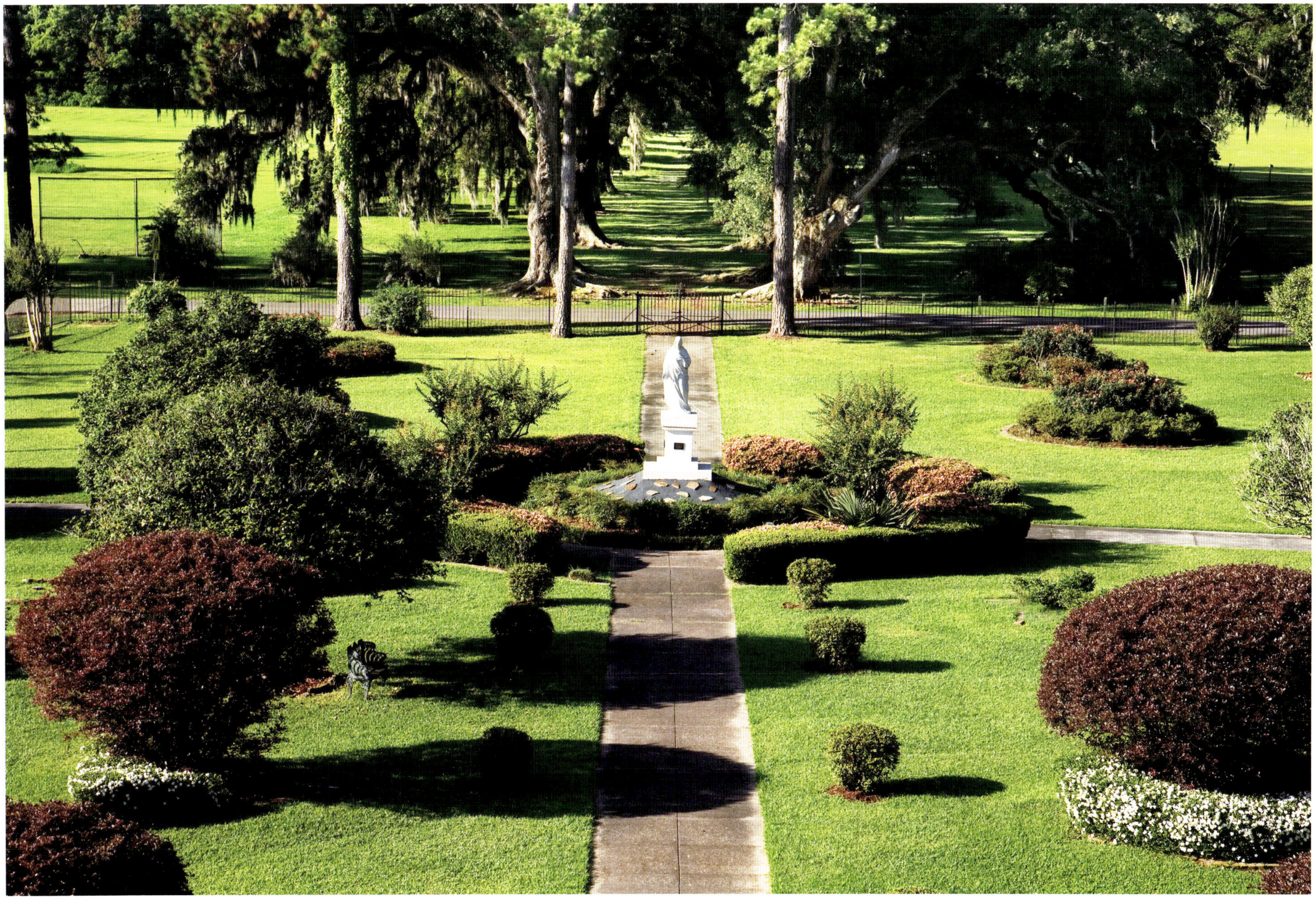

St. Ignatius Crossing

2012

Pre-kindergarden and kindergarten students are directed across Church Street by crossing guard Mac Eaglin in the early morning. Founded in 1890, St. Ignatius offers classes through the eighth grade. It is a Catholic school extolling the core values of faith, service, and knowledge.

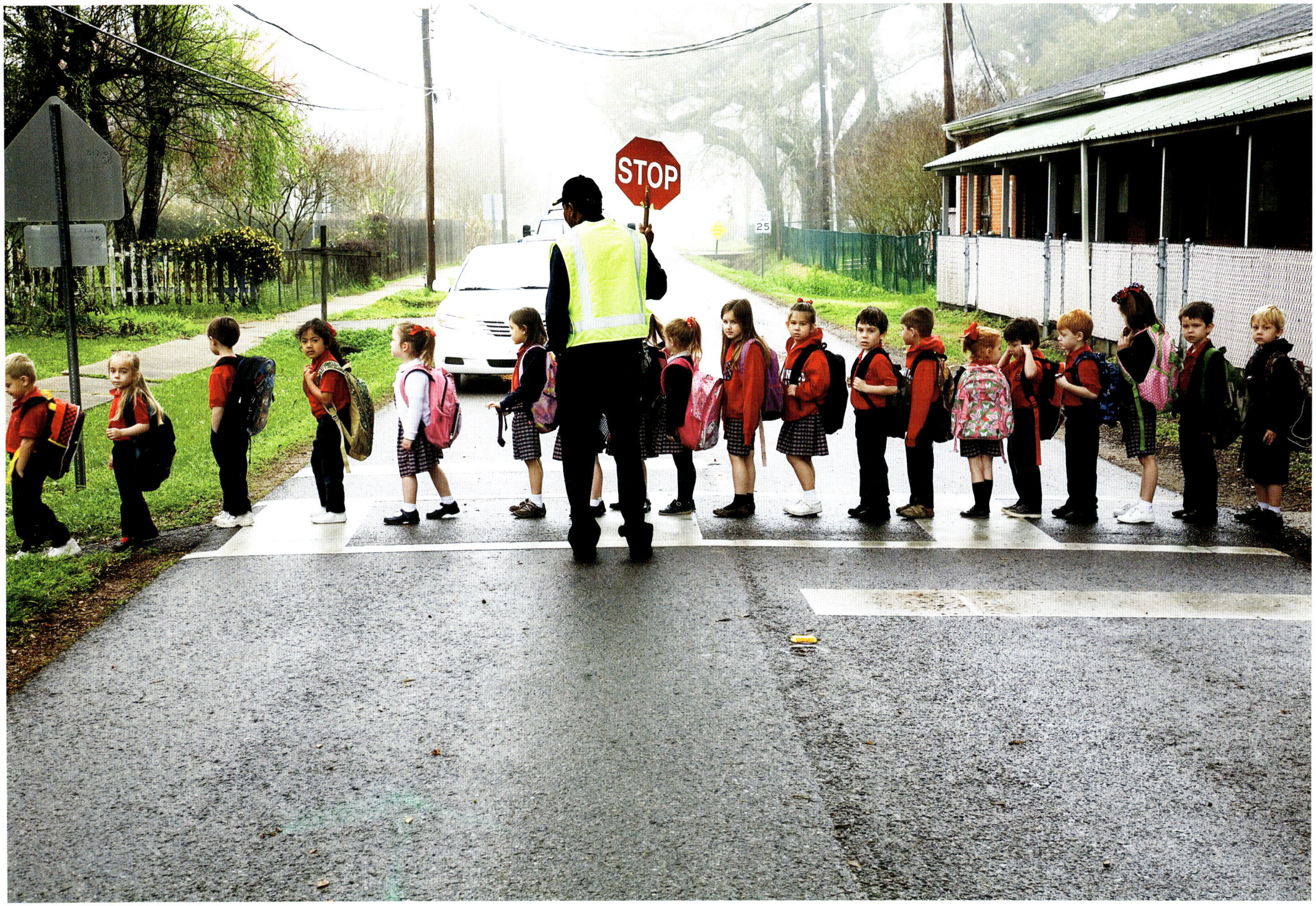
STOP
25

Graduation – Academy of the Sacred Heart
2012

One of the time-honored traditions is for graduates to walk from the main building through the gardens to take their place under the oaks. This ceremony is not only for the graduates; it is for the teachers who taught, the parents who invested, the administrators who managed, and the friends who gave support. These girls are the product of much love and attention.

Founded in 1821, the school is closing in on two hundred years of continuous operation. The dedication and determination of all the staff throughout the years deserves and demands respect. It's beyond remarkable that this institution exists considering its remoteness before the era of modern transportation. The school's reputation is so strong that in many circles Grand Coteau is synonymous with the Academy of the Sacred Heart.

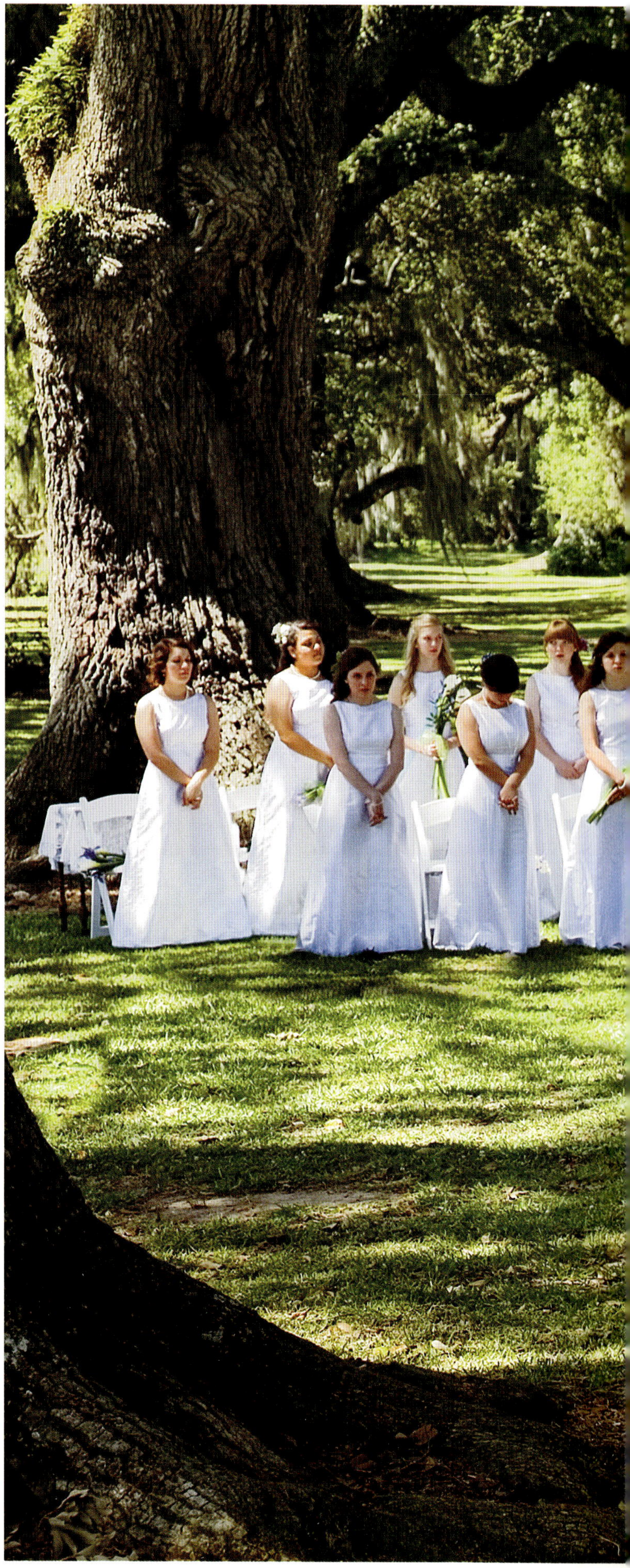

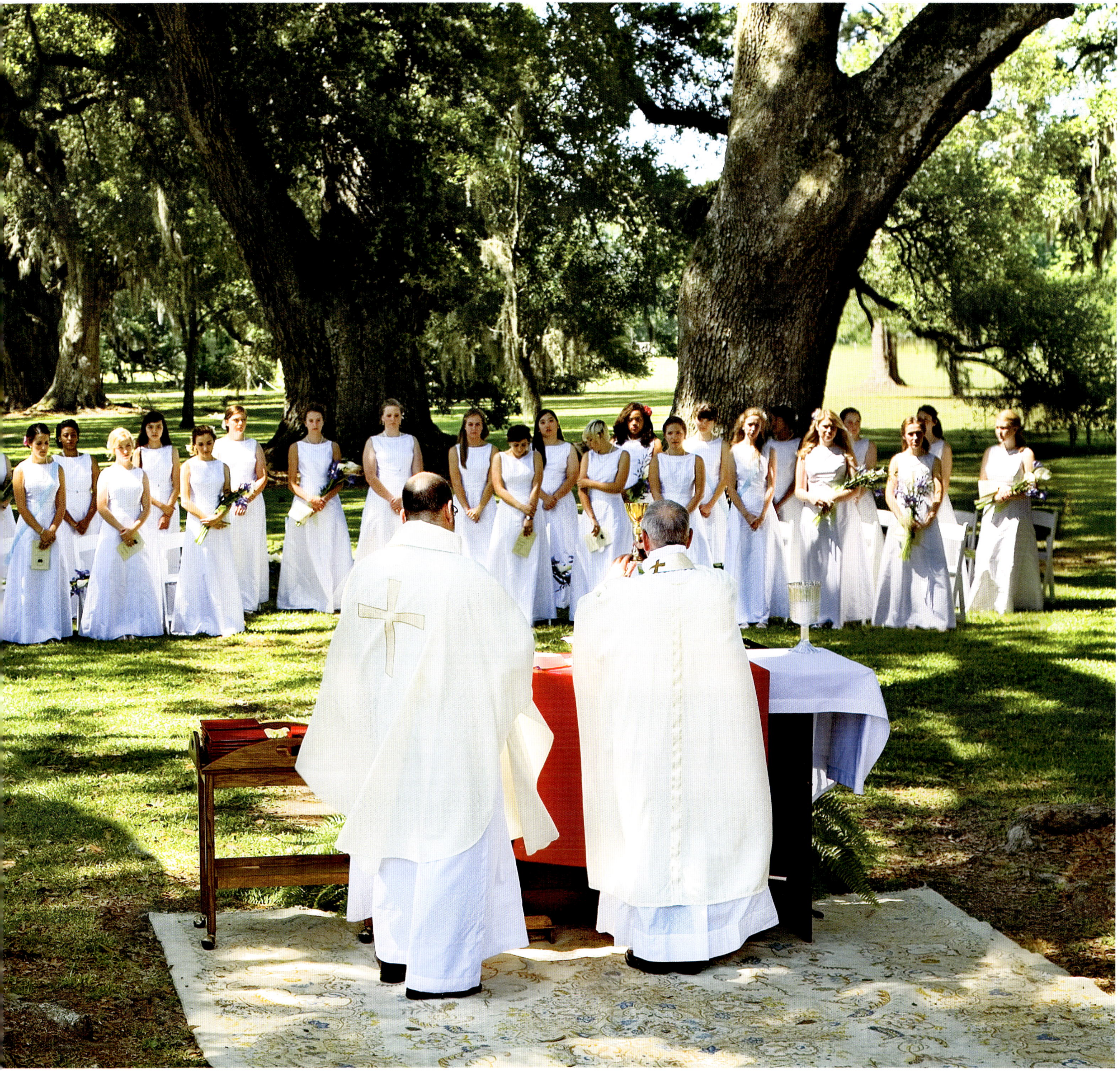

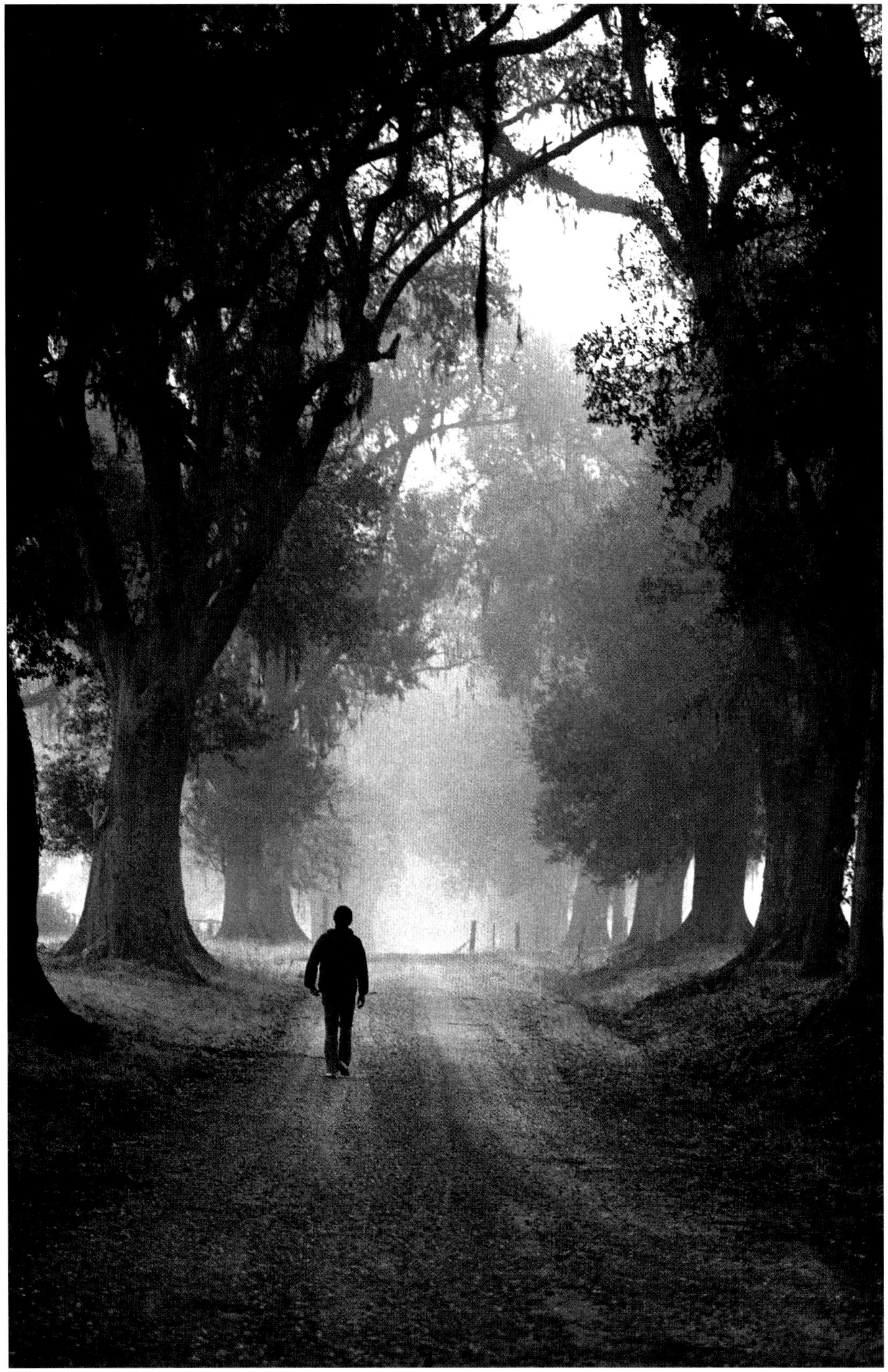

MEDITATION
1978